PHILOSOPHY AT THE CROSSROADS

PHILOSOPHY
AT THE
CROSSROADS

BY

EDWARD G. BALLARD

LOUISIANA STATE UNIVERSITY PRESS   BATON ROUGE

ISBN   0-8071-0523-6
Library of Congress Catalog Card Number 72–130663
Copyright © 1971 by Louisiana State University Press
All rights reserved
Manufactured in the United States of America
Printed by The TJM Corporation, Baton Rouge, Louisiana
Designed by Albert R. Crochet

Every moment the crossroad moves along with us.

—Heidegger, *Was Heisst Denken?*

Preface

This essay is a study of the course and consequences of modern philosophy. It proposes a definition of philosophy and then undertakes to show that this definition is fruitfully illustrated in the work of six philosophers whose writings have been crucial in the development of Western thought. The drift of these discussions is designed to move with the current of history and to end, in the final chapter, with some indication of the point whereto this history has now come. Were this design at all adequately realized, this book might have something to say concerning the future of philosophy. But I lay no claim to skill in the arts of historiomancy or divination.

These chapters do not pretend to offer a history of philosophy. Their aim is different. Their aim is lower in that only a few selected trends, "isms," philosophers, or parts of philosophy enter into consideration. But the aim is higher in that most of those topics and philosophers which are discussed are considered in rather greater particular than is usual for a one-volume history. My desire has been to treat each of the selected philosophers with sufficient fullness so that the points especially to be made concerning him would appear in an adequately developed context. Moreover, each chapter after the first is both a part of the design which I have indicated and a relatively independent essay. My hope is that each of these essays will not only contribute to this design but may also be judged to add something both original and worth saying about the philosophy or the topic in question.

Thus the aim of the book as a whole is to show where philosophy as I define it has now arrived and whither it might go. My consideration of the development of philosophy has been facilitated by the use of certain terms—terms such as "transition," "arché," "psyche," "thymos," "fate," "crisis." These terms will be sufficiently defined, I believe, as the book proceeds. Inevitably one of the ways now open to philosophy will appear to me to be superior to the others, and I shall say so—and why it is so—as well as I am able.

In attempting to achieve these purposes, I have been greatly helped by my friends, students, and associates. In particular, Professor Charles Bigger has at my insistence read and reread each chapter and has helped at every difficult point with suggestions, criticisms, and encouragement. Professors Edward Henderson and David Cornay have read the whole typescript and have assisted me most generously with criticisms and advice. Also Professors Andrew Reck, Carol Kates, Alexander von Schoenborn, and Harold Alderman have kindly and helpfully checked over parts of the book at my request. I owe especial thanks to the Tulane University Council on Research for support while completing the book and to Mrs. Freda Faber for typing the manuscript.

Likewise my thanks are extended to the editors and publishers of the *Tulane Studies in Philosophy* for permission to make use as needed of my articles here indicated: "The Kantian Solution to the Problem of Man within Nature," "The Nature of the Philosophical Enterprise," "Husserl's Philosophy of Intersubjectivity in Relation to His Rational Ideal," and "Renaissance Space and the Humean Development in Philosophical Psychology." Thanks go also to the Duquesne University Press for permission to use my essay "Heidegger's View of Nature and Natural Science," in *Heidegger and the Path of Thinking,* edited by John Sallis.

Contents

CONTENTS

CONTENTS

PHILOSOPHY AT THE CROSSROADS

I

Introduction

§1. IS PHILOSOPHY FINISHED?

Has philosophy now nearly completed its twenty-five hundred years of service to humanity? Has it only a few last remaining tasks of analysis and clarification to perform before its career is ended and the sciences and technology take over the whole responsibility for formulating and solving human problems? It all depends upon what one supposes philosophy to be.

Many people regard the modern sciences as a sort of Zeus who has successfully emasculated his old parent, philosophy, and has taken over the kingdom and set it into order. On the other hand philosophy, though old and often attacked, may not be without present power and use in the world. Again, all depends upon how one identifies philosophy.

I will take the position here that philosophy comes into being as the result of interpreting archaic experience. This definition, when appropriately explicated and understood, is useful in describing some important philosophies. Also, it provides a means for determining some significant relations among these philosophies and between them and a leading philosophy of the sciences. Finally, it throws light upon the position of contemporary philosophy with respect to its function and possible future development.

Philosophy, then, is the interpretation of archaic experience. It is immediately desirable that the notions of archaic experience and of interpretation be specified, although clearly the full development and illustration of these notions are very large tasks for which this introduction can present only the initial statement.

§ 2. PHILOSOPHY: THE INTERPRETATION OF ARCHAIC EXPERIENCE

Today the term "to experience" is usually understood to refer to a transaction of some sort. It suggests in part the passive reception of something whose source is usually not oneself, and in part it suggests an active affecting or a manipulation of that which is received. I shall, consequently, use the term to refer to the operation of the passive-active powers of mind.

But clearly not all of these operations of mind issue in the kind of experience which is grist for the philosopher's mill. Nor is the grist defined by the ancient doctrine of common experience, for there is no settled way of deciding what is common. It seems to me that the experience which belongs least to specialist pursuits and most evidently to philosophy is that which is concerned with the more radical transitions to which men and history are subject. Some of the divisive times in history are, of course, merely rebellions—for example, political rebellions—and tend to the reestablishment of only slightly altered regimes. They are the consequence of reshuffling and redistributing political or economic cards. But the game remains the same. Others are genuine revolutions. They are the result of changing the rules of the game. When radical changes of this kind occur in the life of a man or of a society, then the continuity of this life becomes problematic.

Continuity of life or identity become problematic upon occasions of major transitions in the life of the individual—for instance, upon the transition from childhood into adulthood. The more radical changes occur in the history of peoples as a change-over is made from one epoch to another. Interpretations of these changes attempt to find sense in the apparent discontinuities in such times of transition. It is not surprising to find gaps, apparent discontinuities, or actual incoherencies in those philosophies themselves as they attempt to interpret (do justice to) the multitudinous character of such times of trial and revolution.

A general name is needed for the kind of problem presented by a discontinuity in history or in a philosophy. I suggest that this type of problem be called "transcendental." One reason for this term is that a philosophy concerned with interpreting the times in which radical problems arise must reckon with the fact that once-customary methods for expressing and solving problems no longer work. Thus the poetic methods of pre-Homeric ages no longer sufficed for the more complex demands of later Greece. Again, seventeenth-century physical problems transcended Aristotelian concepts and techniques. Perhaps some of today's human and social problems transcend scientific techniques.

Another reason for classifying this kind of problem as transcendental is that its management requires regression to a fundamental level of thought. At this level in philosophy it is necessary to reconsider and to reinterpret certain basic notions which have commonly gone under the name of transcendentals; these are such notions as "being" and "nonbeing," "good" and "evil," "same" and "other," "one" and "many," and the like. To take an instance, the kind of "being" attributed to man underwent a radical reinterpretation in the seventeenth and eighteenth centuries; and there followed correlative changes in the conception of his "good." Thus, in short, the experience which calls philosophy forth is the experience of the kind of transition which elicits transcendental problems.

The term "archaic" in our definition of philosophy suggests that the kind of experience whose interpretation yields philosophy should be discoverable as far back in time as we care to go. Such is the case, I believe, and it is frequently desirable to return to other times when insights were less obscured by the prejudices which we ourselves happen to share. The term "archaic" also refers to an "arché," or "principle," that which is basic or fundamental, whether old or new, and is that whereon philosophy seeks its foundation, source, or beginning. To be advanced in philosophy is to be at this beginning, or near to it.

Both senses of the archaic element in philosophy may reasonably be intended in historical study; for a chronologically early stage of philosophy can be recognized as such only when it is identified as embodying a certain principle or property. Western philosophy is considered to have begun in the fifth century B.C. just because the thought of this age recognizably embodied such a principle or property. It is important but not easy to identify this principle.

Prior to the beginning of Western philosophy, thought was probably more passive, poetical, and mythic than ratiocinative. This condition has been rather well established by certain philosophers and philologians.[1] Heraclitus, as much as anyone, seems to have been aware of changes occurring in the basic character of his culture. He observed that only by constantly changing does anything either become or remain itself. We may suppose that he saw his own world as engaged in a transition from the somewhat damp world of Homer and Hesiod, whom he thought foolish, into a world of dryer thought. Plato developed the definitive interpretation of this transition. More generally, the effort in the West has been to envisage changes like this one as a development or growth which carries forward what birth, or the *physis* (which is or gives being), had initiated.

A typically modern longing is to see mankind as a whole developing into the one, modern, and perfect society; this development is often called progress and is now widely believed to be made possible only by the applied sciences. An older tradition, however, did not share this single-minded devotion to

---

[1] See Ernst Cassirer, *Philosophy of Symbolic Forms*, trans. Ralph Manheim (3 vols.; New Haven: Yale University Press, 1952), II; and especially Eric Havelock, *Preface to Plato* (Cambridge: Harvard University Press, 1963).

progress through the technical domination of nature and control of society. It had reached no such enlightenment. It thought of human change as a passage among worlds. Heraclitus observed the transition from the world of sleep to the world of waking. This metaphor of transition offers an interesting and suggestive figure for philosophy in its function of reflecting upon its own nature and change and interpreting the history of human change generally.

The ancient world was not always paralyzed by fear of the destruction which radical change must seem to risk. Heraclitus had faith in a logos which "guides all things through all things." And Parmenides in a famous sentence affirmed that genuine thought and being mutually measured each other.[2] This confidence, I believe, reaches its clearest expression in the philosophic intellectualism of Plato. If so, and if I may venture to give it a brief expression, I would state the fundamental and revolutionary conviction in these terms: being is intelligible. Of course this statement of intellectualism is less an axiom than a problem or a series of problems. Is being held to be wholly or only partly intelligible? Is it thought to be intelligible to all men, to the wise, or only to the gods? If to man, to what use of his mind is it intelligible? The intelligibility of being to mind is one of those basic notions or principles whose several senses may express or give rise to so many changes in individual or cultural history. The philosopher interested in interpreting revolutionary transitions does well to keep this conviction near the center of thought.

To suppose that the radical transitions in human life are dominated by an arché or illustrate a principle and to suppose this arché to be intelligible to the philosopher are suppositions which already constitute an interpretation. It is doubtful that one can reach or begin anything with an arché which involves no interpretation whatsoever; however, one may still be critically aware of interpretative activity. Here I shall suppose interpretation to refer to the conviction that the arché which renders

[2] Fragment 5.

radical transitions intelligible is discernible and expressible in some communicable form. Interpretation, thus, is the expression of intelligibility.

Expression is always translation of that which is to be interpreted into other but analogous terms. The analogous terms may be concrete and even personal. For example, Sophocles translated an understanding of human life into a poetic account of a man who, seeking to avoid his fate by one route, encountered it by another. Or the analogous terms may be highly generalized and abstract concepts, such as those common in philosophy. By means of this kind of translation, the philosopher achieves clarity and explanatory power, but he also risks attenuating his relation to the very experience which he wishes to interpret.

Abstract concepts are often deceptively remote from experience, and the philosopher is wise who is critical of his concepts, if for no other reason than that the arché which has often been said to dominate history is inextricably involved with fate or necessity (*anagke*). Fate is that which constrains. This term is introduced here in part because of its strangeness in philosophy and its seeming to suggest something which has been overlooked. The word has wide associations. It has been used to refer to the will of the gods, to that which may rule the gods, to the determining influence of the past, to the laws of nature, or to the intrinsic limitations of the human being. But fate, however interpreted, seems to be a being. Is it, then, intelligible? The obscurity of fate and the fact that predictions concerning its course have so often and tragically miscarried strongly intimate that convictions concerning the intelligibility of the whole of being to philosophers should be twice considered. Fate often dominates human life; perhaps, though, it can be dominated. Or perhaps some other attitude toward it is appropriate. In any event, the philosopher who holds being to be intelligible does well to recollect that the fate with which human-being is involved is often mysterious. Let us say that philosophic interpretation is the art which seeks to understand fate and to communicate about it without slighting its paradoxical quality.

Philosophy as the interpretation of archaic experience, then, is the art which seeks, in the light of a principle, to disengage the intelligible aspects of the compulsion which has precipitated the more radical transitions in human experience.

§ 3. THE FACTORS OF ARCHAIC EXPERIENCE

A man must live out his fate in a world. If his world be not adequate to the demands made upon it, then he must effect a transition into another. An illustration of transition among worlds is offered by the Greek myths which describe the first formation of the cosmos. In these myths a hero (Kronos or Zeus) forces the original parents (e.g., Ouranos and Gaia) to separate, apportions the resultant parts—heaven, earth, and the area between—to the appropriate powers, and then proceeds to the creation of animal and human life and to the inauguration of human society. All the while this creative action is threatened by some fateful power which in time succeeds in reducing the whole structure to its original state. Then the cosmic cycle begins anew. Pre-Socratic philosophy may quite reasonably be viewed as derived almost immediately from this mythic beginning, perhaps by a process of abstraction,[3] or perhaps in consequence of loss of poetic inspiration.

However, another illustration of the elements involved in such a transition, one more relevant to the philosophy of Plato and to modern thought, is to be discerned in considerations of language and their implications concerning the human mind and its functions. It will not be altogether arbitrary, then, to follow this latter route. Moreover, this route is by no means devoid of similarity to the cosmogonic myth just cited and seems particularly relevant when the old story is recalled which says that the gods named the world into being. We turn immediately, therefore, to some linguistic clues concerning the

[3] As argued by F. M. Cornford in *Principium Sapentiae*, ed. W. K. C. Guthrie (Cambridge: Cambridge University Press, 1952), Pt. 2. Cf. the essay "Prologomena" in C. G. Jung and Carl Kerényi, *Essays on a Science of Mythology*, trans. R. F. C. Hill (New York: Pantheon Books, 1949).

nature of the human mind, its relation to the world, and its relation to its fate.

Some primitive languages consisted generally in a mono-sound of complex significance whose specific kind of reference or function could be changed sufficiently for the occasion by the addition of modifying sounds or inflections. The Nootka language of Vancouver Island is such a language.[4] And no doubt primitive thought, like primitive speech, also consisted in complex unanalyzed notions applicable with a minimum of change to many situations. Consciousness, perception, emotion, speech, tendency to action were all merged in one unitary experience. Only gradually were these elements separated and some broad distinctions made. The content of this thought, as we may well expect, had to do with elementary mental experiences, the body and its organs, the world and its resistant character in relation to man, and the practice of the arts which sustain life—agriculture, hunting, weaving. A vast amount of linguistic evidence for the nature and structure of this thought has been collected and organized by Professor R. B. Onians and others.[5]

There is ample indication dating at least from the Homeric age that early man, meditating in his fashion upon human nature, had come to regard it as a duality of parts or of functions which had separated out of a primal unity. There is no suggestion here of a mind-body dualism; no such distinction was made. Yet a distinction was envisaged between whatever there is in man which is permanent, perhaps immortal—his real self—and the changing, consciously experiencing, waking and sleeping, remembering and forgetting self. Consciousness, it seems, and all the thought, desiring, feeling which we distinguish within the mind was lumped together and called *thymos*. This thymos, or

[4] See B. L. Whorf, "Language and Logic," *Technology Review*, XLIII (April, 1941).

[5] R. B. Onians, *The Origins of European Thought about the Body, the Mind, the Soul, the World, Time, and Fate* (Cambridge: Cambridge University Press, 1954). See also F. M. Cornford, *From Religion to Philosophy* (New York: Harper and Row, Harper Torchbooks. 1957), 109f.

conscious mind, was associated with the *phrenes*, which Professor Onians shows was not originally the diaphragm (as Plato thought, *Timaeus* 69) but rather the lungs and neighboring organs. The thymos, or discursive thought (*ratio*), was identified with the breath that uttered it (the Latin term was *animus*) and with the blood or blood-soul. Even as late as Aristotle, it was believed that conscious thinking was a function of the heart.[6] Perception was also a function of thymos and was associated with the area around the chest. Thus *oida*, and its aorist *eidos*, referring to perception, sight, and also connoting emotion, a point of interest in connection with the later meanings of these words in Plato's dialogues, are operations of thymos.[7] Likewise *aisthesis* (sensation) is related to the Homeric *aisthō*, meaning "I gasp, or breathe in."[8] And *nous*, which conceived purposes, was located in the chest or lungs.[9]

The behavior of the thymos was conceived to be continually changing. It was as manifold as the stream of consciousness; it died out temporarily during sleep; and at death when breathing stopped and the heart was stilled, it was finally destroyed.

There existed another factor, however, which contrasts strongly with this changing and mortal part of man. The other factor, apprehended within the human nature, was called the *psyche*, or soul (Latin, *anima*). This is the part which was permanent. It survived death as the *eidōlon* in Hades and was en-

---

[6] *Timaeus* (Archer-Hind translation; London: Macmillan, 1888) 702A; 2–16. Cf. Plato *Phaedo* 96.

[7] Homer *Iliad* iv. 409.

[8] Onians, *Origins of European Thought*, 75.

[9] Homer *Odyssey* xxiv. 474. Bruno Snell, in *The Discovery of the Mind*, trans. T. G. Rosenmeyer (New York: Harper and Row, Harper Torchbooks, 1960), 12, finds in his analysis of Homer's language that "thymos" refers usually to motion (or emotion) whereas *nous* is generally "in charge of intellectual matters," but he notes that this distinction was vague. He is in substantial agreement with the distinction between thymos and psyche which I shall indicate below (see his Chap. 1). Professor R. E. Dodds makes a remark in this connection which is well to recall; he writes, "We must admit that the psychological vocabulary of the ordinary man in the fifth century was in a state of great confusion, as indeed it usually is." *The Greeks and the Irrational* (Berkeley: University of California Press, 1951), 138.

countered in dreams, for it was active in sleep. This is the life principle, given by the gods. This psyche is the water-soul, source of life, power, physical strength, and sex. It is associated primarily with the head, backbone, genitals, and knees. The brain was commonly regarded as the source of the reproductive seed; and other juices of the body (except the blood)—for instance, the spinal fluid, sweat, tears, fat, marrow, anything seemingly wet—were related to the same. Evidently the importance attributed to the head, even since the Stone Age,[10] is thus made comprehensible. Involuntary movements, such as sneezing, blushing, shuddering, and especially the inspirations of the religious genius or poet, were attributed to the psyche and were regarded with awe as a communication from the inner source of power or from the gods.

There also exists a connection between psyche and *daimon* which is important for understanding religious roots of the drama. Evidently the early Greeks closely identified the two.[11] A daimon—for example, Dionysus—was always regarded as divine. The belief in the divinity and immortality of the daimon and in the connection of psyche and daimon, Professor Onians suggests, may be at the basis of the Orphic claim for the divinity of the psyche. Plato also connects psyche and daimon: "God gave the sovereign part of the human soul (psyche) to be the divinity (daimon) of each one, being that part which as we say dwells at the top of the body ... and raises us from earth to our kindred who are in heaven." [12] And in the Myth of Er of the *Republic* (617) each individual is assigned a daimon as a kind of guardian angel. In general, then, human psyche and divine daimon are very closely, though vaguely, related. Jane Harrison provides one account of the development of the daimon of ritual into the hero of drama and saga.[13]

[10] Onians, *Origins of European Thought*, 530–43.

[11] *Ibid.*, 405, note 8.

[12] *Timaeus* 90A. And at 70A the ruling part of the soul is compared with the sacred image which issued commands from the temple.

[13] Jane E. Harrison, *Themis: A Study of the Social Origins of Greek Religion* (Cambridge: Cambridge University Press, 1912), Chap. 8.

The point relevant at the present is that the human psyche or "life" is also a man's instrument for coming into contact with superior power; it is his spark of divinity. As Plato wrote: "The part of the sane man is to remember and interpret all things that are declared, dreamed or waking, by the prophetic and inspired nature; and whatsoever visions are beheld by the seer to determine by reason in what way and to whom they betoken good or ill." [14] Thus psyche and thymos are to each other more or less as inspiration is to routine discursive thought.

These beliefs about human nature, as constituted by the semidivine life-soul, or psyche, and the conscious but mortal thymos, or blood-soul (providing, as it might be expressed, a continuous factor and an intermittent or discrete factor), did not remain unchanged. During the fifth century B.C. and after, probably under the influence of Orphic and Pythagorean doctrines, which taught that more of the person survives death than merely the life principle,[15] the notions of psyche and thymos begin to come into another relation. The brain becomes something more than a repository for the life seed and tends to become the seat of consciousness and of the personal agent. As it were, a boundary is crossed; psyche comes into a much closer, and perhaps a healthier, relation with the conscious thymos or *animus*, until as Plato maintained—if the Myth of Er be taken rather literally—the departed spirits are not merely psyche, bare seeds of life, but they preserve consciousness, memory, a power of intelligent or foresighted choice, and some awareness

[14] *Timaeus* 72A.

[15] Onians, *Origins of European Thought*, 115–16. There are, as I have already indicated, many recognizable indications of these beliefs preserved in Plato. Socrates, for example, raises the question whether we think with the blood (*Phaedo* 96), and in the *Timaeus* (73C and 91A–B) the brain and marrow are said to be the channel through which contact is made with the gods. But in general, Platonic thought represents a change in these beliefs, which brings them into harmony with the developing naturalistic thought, and also makes them more acceptable to contemporary philosophic views. Cf. F. M. Cornford, *Plato's Cosmology* (New York: Humanities Press, 1952), 284–86. The Latins clung to these ancient beliefs more tenaciously than the Greeks. Onians in *Origins of European Thought*, 169, quotes Nonius, "Animus est quo sapimus, anima qua vivimus." Tertullian considers *anima* to be the organ of intuitive knowledge and of revelation. Cf. *De Testimonio Animae* 1 and 5.

of responsibility. Of course it cannot be supposed that primitive man expressly formulated and reflectively grappled with the problem concerning the unity of the self, however its parts be imagined. Nevertheless, he achieved some self-awareness, and we may suppose that the conscious mind as well as the psyche came to be regarded as factors of the same person. What, in short, may be supposed to have occurred is that primitive man, or perhaps any man somewhere along the way of his maturing, learned to cross with increased facility the boundary separating his daily and more or less rational self from his more obscure yet sometimes inspired self.

So much, for the moment, about man and his dual soul. Let us turn to the environment within which human nature developed; how was it conceived? The world is the stage on which man's life is lived and his fate worked out. What is the nature of fate? It seems to be reasonable to expect, as we have actually found, that the beliefs about the body should be reflected by analogy in beliefs about the mind; similarly men's activity in the world—their arts—may be expected to give the cue to their beliefs about the world and its order.

This fateful order, against which the Homeric heroes and even the gods felt themselves powerless to struggle, is not merely the projected image of tribal organizations; nor is it a personified figure of the boundaries between tribal preserves. The notions which elaborate it go back to an even less complex epoch. They draw their first content, Onians has found, from the context of human work, specifically from the weaver's art. Man's fate hangs on "the knees of the gods," for it was on or by the knees that the spinner's spindle was held.[16] The fully developed image is presented in the description of the fateful spinning, *epiclosanto theoi*, "the gods weave." Fate is made or woven by the gods. In Homer, Zeus and the other gods are those who spin fate.[17] Although Zeus is the source of fate, he is not

[16] See *Republic* X. 616.

[17] Onians, *Origins of European Thought*, 393, 409f; cf. *Iliad* xx. 127; *Odyssey* vii. 197.

bound by it,[18] yet he was usually felt to be morally constrained by his own ordinances and allotments in this respect. Later it is the Moirai, the Fates, who weave, and these three sisters may be personifications of parts of the weaving process. Lachesis selected the wool (weighed out for her by Zeus himself), Clotho spun the thread, and Atropos wove the web. The fate thus woven at or before a man's birth is then thought to bind him as if it were literally a net or a cord. In this manner fate constrains man's life. The intrinsic character of fate, then, is its whole or partial independence of the living beings whom it constrains. It is a quasi objective order which embraces man's life, and perhaps that of the gods as well. It constitutes those limits known today by the term "the human condition" and includes being born in a unique time and milieu; also it means the inevitable constraints of living, sex, conflict, and death. It sets up situations which impel men to cross boundaries, boundaries which they fear to cross.

A man's fate is inescapable; it is bound upon him by *peirata*. This term, *peras*, which becomes so important in Plato,[19] was

---

[18] At least in Homer and Hesiod, the Moirai, the fateful spinners, appear to be subservient to Zeus (*Odyssey* iii. 236). They are the offspring of Zeus and Themis: Themis being identified by Jane Harrison in *Themis*, Chap. 8, as a projection onto the universe of tribal customs respecting boundaries and legal regulations. Aeschylus, however, seems to regard Zeus himself as subject to the Moirai (*Prometheus Bound* 515). Plato makes them the daughters of Necessity, of Anagke (*Republic* X. 617C). Evidently the Moirai are agents of a general and pervasive fate whose relationship to other powers, to the will of the gods, to man's free will, is conceived variously at different times.

The root meaning of *anagke* (necessity or fate) is not clear. Onians, in his *Origins of European Thought*, 332, connects it with *agchein*, "to strangle," which preserves the analogy to a binding cord (or serpent) and cites Parmenides, "For mighty *anagke* holds it [reality] in bonds of the *desmoisin* which enclose it around." In the *Timaeus, anagke* has a kind of prerational existence; the chaos that existed before the world was made has its own mechanical movement (*ex-anagkes*) which is persuaded to receive such purposive or rational order as it can embody. The same notion occurs in the myth of the *Politicus* (272E) where Plato pictures fate (here referred to by *heimarmene*) as taking over when God withdraws his hand from the tiller of the universe. Fate is thus a necessity which operates independently of any sort of intentional movement toward an end, though it may be integrated into such a purposeful movement.

[19] See *Philebus* 23f. In *Politicus* (309B–C), the kingly artist is said to use true opinions as the bond with which he binds the soul to the divine. (The term used here for bond, to *xyggenes*, is also used in connection with spinning.)

also used in connection with spinning. It meant thread or woof
thread, a spun rope, or even a knot. It came also to refer to the
cord or thread by which a man's fate was fastened upon him
and whose presence is betrayed by its effects.[20] No doubt a
cord or thong with which a man could bind things together (a
bundle of sticks, a group of prisoners) so that he could treat the
many as one was a most valuable instrument and an impressive
source of power. To the primitive mind it could well seem to be
a godlike instrument suggestive of the way in which the universe is held together or formed. Later *peras* came to mean
boundary, limit, or form, approaching the sense in which Plato
used the term. The figure of fate as a woven bond or ligature
which limits or circumscribes a man is expressed in many ways.
One recalls the ring binding a marriage, a king's magic ring, the
collar signifying slavery, a belt with its many meanings, and
especially the crown of oak or ivy leaves which specified the
status of its wearer, or a kingly crown which quite literally
bound the psyche. Thus psyche is limited, sometimes con-
stricted, by its fate.

Naturally, then, psyche is particularly attentive to intimations of this fate. An image running through Homer suggests
that in the web which binds a man the warp threads are time
or length of life. This time is to be understood as qualitative
time, time as lived, its hours differentiated by the varying contents of experience. The woof threads are fate, the ordained
events themselves. The tapestry thus woven and bound upon a
man, by design of Zeus, is unchangeable. Yet within limits—
undefined limits, it is true—there was sometimes conceived to
be freedom. A man could render his fortune worse by his ill
choice, but just how and to what degree choice could affect fate
was a problem which ancient man could scarcely reckon with.
Still, by exercise of his thymos or ingenuity he could adjust himself more appropriately to his fate.

[20] Onians cites the Greek epigram, "Such is the wretched life of mortals, so
unfulfilled their hopes, over which the threads of the Moirai hang." *Origins of
European Thought*, 337.

Now, bringing these several notions together for the present purposes, we may think of psyche as offering, in times of stress, inspirations which then may be reasonably interpreted (by thymos) and the interpretation used as a guide to action possibly in greater harmony with one's fate.

Much of this lore concerning man's relation with fate is summarized in a cosmic figure of some interest. Okeanos, over which the heavens bent like the inside of an eggshell, was the primal sea from which, as Thales recalled, the world was born. It was said to lie around earth's shores like a serpent.[21] As the source of the world and its life, this water, Okeanos, is the psyche of the universe and the source of the human psyche. At the same time, since it lies around the world, limiting it and holding it together, it is the world's fate. Thus at this point the notions of life, innermost nature, and predetermined fate become conjoined in a manner which presages later beliefs.

These convictions of the primitive Greeks are shown by Onians to have been extraordinarily widespread. Like primitive tools, primitive beliefs seem to have been all of one stamp the world over. This is an astounding fact. Why this is so we can only speculate.[22] Perhaps once a single culture came to dominate a people who later spread and populated or conquered the world. Perhaps all peoples faced with a given type of problem at a given stage of their history react in similar ways. Whatever the explanation of this fact may be, the prevalence of this body of beliefs is ancient enough and is sufficiently widespread and its content sufficiently explicit to justify our suspecting it to be related to the archetypal datum of men's thought.

[21] The serpent, as everyone knows, is a phallic symbol. Also it is a symbol of death. Snakes were supposed to haunt graves and perhaps to be a form which the dead assumed. Onians notes the ancient belief that the spinal marrow, repository of psyche, was thought to turn into a snake after death, a belief suggestive of the resemblance between the spinal cord and a snake's skeleton. *Ibid.*, 206.

[22] See Joseph Campbell, *The Hero with a Thousand Faces* (New York: The World Publishing Co., Meridian Books, 1956), on the common character of myths.

An image emerges from this summary which is by no means without later and present power, although it has been variously interpreted and transformed. This is the image of a man exercising a simple art and at the same time, through its agency, coming in many other ways into significant contact with himself, with others, and with the world. The art might be spinning and weaving cloth of wool. But from this simple routine, carried out according to rules handed down by tradition, a universe is born. The cloth, as it magically takes form under the artisan's hands, not only has practical values which preserve life, but it acquires meanings which relate him and it to the animal life from which its material came and to the environing universe itself. The cloth is not only woven but interpreted. It becomes the web of a mysterious fate within which he himself and his humble weaving are woven and ordained images and within which he is to make his place and his peace. Likewise, as the web is at once a manifest and useful object in his hands, yet expressive of the unmanifest and awful power beyond, so the weaver too is not merely a consciously active and thinking self (a thymos); he is also a something or a part of something (the psyche) which touches on the mysterious source of life and power which he must somehow use and serve. Against this background of belief, Plato's image in the *Politicus* of the statesman weaving the two different kinds of human souls into the fabric of the state takes on a rather special interest and grandeur and opens the way to rendering the ancient fate somewhat less blankly mysterious.[23] The weaver and the woven, fate and man, thus become the material for reflection.

The elements thymos, psyche, and fate that are associated with early beliefs concerning human-being and life may now be assembled in an initial expression of the datum of philosophy: Philosophy, we say, is the interpretation of archaic experience; this experience is the experience of crossing boundaries. What

---

[23] 279B *passim*. Also compare the remark in the Cornford translation of the *Sophist* (259E), "any discourse we can have owes its existence to the weaving together of forms."

is the nature of these boundaries? For one thing, they are always already there. Mythically we may say that fate has set them up. In the effort to continue life within them, an unusual difficulty is encountered. The ordinary daily rationale of life, the embodied thymos, is not enough to cope with the difficulty. Then a boundary must be crossed; fate—such is its ambiguous character—compels the crossing. Thereupon primitive man turns to the source of inspiration, to psyche. But psyche, being semidivine, is also taboo; it has to be walled off from ordinary life and can only be approached with awe and appropriate purity. The transition over the boundary from thymos to psyche is regulated by its own kind of necessity. Man must learn to deal with this determined order which resists his fantasy, flouts his conventions, and drives him to the search after wisdom; he must learn to deal with it if he is to come into a profitable connection either with himself, with others, or with the world.

Although the present section should be regarded as belonging to the order of myth, still it does make an approach to our thesis. This thesis holds that something analogous to psyche, as well as to the more rational and familiar thymos, belongs to the human person and is functionally related to his need to live in a world or to make a transition among worlds. Likewise, each of these organs is reflected in a correlative use of language; poetry and myth are the language of inspiration whose organ is psyche (or some intuitive function of mind); discursive, ordinary, and more or less logically organized speech is the language of thymos.[24] Both organs, both kinds of speech, must be duly included in a view of the whole. But the effort appropriately to include psyche and to understand its language requires precisely the crossing of the boundary which separates thymos (*ratio*) from psyche—a dangerous transition, but one which nevertheless has to be repeated in different epochs as different kinds of dangers or different elements of fate threaten to de-

[24] See Snell, *The Discovery of the Mind*, 224. "Mythical thought requires receptivity; logic cannot exist without activity. Logical thought is unimpaired wakefulness; mythical thinking borders upon the dream, in which images and ideas float by without being controlled by the will."

stroy the integrity of the self and of the world. Many of the philosophers of our tradition offer views of these transitions, or ways to avoid them, or ways to effect them.

Psyche is still a good name for the passive or receptive aspect or function of mind, that which receives inspiration or intuition from a source seemingly not itself. Plato represents the poet as the passive recipient of inspiration from the gods; also he describes the initial stage of philosophic thought as a recollection of that which had somehow been already given to mind; some later philosophers have limited the given to the operations of sense or to perception, and others have confined sensing severely within the boundaries of a narrow status quo. Just what this passively received given may be is variously viewed at different times, but that there is such a given seems quite generally to have been believed.

Similarly thymos, *ratio*, discursiveness, and such terms will denote the active function of mind, its more familiar and presumably logical problem-solving and interpretative operations. Reason in the broad sense includes both of these powers, but in the narrower modern sense it refers primarily to this same thymos or to its principles. There is, I may add, some precedent for my linguistic innovation. The word "thymos" is contained within the term "enthymatic," which refers to the presence in the mind of something necessary for a syllogistic argument.

Psyche and thymos still usefully refer, though in varying emphases and in changing relations and proportions, to our primary means for dealing with the initially—and always, to some extent—irrational forces of constraint or of radical change. Man, it seems, is victimized by the powers of fate, unless he can use his powers of mind to adapt to them more harmoniously and see himself across the more challenging boundaries.

Heraclitus remarked, "The sun will not overstep his bounds, for if he does, the Erinyes, allies of justice, will find him out." But with man the matter is more puzzling, for the boundaries of the human both within and without him are ambiguous and must be approached questioningly.

Man's fate has been a series of efforts to change his fate. He has sought at the least to think through the paradoxes of his fate and to render them thus a little less opaque. This "thinking through," eventuating in an insight, is a process of interpretation. I mean to suggest that interpretation itself is a peculiar kind of transition; in this instance it is the crossing of the boundary which sets apart the use of mind that achieves insight into fate from the more familiar use of mind that translates such insights into practical terms which can be rendered effective in the world.

How marked and definite is this boundary within the mind? Ancient writers sometime seem to hold to two centers of man's life: the gods, to whom psyche has access, and the things and events of the everyday world, with which thymos deals. After the Renaissance these two centers seem to approach each other, and psyche is curbed to the service of thymos, almost identified with it. The world and man become anthropocentric.

Even the most canalized culture, however, requires some inspiration, some crossing of the internal boundaries. In any event, geniuses sometimes arise, receive inspirations, and render them effective through discipline. A somewhat specialized illustration of these two uses of mind is Jules Henri Poincaré's sudden intuitive and inspired grasp, as he stepped on a bus in Coutances, of the identity of a group of Fuchsian functions with a non-Euclidean geometry. This was a sudden, unreasoned, and immediate grasp, whose technical detail he later elaborated at leisure.[25] In other than mathematical thought, an inspired beginning may be distinguished from a disciplined continuation and use. Philosophy, I suggest, can also be described as inspiration submitted to rational and disciplined thought. Interpretation, in other words, is inspiration disciplined by logic.

[25] *Science et Méthode* (Paris: E. Flammarion, 1908), Chap. 1; and see Arthur Koestler, *Insight and Outlook* (Lincoln: University of Nebraska, Bison Books, 1965), Chap. 18 *passim*.

But interpretation becomes philosophic especially when it takes archaic experience, the experience of crossing fundamentally significant boundaries, as its datum. Surely a crucial boundary to be crossed is precisely that between inspiration and disciplined thinking. The philosophic sense of *physis*, with its allusion to birth, is a reference to that initial inspiration which originates a way of human life; its reference to subsequent growth has in the West been the concern for continuation in disciplined reason.

The reverse is also true: philosophy is careful, analytic thought only when this latter is enlivened by some effective inspiration. Thus philosophy arises from the interchange between inspiration and disciplined thinking. Philosophy is, in short, inspired reason. It will also be useful to speak of philosophy as a movement back and forth between myth and more precise doctrine. It must be emphasized, however, that philosophy arises from such an interchange only when the whole context within which life (cultural or individual) actually goes on is brought into question; then a whole world is undergoing significant change. When this kind of change is feared and avoided, some conventional notion of inspiration or of discipline may be taken for granted; then the interchange between them is limited within these initial, if inexplicit, conventional boundaries. And then all that which remains outside these boundaries persists in the guise of an unknown, arational, and, accordingly, revengeful fate.

There appears to be reason for believing that the modern world has for a long time been accumulating unknown or forgotten material which may be expected to return upon us in the form of a revengeful fate; at least this is the conviction attributable to one contemporary philosophical tradition. Certain aspects of this conviction invite investigation. The general problem concerns the nature of the self and its relation to its world. More specifically, however, the point of attack often narrows down to the question concerning the relation between the mind's receptive and active powers and their function in experience. One may inquire, for instance, whether or under what circumstances the receptive or psychic powers of mind are altogether independent of the active or thymic ones; whether or how one of these is derivative from the other; whether or how one may or should be made to subserve the other. Inquiry along these lines, I think, reveals aspects of the human being which have in the course of history been ignored or forgotten and so relegated to the nonrational.

§ 4. CONCERNING THE PLATONIC INTERPRETATION

Plato interpreted the transition out of the age of poetic intimacy with the gods of pre-Homeric and Homeric times into his own epoch as a movement away from ignorance and barbarism and toward greater proximity to reality and the Good. His philosophy is also, as *Republic* III and X reveal, a devaluation of the poetic means of communication with the gods. This Platonic interpretation and its succession of reinterpretations have been determinative of our epoch in history. It is, therefore, advantageous to pass in brief review the essentials of his doctrine and to observe also certain of the transitions effected and attempted within his philosophy. My remarks are offered not as a study of Plato but rather as an illustration of the ideas about philosophy indicated in the preceding sections; also they are offered because Plato takes an important stand on the problem concerning the relation of psyche to thymos and concerning their involvement in the world. Thereby the Platonic philosophy opens the way to modern philosophy and to the theme which will occupy subsequent chapters.[26]

That Plato distinguished between the mind's receptive and active powers is evident. Whatever his terms, he was certainly aware of the geography of mind as outlined in the preceding section. Reason for him is a disciplined and mutually cooperating use of both psyche and thymos, though not so much

---

[26] Of course Aristotle is also involved in the initiation of the modern world. However, it will be convenient to discuss his philosophy only where specifically relevant to particular topics. See §§ 16 ff.

to avoid fate as positively to respond to the eros of the Good.

In *Republic* V and VII, Plato divided the powers of the mind into several levels. Its highest level, *noesis*, represents the immediate grasp of or insight into principles or ideas, for instance into the idea of the Good. But the way to this grasp, this recollection, is provided by an intellectual activity (*dianoia*) which disciplines both perception and mental action by the standard of that which insight reveals. These two functions render intelligible, so far as possible, the inchoate experience and irrational opinion of the mind's lower levels of operation. Thus the mind's active powers are brought by means of a carefully conceived intellectual discipline to subserve the interests of its receptive powers, especially in respect of the ability of these latter to entertain insight into the human good. In this manner knowledge becomes virtue.

The same evolution is expressed in the *Phaedo, Meno,* and elsewhere by the doctrine of recollection. There, as the myth is interpreted, the mind, like an intellectual eye, perceives the ideas, but only obscurely. It is as if this insight were always immediately given, yet were initially darkened. Thus intellectual intuition is confused until a dialectical activity trains, so to speak, the vision by purging it of ignorance and forgetfulness. This dialectical purification is also a *paideia*, a growth in virtue. For it reveals the true human nature, the end of man's striving. The vision of this Good is at the same time a rectification of the will and, since no one errs willingly, the perfection of character. Thus again, the active powers of mind are subordinated to the intuitive ones by means of an intellectual discipline. One may, I believe, conceive of this movement whether described in terms of the divided line of *Republic* V, or of the Cave of *Republic* VII, or in terms of the doctrine of recollection, as an intellectualization of ancient ritual forms which were, no doubt, well known both to Plato and to his audience.[27] Insights into the idea reached by dialectical means replaced contact with the

---

[27] I have tried to develop this point in my article "On Ritual and Persuasion in Plato," *Southern Journal of Philosophy*, II (1964), 49–55.

sacred achieved by ritual purification and ceremony. Thus the hero of chthonic religion became the hero of reason.

This solution to the problem of the unity of mind was, however, unstable. At least two difficulties arose to render this subordination of dialectical activity to contemplative intuition hard to envisage clearly. The first and perhaps basic difficulty is the well-known problem of participation. The second devolves from the increasingly mathematical character of Plato's dianoetic thinking which his appreciation of the intellectual value of clarity, and no doubt of other factors, rendered inevitable.

The problem of participation points generally to the need for an adequate description of the relation of the particular instantiation to the universal. Several forms of the problem are exhibited in the first part of the *Parmenides*. The form of the problem relevant here follows from the discontinuity of the educational process undergone by the philosopher as he moves along the divided line. How can dialectical activity actually induce vision of the idea? There is no guarantee, as dialogue after dialogue illustrates, that the discipline will issue in insight. Poincaré's intuitive solution of his problem, mentioned above, seemed to him and to others to be quite mysterious. No less difficult is it to see how the Socratic dialectic of the *Meno* leads the slave boy to solve his mathematical problem. Socrates' position, in effect, is this: If the boy submits to a purifying questioning, then he will find that he knows the solution to the problem. Now, the boy does find the solution. But it does not logically follow that the questioning discovered it. In fact, the same sort of questioning directed upon Meno had been ineffective. Meno got no further than the experience of the "torpedo shock," the recognition of his own ignorance or forgetfulness. Though this shock is a beneficial crisis of knowledge and an advance over an ignorant ignorance, still it is not the desired insight into the knowledge which is virtue. Certainly the relation of idea or of a universal concept to the particular illustration is not a deductive relation. What relation, then, is it?

In the *Republic* VII the idea of the Good, to which the mathematical discipline is said to lead, is concluded finally to be beyond knowledge (509B). Quite reasonably, then, Socrates disclaims knowledge about it (506f; 517B). But immediately the question arises how this idea can be related to the intellectual discipline supposed to reveal it. In my opinion the notion of good becomes ambiguous at this point. In one of its senses it refers to the highest or architectonic idea to which the dialectic may point but which it does not reach. In another sense "good" is a transcendental term, pervading the whole of being and possibly unifying the value aspects of all beings. In this sense the intellectual means to the Good is itself good. This means never becomes identical with the idea; nevertheless, the transcendental sense of "good" might have been found useful for specifying a kind of continuity among the levels of the divided line—between Good as idea and as end, and good as means to this end. In other words Plato could have pursued this route further toward solving the problem of participation. And in fact the *Sophist* does go somewhat further in this direction by distinguishing meanings of two other transcendental terms, "being" and "nonbeing." Still I cannot see that Plato reached a full solution to the problem of participation as it was stated in the *Parmenides*.[28]

The indeterminate state in which Plato left the problem of participation was not without effect upon other Platonic problems and their management. For instance, in the *Phaedo* Socrates recounts how he faced up to the question whether to pursue a fairly clear-cut, even if primitive, sciencelike knowledge of the world, or whether to turn toward himself and to pursue an elusive and uncertain knowledge of the psyche and of the Good. He rejected the former course and elected the latter.

[28] Some writers, however, believe that he did solve this problem. See Hwan Chen, "On the *Parmenides* of Plato," *Classical Quarterly*, XXXVIII (1944), 101–44. I have indicated an answer to Chen's argument in my *Socratic Ignorance: An Essay on Platonic Self-Knowledge* (The Hague: Nijhoff, 1965), Chap. 4. Professor Charles Bigger holds that Plato provided all the concepts required for the solution of the problem, and he goes on to show how a solution might have been reached. See his *Participation: A Platonic Inquiry* (Baton Rouge: Louisiana State University Press, 1968), Chaps. 3 and 4.

Perhaps we can see on Plato's or Socrates' part some dissatisfaction with this decision, for in the later development of this philosophy an effort was made to pursue both of these two kinds of knowledge and to relate them to each other. Knowledge about objects in the world, especially mathematical knowledge of the harmonies embodied in worldly and celestial objects, came to be interpreted as the means to insight into the Good (*Republic* VII). This mathematical note is often emphasized in the later dialogues. Perhaps Plato's appreciation of the pervasiveness of the mathematical relations was increased as he learned more about mathematics. At any rate, he observed that measurement and calculation provide the means for managing the vague and seemingly contradictory properties of visible objects.[29] He wrote that all the arts are dependent upon measurement of quantity (*Politicus* 284D). And in the *Sophist* (238B) he remarks, "Numbers must exist if anything else does." But the full extent of the participation of the world in mathematical form becomes evident only in the *Timaeus*. The important element in this latter dialogue is the mythical account not only of the participation of the cosmos in mathematical harmonies, but of man's participation in them also. Man can and should become in this respect an imitation of the cosmos. Indeed, the *Timaeus* is a sort of dialogue between the cosmos and man, a dialogue which concludes to the need and desirability of continuing the same dialogue in the life and thought of every person. Moreover, a continuation of this dialogue in thought is also a continuation of it in life, for an understanding of the mathematical harmonies of the universe is said at the same time to be a correction or an attunement of the internal harmonies in man. Hence this study constitutes the way to human perfection and virtue. It provides the meeting place of the intellectually conceived and the actually embodied harmony. Plato writes, in Jowett's translation:

> The motions which are naturally akin to the divine principle within us are the thoughts and revolutions of the universe. These each man should follow, and correct the courses of the head

---

[29] *Republic* VII. 523F, X. 602; cf. *Epinomis* 977D–E.

which were corrupted at our birth, and by learning the harmonies
and revolutions of the universe, should assimilate the thinking
being to the thought, renewing his original nature, and having
assimilated them should attain to that perfect life which the gods
have set before mankind, both for the present and the future.
(*Timaeus* 90C; cf. *Epinomis* 988A)

At this point means and end merge. The intellectual means
produce a moral effect; the final use of the mathematics of the
universe is to produce the desirable human change in the
movement to maturity.

The Platonic arché, the principle of continuity which renders
possible the crucial transitions in human life without loss of
identity, thus becomes evident: it is the mathematical form
embodied both in the cosmos and in man. By giving the Good
common to both the cosmos and to man a mathematical character, Plato was able to point the way to a solution of the problem of connection, his transcendental problem. This manner of
treating the problem is most important in terms both of its
subsequent influence and of its deficiencies.

Something like an acceptance, at least in principle, of this
solution can be followed throughout much of the medieval
age from St. Augustine up to Kepler. These philosophers, like
others, saw the whole universe and all human activity as
teleologically directed toward the human good. This good was,
in general, the perfection in man of the image of the Trinity.
But in addition, the mathematically inclined philosophers believed they found a peculiar relation between the Second
Person of the Trinity and mathematical law, for mathematical
law seemed to be the clearest expression of Reason itself, the
Logos. Thus, through pursuing an understanding of the mathematical logos of all created things, one both glorified God and
perfected the Image within oneself. Again mathematics was
measured by its moral and humanistic use.

These firm convictions about the moral and divine structure
of the universe are precisely those which encountered a crisis
during the Renaissance and finally collapsed. Part of the complex reason for this catastrophic collapse no doubt lies in the
inherent instability of the influential Platonic answer to the

question concerning the relation between the active mathe-
matizing mind and the intuitive or receptive mind. This instability is inherent in Platonism because it follows from the
failure of this philosophy to effect an intelligible transition
between ideas and particulars, concepts and individuals. In
addition, there are circumstances surrounding this instability
which are immediately related to its eventually evident weakness.

The very fact that the Platonic views on man's mathematical
perfectibility were expressed by Timaeus in a myth may suggest to some that these views are mere imaginative play.
However, Plato's choice of this mode of expression may also
testify to his conviction that the problem of participation can
be managed only by mythical or poetic discourse. For this kind
of discourse is, or can be, persuasive. And it seemed that the
problem could be managed only by persuasion, itself a means
to participation, rather than by deduction or by regular manipulation of precise concepts, since precise concepts of this kind
were not then available. Indeed, the initial task requires the
setting up of a context in which precise concepts could be
formulated. However, Plato's choice of method and form of discourse indicated that his solution was not unique; otherwise
persuasion would not have been necessary.

As the Demiurge persuaded the cosmic receptacle to receive
and to embody the mathematical harmonies, so Plato persuaded
others. The consequence of his persuasion was to spread the
conviction of a very close relation between the approved uses
of thymos and psyche. If the actively thinking mind is in its
better and more skilled moments a mathematically thinking
mind, and if this kind of clear harmonious thought interprets
and "corrects" the psychic movements and so perfects the man,
then this perfected man thereby becomes an embodied mathematical intellect. Here something like an apotheosis of intellectuality is approached. And here the ideal of rationality
becomes explicit, the ideal which Husserl was later to judge to
be the crowning achievement of civilized man. This kind of conclusion is inevitable if, as Plato seemed to hold, the intellec-

tual means become in this instance identical with the human end. In addition, man is not only identified with his intellect; his intellect is fixed. It has, or should have, just the definite structure attributed to the cosmos. Looked at in this fashion, and judged by hindsight, the Platonic tradition moves without difficulty into the Cartesian one: The ideally developed man is the mathematical physicist.

This Cartesian view also points backward to a weakness or narrowness within this version of Platonism. Is man indeed primarily his intellect? Is his nature fixed so definitely as this cosmic-ethical model suggested? So narrow a determination of the direction of human growth may automatically reject indefinitely many other possibilities dormant within man. These rejected and forgotten possibilities could eventually become menacing. However, the narrowness of this view and its consequences could not be fully appreciated until after they had been accepted and their effects exhibited in life.

Conversely, this aspect of the Platonic tradition points forward to a significant conviction of modernity. If the good man is he whose mind is formed on this mathematical model, then human rationality may eventually seem to be exemplified only in the thinking which most closely resembles mathematics. To be knowable, an object or an event must be translatable into mathematical terms. If so, then Plato's dictum in the *Republic*, "the perfectly real is perfectly knowable" (477A), could be given the seventeenth-century twist: What is perfectly clear to the (mathematical) intellect must be real. Therefrom it was but a small step to conclude that the master intellect would be the master of reality.[30] Thus a path was beaten from the conviction that knowledge is virtue to the axiom that knowledge is power.

[30] I shall often use "intellectual" and derivative terms to refer to the metaphysical conviction that being is intelligible, or more specifically, that being is identical with being as seen, or with being as accessible to the human mind. Subordinate senses of intellectuality are generated by different meanings of mind, by different contexts, or by different and more specific meanings of being, as the sequel will illustrate.

If in consequence of this movement of ideas, the modern world retains the thesis that mathematics is the means to the Good, it retains it in a simplified and uncritical manner. Since the Good is above knowledge, it becomes for many thinkers subjectively determined; and the usual subjective determination, the general desire, is directed toward the control and exploitation of nature by means of applied mathematics. This confidence in the good of mathematical study of nature is a truncated Platonism. It tends to accept for example the technical evaluation of mathematics. A popular belief holds that by training in the mathematical sciences the engineer can design the industrial machinery which, it is supposed, will then produce goods. And inherent in these goods—in gadgets, creature comforts, and laborsaving devices—is the Good for both society and the individual.

This last observation to one side, my point is that the complex relationship of Plato's philosophy to the Western tradition may be seen as reflecting a tension within that same philosophy. This is the tension between Plato the father of science and Plato the philosopher upon man and the Good.

Plato himself, however, sought to restrain discursive thought within a context limited by a myth whose persuasive power was to be maintained, if we recall the *Laws* (738, 799, 967ff), by ritual. Still it is difficult to term the resultant philosophy a myth since it does retain nonmythical and scientific content and functions. Also, as I have already suggested, it is not a theoretical unity, for it contains a nonrationalizable dimension, the gap between imitation and idea, and envisages a nonintellectualized end, the idea of the Good. Just this tension between the two tendencies of this philosophy, preserving the contrast between the thymos and psyche, has lasted till our own times. Its remnants are still perceptible on many levels and in many aspects of Western culture, for instance in some university departmental and faculty organizations where the humanities and the sciences occasionally generate fruitful conflicts but more often merely ignore each other.

It will not be amiss to include here the mention of an old story. The story tells of a man moving down a road—possibly a culture hero moving through history. As he walks down the road, the sides begin to slope away. He moves on and the sides slope even more sharply. Soon each side becomes a sheer cliff dropping away into shadows. And the road, as it winds on, continually becomes more narrow. Finally, the pathway contracts to a razor-sharp edge and the traveller is sliced in two, like Aristophanes' man, and falls down on both sides into the obscure and misty depths.

§5. SOME QUESTIONS

Plato's interpretation of the transition experienced earlier in his time out of an age of poetry and into an age of a more intellectual life developed a tension, as I have tried briefly to show. The mathematical forms encountered on the way up out of the Cave are interpreted as a necessary step toward the Good. However, mathematical forms and the idea of the Good at first appear to be quite different, even incommensurable. A mathematically unreconstructed Platonist may ask: Can the Good, being beyond knowledge, be conceived as an end? Do pursuit of mathematics and of discursive rationality in general constitute the only way to the Good? Are not the mathematical forms and the Good actually identified in Platonism despite their apparent incommensurability? Finally, one may also ask whether "good," like the transcendental notions of being, one, and the like, could not refer to certain pervasive properties of the world—of the Good conceived as the highest Idea, and of other ideas as well—suggesting thus a nonmathematical means of uniting the apparently discrete parts of the Platonic metaphysics. To an extent, we must answer yes to each of these questions. But these answers are not all compatible with each other. We must, therefore, conclude that the combination of mathematics with the Good was an unstable combination whose final synthesis depended upon faith in Timaeus' myth in which we are persuaded to envisage the Good.

Western thought, rightly said to constitute a series of foot-notes to the philosophy of Plato, elaborates, clarifies, often simplifies, or omits parts of this initial datum. Where, however, Plato had left problems problematic, later philosophers often provided definitive answers. Descartes legitimated the hegemony of the mathematical intellect and opened up the possibility of determining the human good by way of changing the world through the instrumentality of the sciences. Hume, the Enlightenment, and their successors in Marxianism and logical positivism carry these trends to their paradoxical conclusions. But Kant, the Romantic tradition, and recent phenomenological philosophy oppose these latter tendencies by seeking to recapture some sense of the distinctiveness of man and his need for internal change. Latterly the function of psychic receptiveness has been recognized and even given a predominant role.

Dealing with these matters, interpreting the character of the actual and desirable relations among the elements of archaic experience may, perhaps, open a philosophical way through the labyrinth of history. But this way is not to be opened all at once. The difficulty which we have witnessed in the Platonic interpretation of archaic experience may be summarized in symbolic form in terms of a pair of crossed lines. This symbol is dual; it resembles not only a cross with its cons of funded religious significance and its reminder of guilt, personal sacrifice, death and rebirth, and the gradual transformation in men from cannibalism to culture, but at the same time it brings to mind a set of Cartesian coordinates whereon the curves of nature may be mapped. In either sense the figure provides a mnemonic device which recalls beliefs about man and nature which in part are as old as the cave drawings of Lascaux and in part as modern as Descartes or Carnap.

The crossed lines, moreover, recall a crossroads or a division of ways within a labyrinth; such a division is offered by the two ways of thought and feeling associated with the two interpretations of archaic experience which were just indicated. They bring us to a crucial point. Is only a single one of these two

interpretations of the crossed lines meaningful? Are both interpretable within a single all-inclusive universe? Or is there some
third way, perhaps a mystical one, which cuts directly through
these complexities? If in fact philosophy does stand in some
manner on the boundary line between myth and science, between poetic inspiration and discursive thinking, then it would
seem to be already implied that both meanings of our symbolic
crossed lines, in their very different ways, need to be taken seriously, and that a desirable function of philosophy is to make a
transition between the two or to include, if possible, both in
one whole interpretative scheme in accordance with the ideal
which animated Plato and might be continued in the humanistic tradition. Certainly we shall not begin by presuppos-
ing the popular eighteenth- and nineteenth-century dogma of
historical progress from myth to science; an equally valid progress may well move in the opposite direction.

Perhaps the issue comes to this: whether men are best advised to seek their chief satisfaction in changing the world,
guided primarily or entirely by the sciences; or whether they
should direct their efforts toward effecting dramatic changes
within themselves. Are the two choices mutually exclusive?
This question points to another: Is man an object within the
world such that he can be understood and predictably and de-
sirably changed by use exclusively of scientific techniques? Or
does he in principle escape inclusion within any science or collection of sciences? Probably, in fact, a selection of either
choice would entail some needful action to be taken with respect to the omitted or minimized alternative. Ignoring such
omitted alternatives is an invitation to catastrophe and tragedy.
The return to archaic experience is a move toward avoiding
such omissions.

II

Descartes: Two Sources of Modern Philosophy

§6. AFTER PLATO

After the crystallization of Greek thought in the Platonic-Aristotelian tradition, the decisive personality in the history of modern Western thought is Descartes. Perhaps, however, the times were more ripe for Descartes than they had been for Plato and accordingly tended to force the Frenchman into a pivotal position. His commanding position stems from the function which his philosophy played in articulating and thus in directing the transition between two doctrines of man and of the cosmos. He rendered the issues clear and successfully transferred persuasive power from the older to the newer doctrine. The degree of his success was perhaps puzzling even to himself. This puzzlement is reflected in the two contrasting kinds of philosophical interest which follow upon his work.

First, Descartes made possible the directions of thought explored by Spinoza and by Hume. Spinoza, seeking to understand the unity holding between the mind and the whole of nature, a unity seemingly compromised by Descartes, projected a study of man as if he were studying lines, points, and solids, as the famous description of *Ethics* (III, preface) has it. But so literal a mathematical interpretation of man was concluded by later philosophers to be a blind alley or to involve a downright misunderstanding of the nature of mathematics, a misunderstanding which Leibniz did much to clarify and to correct. Hume, on the contrary, envisaged the possibility of an empirical study of man just as if he were an object in nature continuous with other objects and hence accessible to scientific explanation, and even control. His study, involving a kind of spatialization of the person, proved to be one side of the wave of the future. The other side of this wave is represented by the second aspect of Descartes's influence. Here Descartes seems to anticipate some of the effects of his epistemological doctrine and to regret them; consequently, and as if in compensation for these effects, his thought also turned in a transcendental direction. In this latter respect he was a forerunner of the tradition which is most closely associated with Kant.

In order to display the transitional function that Cartesian thought played in the filiation of modern philosophy and illustrates in itself, it is needful first to be reminded of the developments in the sciences of that era. These caused Descartes to incline away from the Scholastic-Aristotelian tradition in which he had been reared and within which he despaired of finding the intellectual certainty which his liberated and skeptical age so earnestly desired. It will then be possible to see Descartes's problem and the complex kind of certainty which he reached as well as the dual role which this thought played in determining the subsequent courses of philosophy.

§7. HUMANISM AND SCIENCE

Why did the medieval age disintegrate? Some historians have pointed to science and the scientific method as one of the destructive elements. But if it is true that the disintegrating factor introduced into the medieval intellectual world was the discovery of the scientific method of discovering and formulating possible recurrences in nature and then confirming them by way of controlled and impersonal observation, it should be remembered that this method was not altogether a stranger to the older tradition. Certain of its constitutive elements had

already emerged in Greek philosophy. Likewise, other important elements of this method were not altogether unknown to
Renaissance humanists. These humanists—John Colet, Erasmus,
Henry More, for instance—utilized this method in the service
of Biblical criticism and interpretation.[1] In fact the new method for getting at the sense of ancient texts, as proposed by
Erasmus, first rejected traditional interpretations defended by
theology and then enjoined a remarkably scientific use of
grammatical, linguistic, biographical, and historical knowledge
in order to determine the meaning of the text in question.
However, the humanists' interests remained humanistic; they
were concerned not to discover the mathematical laws of nature
but to determine the meaning of ancient writings through
checking their hypotheses by all the observational means at
their disposal. Accordingly, they laid emphasis not upon use of
the scientific and mathematical intellect as their way to discovery, but upon imagination and memory. And the end which
they sought was not the mastery of nature but the unprejudiced understanding of these writings; their ultimate goal
was the cultivation of the rationality of man by religious and
philosophic study. Their general philosophical position, unlike
Descartes's, is precisely not at odds with an Artistotelian one.
They continued to construe human rationality broadly, according to their Hellenic bias, as inclusive of all the human faculties, imaginative and inspirational, as well as more narrowly
intellectual.

Within limits, it could be said that the seventeenth-century
scientists applied these humanistic techniques to what Galileo
described as the reading of the book of nature. However, the
book of nature was written in the mathematical language; this
difference of language is decisive. Not historical and imaginative techniques therefore, but mathematics and measurement
had to be used by the intellect to decipher this natural notation. Not the imagination, not inspiration, not memory and

[1] See Fredrick Seebohm, *The Oxford Reformers* (New York: Longmans,
1911).

tradition, but the discursive powers of controlled and exact reasoning (thymos) was the decisive mental faculty.[2] A consequence of the decision to depend upon this kind of thinking was the high evaluation of the mathematical intelligence which directed it and a correspondingly lower evaluation of other faculties, imagination and sense, which seemed to resist and even to violate mathematical usage. An analogous reevaluation of the properties of objects and of the cosmos also followed; quantitative properties became more important and more real than qualitative or valuational ones. The issue involved in the application of the scientific method during the seventeenth century may be described as the battle of the giants over the nature of man and of the cosmos. The fate of man—perhaps more accurately, convictions about the nature of that fate—hung in the balance. And moreover, a typically modern use of scientific knowledge began to be envisaged. The fate of man, it was beginning to seem evident, was not so much to cultivate his whole rational nature as it was to dominate the natural world in his own interests by means of a mathematical and objective science. In Descartes's philosophy the possibility and even the necessity of this new fate is established.

The nascent modern science of the cosmos was arrayed against the Aristotelian-Scholastic physics. When the struggle took form within Descartes's philosophy, it initiated the two trends which since have dominated modern philosophy. These two trends are observable in Descartes the militant mechanist, who opened up the context for scientific and naturalistic thought, and in Descartes the nostalgic humanist, who in part anticipated the transcendental turn in philosophy which opposed militant mechanism.

---

[2] From time to time throughout this book I shall continue to make use of the terms "psyche" and "thymos." These terms were explained in Chap. 1 § 3, and used to refer to contrasting mental or spiritual powers. They cannot be defined universally, but they can be given analogous meanings in different contexts.

§8. ANTHROPOMORPHISM AND ITS REJECTION

The Aristotelian concept of the object, like the Platonic, originated with consideration of human artistry and growth. Nature, said Aristotle, is a good artist (*Physics* 199a). It is, thus,
not so much that man is like nature as that nature is like man.
Both are "inner directed." Like man, any object is to be conceived as possessing a material component (that which is to
be developed in the artlike process of coming to maturity) and
a formal component (that which comes to be effective during
the maturing process). Man, then, is a composite substance of
form and matter, and so in principle is any other Aristotelian
object, however specifically different from man it may be. The
motion of any object is some sort of actualization of its material
potentialities in its approach to its immanent end or to its ever
fuller embodiment of its specifically relevant forms. The archetype of the Aristotelian object is the organism moving through
its life history in process of reaching specific self-realization.
Man, too, is such a substance and moves toward his own maturity in a cosmos like himself, his natural home localized on
earth, the center of this cosmos (a unique and definite—if not
especially "high"—position). In this pre-Copernican universe
man is commensurable with his world.

Aristotelians have always held their philosophy to be the
philosophy of common sense *par excellence*. In this context
common sense may be accepted as referring to what has lately
been called the life-world. At the level of lived experience, of
immediate or unreflective engagement in the tasks of living,
fact and value are not yet distinguished. The fact that the
knife edge is sharp and cuts meat is no more basic, no more
real, no more "objective," than the need to cut the meat. One
uses tools just because they are useful instruments for accomplishing the end at hand. The Aristotelian causal analysis renders explicit the elements within this experience; then it extends them to nature. It renders explicit the being of values in
the world in terms of the motion to maturity intrinsic in every

organism and even in the world itself. Each substance is a fact moving to actualize its essential value.

Within this cosmos, composite substances can be seen to be arranged in a continuous hierarchical order of possible perfection or value, leading up to and away from man. It is important so to arrange them, for this order determines man's place in the cosmos, and his place points to his own value and ethical function.

On one side, man is related to inferior substances through a series of souls, or forms of organized bodies, of decreasing complexity and power. On the other side, he is related through a series of souls of continuously increasing power and actuality until the end is reached in the simple and purely actual substance, the final cause of all activity. The dialectical astronomy of Plato was thus filled in by substantial intelligences guiding the Aristotelian spheres along their Ptolemaic cycles and epicycles. And accordingly, man could sense himself at home in this universe within whose continuous chain of beings he was a necessary link.

Up to a point this universe functioned for man, and he for it. To it *nihil humanum est alienum*. Without him there would have been a gap, an imperfection, in the universe. This position in the chain of beings indicated the human function: practical in relation to those substances below it, speculative in relation to those above it. In his practical activity, man imitated his own irrational but rationalizable faculties to their maturity in virtuous action. In his higher theoretical activity, he cultivated the speculative virtues of contemplative wisdom, fixing his intellectual gaze finally upon that which is most perfect, in imitation of the pure activity of the Supreme Being.[3]

Probably life in this universe was rather rich. Substances which men manipulated in their artistry "really" had (or

---

[3] Aristotle is rather cryptic in his account of the active intellect's access to speculative first principles. This access seems to be an intuitive activity of mind (*De Anima* III. 5) and to imitate the eternal thought of the unmoved mover. It may be associated with the activity of psyche as described in the preceding chapter.

could have) the values and qualities which they were experienced as having. There was a difference in the object between maturity and mere potentiality. There was no fact apart from value. Accordingly, man possessed an end which belonged to him by nature and to which he moved in his individual development, not only as he cultivated the moral virtues, but especially as he grew in skill in the contemplation of metaphysical substances. Further, insight into these metaphysical or transcendent substances and into the principles and order of the whole universe provided a defense for moral convictions as well as the goal for human activity, common and individual.

This is the universe which Bertrand Russell with gratuitous condescension has likened to a neat Dutch interior. It is the anthropomorphic world which Descartes, perhaps hesitantly—yet effectively—destroyed. Descartes's rejection of anthropomorphism recalls on more than one count Plato's rejection of poetry: Both philosophers are reluctant in their exclusions, and both allow the hidden return of much of that which they had explicitly excluded.

Of course there were movements on many fronts toward the destruction of the medieval cosmos, not the least of which was the gradual elimination of the effective power of the religious institution which had adopted and "theologized" it. Descartes's philosophy carried the cutting edge of the intellectual attacks on this institution and its tradition and expressed the alternative to it.

These attacks were aimed at liberating man from the beliefs, discipline, and authority of the religious institution and at leaving him finally his own ruler. This freedom, like any other, brought with it a responsibility which awakened anxiety. But other sources of anxiety lay dormant in these attacks. Weakening of the power of the religious institutions incurred also the loss of the source of confidence in the ends and values which ordered human life. Likewise, it incurred the loss of the basis for confidence in human knowledge. The successes of Descartes's attacks upon institutionalized beliefs oriented his search for another, a scientific source of certainty; his successes were also an origin of problems.

The final effect of these attacks was twofold. First, they eliminated the hierarchy of forms which stretched from man to the Supreme Being and led man's theoretical gaze by a continuous route towards a contemplation of pure activity. This elimination proceeded in two stages: (1) by way of the new Copernican astronomy it destroyed the intermediate spheres which had provided an imaginative bridge over the gap between earth and the empyrean; (2) Descartes's denial of the analogy of being was tantamount to the denial of any access to knowledge of the substance of God (*Principles* I, 52). Second, these attacks eliminated the souls which were intermediate between man and the substances composing physical nature.

After the destruction of the Scholastic convictions concerning the substances above and below man, Descartes was faced with the complex task first of rethinking the nature of man, of the divine substance, and of physical substances; and second, of discovering some way for transcending the gaps which were interposed between man and the divine substance on one hand, and between man and physical nature on the other. It is interesting that Descartes conceived these problems partly in terms of a need for a ground of certainty in knowing and partly in terms of a doctrine of substance. He, no more than the greater part of both older and contemporary philosophers, could avoid thinking in inherited molds, just the molds which, in a different guise, he sought to destroy.

Descartes's formula for destruction is controlled skepticism. Skepticism had in part already undermined confidence in the Aristotelian world just mentioned. But the Cartesian skepticism is not the indiscriminate doubting which characterized some Renaissance writing and which Montaigne ascribed to the sickly skeptic. Descartes knows very well where he is going in the first two parts of the *Discourse* as he, like the priestly leader of a chorus, leads his seventeenth-century readers through the labyrinthine intricacies of Scholastic education and culture, in-

dicating the dead ends at each turning but carefully pointing
out the unexplored opening, mathematics. The metaphysical
part IV of the *Discourse* hardly does more than indicate the
viability and certainty of this route to truth. However, parts
V and VI advertise it in a thoroughly modern manner; they lay
out the universe of mathematics-become-objective in a way to
entice the mathematician by its elegant simplicity, the average
mind by its promise to make us "masters and possessors of nature," and the philosopher by suggesting that wisdom and salvation somehow lay that way. It is not until we come to the
Meditations that the full nature and difficulty of the problem
are made evident.

The method of doubt as he explains in his reply to the sixth
objection leads to the diagnosis just indicated; the previous tradition is vitiated by anthropomorphic thinking—the natural
mode of childish thought—and is not removed but powerfully
reinforced by Scholastic philosophy.[4] The Scholastic philosopher, like the child, finds real qualities in nature; he thinks values exist in substances, and he thinks things develop reasonably
or teleologically by their own nature.[5] The doubt of the *Meditations* sweeps all this and more before it. It moves in three
stages. The first stage, rehearsing the skeptical observations of
antiquity, throws doubt upon the reality of appearances: Perhaps all our experiences are illusory; it is logically and perceptually possible, for example, that what seem to be people may be
disguised machines. In the second stage, the figure of a malign
genius allows us to doubt the existence of anything of which

[4] Reply to Objections VI. See *The Philosophical Works of Descartes*, trans.
E. S. Haldane and G. R. T. Ross (2 vols.; reprint edition; New York: Dover
Publications, 1955), II, 251–57. Hereinafter I shall refer to these two volumes
as *Works* I or *Works* II. *Works* II contains the Objections and Replies.

[5] See comments on this point in Etienne Gilson, *Discours de la Méthode,
Texte et Commentaire* (Paris: Vrin, 1925), 199. That Descartes regarded his
philosophy as a refutation of Scholasticism is made clear by his letter to Mersenne
of December 22, 1641, contained in *Oeuvres de Descartes*, ed. Charles Adam
and Paul Tannery (12 vols., Paris: Cerf, 1897–1910), III, 464 *sq.*, hereinafter
cited as *Oeuvres*. See also Alexandre Koyré, *Entretiens sur Descartes* (New York:
Brentano, 1944), Chap. 2; and Etienne Gilson, *Etudes sur le Rôle de la Pensée
Médiévale dans la Formation du Système Cartesian* (Paris: Vrin, 1930).

we previously were confident (even the disguised machines may be figments of a dream). And finally, the hyperbolical doubt, expressed in terms of a deceiving deity, suggests the possibility that there is a sense in which even the truths of mathematics are contingent; even the rationality of the universe, mechanical or any other, may seem to be open to suspicion. Can the doubt really proceed to this third stage? A reservation must surely be made: Descartes knows very well where he is going; he knows what doubt is, and he has sufficient grasp on the nature of knowledge to recognize that he does not possess it. He always knows that in principle all the things which we conceive clearly and distinctly are true in the very way in which we think them (Synopsis of the *Meditations*, *Works* I, 140). The problem is to know just what those things are which we conceive in this manner. He must admit, for instance, that the memory of a clear and distinct idea is not identical with that idea itself.

The knowledge of which he is in doubt is absolute knowledge; this is the knowledge whose truth depends upon nothing outside the evidences accessible to the knower and which, therefore, is independent of revelation or of its guardian institution. Still, the means by which he persuades himself of deficiency in this regard have seemed to many philosophers to be last resorts. Although the skeptical doubt may be healthy enough, nevertheless, the malign genius, who may bring it about that nothing exists, is surely an exaggerated hypothesis. But especially the deceiving deity, who may poison all wells, appears to bring all possibility of rationality into question. Why is Descartes persuaded that he must go to these extremes? The answer to this question will, I think, bring more clearly into focus the nature of the Cartesian quest. It will bring into evidence the character of the certainty which this quest envisaged and which alone would put an end to doubt. Also it will emphasize the ambiguous character of this certainty, and perhaps the ambiguous character of Descartes's whole philosophy.

§9. THE PROBLEM OF CERTAINTY

We may begin by wondering why the doctrine developed in the *Regulae* was not sufficient to meet Descartes's philosophic requirements. Why did he feel the need to elaborate the doctrines of the *Discourse* and the *Meditations*? For consider what in fact had been accomplished in the *Regulae*.

In the *Regulae* the basic elements of the method already used with such dramatic success by Galileo were clearly set forth and generalized. Descartes saw that questions involved in the application of mathematics to problems of natural philosophy were questions concerning order and measure. The ideal clarity of mathematics, so he argued, was represented best in ordered series of numbers, series where the same ordering relation was continually repeated, so that understanding the relation holding between two easily grasped numbers of the series led to understanding the whole infinite series. Descartes's example is the series 3, 6, 12, 24. . . .

The next step is to observe that upon selecting a standard unit of measure, then lengths and geometrical shapes could be expressed analogously as series. Also the necessary operations —addition, subtraction, multiplication, and division—could be expressed by appropriate operations on simple geometrical figures and represented in the literal notation of a generalized arithmetic. Thus, for example, the problem of determining the square root of a number could be expressed as the simpler problem of determining the mean proportion between unity, or the measure, and the given number (in algebraic notation, it requires finding x in $1 : x : : x : a^2$).

Then a crucial step is taken in Rule XII by the assumption that "the infinitude of curves suffices to express all the differences in sensible things" (*Works* I, 37). This is to say that mathematics is sufficient for the exact description of all the objects constituting nature. In the *Regulae* Descartes used for illustration the mathematical description of harmoniously vibrating strings (Rule XIII in *Works* I, 49f); the numbers representing the ratio of the measurements would turn out to be a selection from a simply ordered series of ratios. In addition the essays following the *Discourse* offer other and more elaborate illustrations. For instance the second book of the *Geometrie* shows that many "mechanical curves" (i.e., curves drawn by suitably constructed machines) could be precisely described by the new mathematics, expressing thus in a completely general form the law of the machine. And another essay in this remarkable collection proceeded to prove mathematically that a machine constructed to make parabolic lenses actually did produce lenses having parabolic properties.[6] Were these achievements not sufficient to show that the claims made for the power of the mathematical method were substantiated in significant ways and could reasonably be expected to be substantiated even further? Surely, in a more thorough way than Galileo ever supposed, "the door is now opened for the first time to a new method fraught with numerous and wonderful results."[7] Why, then, the continued longing for a still further certainty?

A reasonable supposition is that Descartes's failure to complete the *Regulae* arose from his growing recognition of the subtleties involved in the problem of certainty. How could he be sure that his thought could bridge the gap between the mathematical and the physical world? In the first place, only mathematical objects, numbers, figures, quantities, or other ideas like these are intuited or known directly. In the *Regulae* (Rule XII) Descartes seemed at first to believe that nongeometric and nonalgebraic objects—those which could enter into cause-effect relations—also possessed simple natures that could be directly intuited and understood mathematically (or quasi-mathematically). But the doctrine of simple natures was never fully developed and was later dropped. Descartes's conviction

[6] *Oeuvres* VI, 211–28.

[7] *Dialogues Concerning Two New Sciences*, trans. Henry Crew and Alfonso de Salvio (New York: Macmillan, 1914), 234.

grew that however certain mathematics might be in itself, there was no *mathematical* reason for the conviction that in principle the infinitude of mathematical curves would suffice to account for all the differences of sensible things. The certainty of his knowledge of the external sensible world, in other words, could not immediately be seen to be the same as the certainty of his knowledge of mathematics. In *Discourse* II he observed that algebra embraced "only matters the most abstract, such as appear to have no actual use" (*Works* I, 91), and in *Discourse* IV he noted that in the demonstrations of geometry there was nothing at all "to assure me of the existence of their object" (*ibid.*, 103). The same point is reiterated elsewhere, for instance in *Meditation* I (*Works* I, 147) and *Meditation* V (*Works* I, 179f).[8] In general, the external world is not immediately known with mathematical clarity.

The requisite, therefore, was some means for rendering acceptable and persuasive the conviction which lay behind the *mathesis generalis*: This is the conviction that there does exist a possible correspondence between the timeless necessities of mathematics and the essential permanent properties of the objects in the existent world and that, moreover, this correspondence could come to be known in particular instances. There must be some intermediate faculty or function, then, which would provide for translations back and forth between the intellectual certainties of mathematics and the physical world. Thus Descartes first envisaged a solution to the transcendental problem by discovering an intermediary bridgelike faculty or function which would connect the mind with its object. However, Descartes's selection of the faculty of sense and imagination (Cf. *Meditation* VI, *Works* I, 186, 191) to perform this bridge-

---

[8] Also, Descartes's view that his mechanical philosophy is only an hypothesis and that the sciences are "romances about nature" are further conclusions from this same line of thought. See my article "Descartes' Revision of the Cartesian Dualism," *Philosophy Quarterly*, VII (1957), 249–54, where it is argued that the sciences of nature have only an "as-if" status for Descartes. Another view is advocated by Profesor R. H. Popkin in *The History of Skepticism* (New York: Harper and Row, Harper Torchbooks), 151 ff.

like function immediately led to a problem from which only the divine certification could extricate him.

The difficulty was that initially the doubt had pointed directly to the separation between clear and distinct ideas and the world as represented. Furthermore, this separation occurred just because memory, imagination, and sense were of themselves anything but clear and distinct. Indeed, Descartes recognized in them the faculties upon which Scholastic philosophy had relied and had been led to produce, in consequence, an anthropomorphic philosophy which deceived and continued to deceive the whole of the humanist and theological world. Thus the literary devices of Descartes's opposing himself—hero of the nascent modern world—to the malign genius and to the deceiving deity resolve into the opposition between the mathematical intellect and its possibly insubordinate aids—memory, imagination, and sense. Descartes understood the problem as requiring him not to eliminate but to reevaluate these aids and their possible subordination to the intellect. There would then follow the practical problem of disciplining them to this subservience.

The problem of certainty, therefore, led Descartes to seek to discover a clear and distinct perception of the appropriate unity of the subordinate mental faculties and the intellect. This unity should guarantee the possibility of transition between mathematical ideas and perceptual experience of individual objects. The actual resolution of the problem moved by way of the cogito and the demonstration or intuitive grasp of the existence and nondeceiving nature of God. The first step in the transference of the certainty of mathematics to knowledge of the object-world was to be accomplished through the mediation of self-certainty. Eventually it was to be concluded that the objectivity of the object—its essential being—is identical with the clarity of its representation to the intellect. In other words, being, for Descartes, is not merely intelligible; it is mathematically intelligible being. And the certainty of this identification is to be found in the very source of Reason itself.

§ 10.   THE COGITO

The cogito is in part a reflection upon the way in which the knowing self is related to its knowledge—for example, to its supposed representation of the world. Primarily, however, it is a reflection upon the apprehension and nature of the self.

Of late there has been a spate of writing about Descartes's soliloquy of the self about itself, but these recent reflections are not of much use for our purposes since the typical modern concern with the cogito is with its grammar and logic. The questions are debated whether it is proved or not, whether it is an analytic or a synthetic proposition, whether its denial is a self-contradiction or not, whether it is a performative utterance or some other sort of utterance, and the like. Although these problems may be interesting in themselves, many of them scarcely advance our understanding of the world—our world—which received its basic definitive form from Descartes's beginning and from later Cartesian workmanship. The debate about these problems presents an exercise in the achievement of clarity and is an exemplification of the Cartesian spirit in philosophy. Since, however, our task is to understand this tradition rather than to continue it, let us seek to determine the function which the cogito, whatever its grammar, performed in Descartes's philosophy.

It is important, I believe, to see that the cogito has a dual function; it is at once epistemological and ontological. These two functions of the cogito correspond closely with the two sides of Descartes's whole outlook, which turns forward to the modern world and yet, despite its rejection of Scholasticism, harks nostalgically back to the medieval.

We have seen that the physical or external world is ultimately unknowable by way of mathematics taken alone, for knowledge of mathematics is the work of the intellect, and the only mode of access to the external world is through sense and imagination. But imagination and sense lack the character of clarity and distinctness by which the intellect can recognize truth.

Thus the essential of the method must lead to the discovery of a connecting link between the intellect and common experience (the contents of memory, of imagination, and of sense). The outcome of this search should be a certification of some of the uses of the lesser faculties of the mind.

For a philosopher engaged in aiding and interpreting the transition out of the medieval and into the modern world, the appropriate source of certainty concerning the nature and authority of this connecting link could be nothing less than God, the origin of the natural light of the intellect. The way to the recognition of this certainty could only be by way of some belief. This belief or proposition should be accessible to the man of common understanding—an inhabitant of the Scholastic or the skeptical world of the Renaissance—and also to any being possessed of the natural light. There was at least one such proposition whose meaning could be made intelligible to any man and whose meaning would also entail its acceptance as true (i.e., whose meaning would be or would supply its own evidence). This proposition is the *Cogito sum* of *Meditation* II. It is interpreted in Replies to *Objections* II as "I, while I think, exist" (*Works* II, 48).

The cogito is particularly apt for performing this connecting function, since the elements which enter into it — thought and existence—are prereflectively known to all men, Descartes believed (*Works* II, 241). Of course at this prereflective level, thought is obscure, childlike, and confused; it tends to the anthropomorphism which he combated. Nevertheless, he was confident that such thoughts are susceptible of reflective clarification. The reflective recognition that "to think is to exist" represents such a clarification. It bears the mark of truth and has no need for being guaranteed by any other principle. Its certainty is, for instance, independent of knowledge of objects; it is also independent of other philosophical or theological premises. As Descartes pointed out to those who supposed he was arguing in a circle, "he who says 'I think, hence I am, or exist' does not deduce existence from thought by a syllogism, but, by a simple act of mental vision recognizes it as if it were a thing known *per se*." [9] To think, then, *is* to be self-aware. The immediacy of this self-recognition does not require any further verification. The guaranteeing of the truth of the cogito by God is required only for the memory of this act of mental self-vision (*Meditation* V, *Works* I, 183f).

Now, the importance of the cogito lies in the two meanings assigned it. First, as self-certainty, it is the archetypal form of certainty. Second, as self-consciousness, it is the exemplary nonobjective being.

Consider that the self-conscious character of the self invites and enables a further investigation into the nature of the self (see *Meditation* II). This inquiry is a crucial one in the eradication of anthropomorphism. For anthropomorphism is the confusion of self with that which is not the self. Since anthropomorphism is the inadvertent attribution to body of that which belongs to soul, then the first philosophic task must be the clear identification of the nature of the self. Only after this identification has been made can body be completely distinguished from soul. Reflection on the cogito thus offers a negative definition of objects, objects being the sort of thing of which thought or consciousness is in no way predicable. Consequently, the cogito marks the beginning of the path leading from ordinary obscure experience to clear and distinct thought about objects purged of anthropomorphisms. And thus also, certainty about the self, its existence and nature, is prior to certainty about objects. As Descartes wrote to Mersenne, "It is impossible that we could ever think of anything unless we should have an idea of our own soul at the same moment as a thing (*une chose*) able to think about everything of which we do think." [10] In

----

[9] *Works* II, 38. He also remarked in a letter to the Marquis of Newcastle, in March or April of 1648, that this cogito "is a proof of the capacity of our souls to receive intuitive knowledge from God." See *Oeuvres* V, 138. The functioning of psyche is to be recognized in such an intuition.

[10] Descartes, letter of July, 1641, *Oeuvres* III, 394. See also *Principles* I, 12.

short, consciousness of anything is always and primarily self-consciousness, and this self-consciousness is just what in principle fails ever to characterize objects.

This self-consciousness, likewise, is that by reason of which the self-certainty expressed in the *cogito sum* is recognized. And this same self-certainty—this clarity and distinctness of the self-affirmation—is the first and most characteristic mark of truth. Henceforth, the certainty of anything is regarded as a modification of this primary self-certainty. Thus the further development of this view lies in discovering ways of extending this basic certainty to the apprehension of other things.

Descartes, pursuing further reflections on the nature of the self, moved quickly to the conclusion that the soul is substantial —a *res cogitans* (*Meditation* II, *Works* I, 152f). This is an ontological decision, and a fateful one. For, in identifying the soul as a substance, it inevitably came to be closely associated with physical substance, just that from which Descartes was at the same time anxiously concerned to separate it. This decision is also fateful in that the operation of the soul, its *cogitans*, is understood as perfectly clear and distinct thought. Such thinking is the very being of the soul and provides a prior determination of the kind of objects which the soul can be related to and know. We shall return to these ontological aspects of the cogito in a later section.

From this point on, the study of Descartes requires two levels of interpretation, one emphasizing the *cogito*, the other emphasizing the *sum* or the *res cogitans*—the one primarily epistemological, the other primarily ontological. This dual face of the cogito reflects Descartes's own division of mind, at once enthusiastically anticipating the new world of science and at the same time fearful of its consequences. We may imagine the cogito as a sort of gateway which unites the two worlds; or perhaps it is a ritualistic pronouncement (in this way a "performative utterance") which officially made of Descartes a modern man; likewise, it converted the old world, at least partly, into the new.

§11.   THE EPISTEMIC FUNCTION OF THE COGITO AND THE
TRANSCENDENTAL PROBLEM

In its most obvious and usual sense, the cogito is taken as the
incontrovertible self-certainty since it offers evidence for its
truth upon every occasion either of its assertion or of its denial.
Thus its denial might be termed "pragmatically self-refuting." [11]
A person must, in fact, exist whether he thinks he exists, or
whether he asserts that he does not exist. The self-certainty of
the proposition turns upon its being asserted. As a proposition,
its being what it is depends upon the being of mind; given the
asserted proposition, then, the existence of mind is necessary.
The proposition points to this necessity (its grammatical or
logical form is probably of slight philosophical importance).
Now the ontological dependence of this proposition upon the
consciousness that thinks it is the analogon of the relation of all
representations to the mind. This ontological relation, to which
we must return in the next section, is the basis for the epistemological one.

For the present we shall be concerned to consider first the
basic certainty (certainty about the existence of the thinker)
and its explication either by subsequent intuitions (as in the
intuition of the existence of God) or else by its application in
subsequent judgments concerning existence and existent objects. This latter is the line of thought from which the transcendental problem emerges in its most frustrating form.

To develop the epistemological value of the first truth,
Descartes moves in *Meditation* III to assert that the cogito bears
the mark of truth—clarity and distinctness—which may thereupon be used as a criterion for detecting the truth of still other
propositions. In the same *Meditation* the criterion is put to
work to detect the truth of the affirmation of the intuition of the
existence of a nondeceiving deity. This latter—which I shall
call the metaphysical principle—is in turn put to work in the
last three meditations to determine the nature of falsity and to

[11] John Passmore, *Philosophical Reasoning* (New York: Scribner, 1961),
60–64.

validate, within appropriate limitations, the use of memory, imagination, and sense in securing true representations or knowledge of the external world.

One of the crucial consequences of this interpretation is indicated in *Meditation* IV which treats of the will and of its infinite reach and of the possibility of restraining its affirmations to that which the intellect sees clearly and distinctly to be true. The important consequence is that an intellectual discipline of the will is indicated; this is a scientific discipline which will restrain all affirmations, whether pertaining to recollection or to imaginative or sensuous perception, to just those assertions which the intellect sees separately, distinctly, and with mathematical clarity to be true. Those alone would certainly be certified by the Divine Perfection since "it is self-contradictory that men should be deceived by God." [12]

In *Meditation* V the metaphysical principle is put to work to certify to the validity of the memory of clear and distinct ideas. Then in *Meditation* VI the crucial step is taken. This step shows that through sense and imagination, which represent external objects to us, truth about the external world can be perceived. But this truth is not exactly what the senses report. For after the contents of sense and imagination have been submitted to criticism by the standard of truth, the true contents are limited to what can be clearly and distinctly perceived—that is, only to "the things which speaking generally, are comprehended in the object of pure mathematics" (*Meditation* VI, *Works* I, 191). Consequently, Descartes could say, "Toute ma physique n'est autre chose que géométrie." [13] It is also to be recalled that everything which is not mind but is di-

[12] Replies to Objections VI, in *Works* II, 245; and Descartes writes to Gibieuf that if God were a deceiver, then "we would have no rule to assure us of the truth" (letter of January 19, 1642, *Oeuvres* III, 478).

[13] Descartes to Mersenne, July 27, 1638, *Oeuvres* II, 268. Thus mathematically disciplined perception is the opening to truth about the world. But of itself, perception is only "obscure idea"; that is, perception and conception are continuous. Likewise, they are continuous for the British empiricists, only the latter tended to see the concept as a "faded copy." This continuity of sense and concept was not broken until Kant broke it.

visible and hence is external to mind is the proper object or referent of physics (*Works* I, 196). Consequently, all being which is not mind is defined by its relation to mind, and the mark of reality is mathematical clarity and distinctness.[14] In this way, the universe of knowable (or real) objects is limited a priori to mathematically knowable objects. Almost in a single stroke we are confronted with the projection of the mathematical mind. This projection constituted the world understood as a reified mathematical machine; it was to run a most dramatic and fateful course during the next few centuries.

This is the world known ahead of time to be submitted to exact laws. Disciplined experience in this world can provide through techniques of measurement exact illustrations of these laws. And although it will only gradually be realized, experimentation now becomes possible (experimentation being the design of a course of experience which will provide confirming or disconfirming evidence for a hypothetical law). Science in the specifically modern sense is now and for the first time possible.

If, now, the physical world is the one which is presented to man's perception (and this is the Aristotelian world), then Descartes's *Le Monde* of mechanics, like Newton's universe of causally interacting masses, is known only indirectly, only as "re-presented"; it is inferred, not perceived. Thus it is physical only in a borrowed sense. Its real objects are not substances like man, having various but definite potentialities of development toward their maturity. Rather they are singular bits of extension, significant only as quantified. These mathematically interrelated singulars make up the world which is the object of knowledge. The new physics is knowledge of a new world which is beyond the physical or perceptible world. The meaning of the term "physical" has undergone a significant shift. Thus, in

[14] This view, that the physical object is defined by way of its relation to the mind, is sometimes referred to as "anthropocentrism." See A. G. A. Balz, *Descartes and the Modern Mind* (New Haven: Yale University Press, 1952). Thus Descartes's philosophy effects the transition from anthropomorphism to anthropocentrism.

a mixture of traditional and modern terms, it is correct to say that the effect of Descartes's philosophy was to identify physics with a metaphysics.

Galileo had said that nature is like a book written in the mathematical language; Descartes was now saying that the natural world is nothing more than what is written in that language. It can be open to no other interpretation. Here we are given the deanthropomorphized world of extension—of fact purged of the qualities, values, and the movements toward ends which the undisciplined minds of children and Aristotelian philosophers had projected upon it. This world may be valued by man, for instance, as an object worth study. But in itself this new world is merely extension diversified by figure and movement (movement now being defined as translation from place to place). It can no more be measured in terms of value than values can be measured by a unit of length. The extended world of objects is outside consciousness. Only knowledge, divinely certified representations of it, is in consciousness. Thus the world is outside human value; hence its study ought, as it was expressed later, to be value-free.

The cogito in its epistemological function is the entryway to this Cartesian universe where the knowing subject is known independently of, and set sharply off against, the reified mathematical mechanism which is to be objectively known. To achieve scientific certainty, the intellect by way of the will disciplines memory, imagination, and sense to the mathematical usage. May we think of the relation of the intellect to its aids as something like the relation within scientific academies (which Descartes was so interested in establishing) between their heads and their subordinate members and assistant workers? Perhaps this analogy holds better with respect to the scientific élite which Saint-Simon and Auguste Comte later imagined to discipline, organize, and rule the masses in the wholly scientized society. Descartes, however, still remained within the tradition of classical individualism and saw in the mathematical-intellectual discipline only the means of achieving the knowledge and mastery over objective nature (nature being understood to include animal and human bodies), while men as the knowing subjects remained strictly outside the realm of mathematicized material substance. Men thus do not come within the initially defined purview of Cartesian natural science. They do not belong within the Copernican-physical world.

Of course, giving the self a status outside physical nature meant that the self lived within a world quite unlike and beyond itself, a dead, valueless, mechanically determined world. It is, moreover, true that this external world is not even knowable in itself but is knowable only as a guaranteed representation. In this respect, also, it was all the more remote. Philosophers following Descartes, and indeed Descartes himself, were quick to sense this difference between the self and the world as an alienation. That is, it was difficult to live in—or reflectively, to suppose that one lived within—a value-free mechanism. The imagination seemed to resist this mathematical determination. For everyday experience has to do with things understood and perceived as tools; it has to do with having or lacking use-values of various kinds, with having or lacking aesthetic, moral, and other values. Thus the intellectualized metaphysical world-as-machine seemed to be impractically remote from the world which men of common sense spontaneously believed themselves to inhabit. The conviction, then, that one "really" does live, despite appearances, in a valueless mechanism could be accepted only at the cost of resigning oneself to a sense of alienation, of remoteness, or of natural exile, from the more human world of value-laden appearances where significant choices might be made. This radical disconnection of the self from the universe of objects, even from its own body, is a general expression of the form which the transcendental problem has assumed in modern times.

The succession of efforts to unify what had thus been put asunder and to cure the sense of alienation either by absorbing man within the mechanical world or by discovering the latter within man need not detain us at the moment. The interesting point is that Descartes himself seemed to be aroused to anxiety by the unresolvability of the transcendental problem within this context and by the alienating effect of this unresolvability. At any rate, the cogito was also given another function that may be interpreted as moving toward another kind of understanding of man's relation with the new world. This is the cogito's ontological function. Let us consider this ontological aspect of Descartes's philosophy, remembering that it was developed not in separation from the epistemology to which we have just attended, but step by step along with it.

§ 12.   THE COGITO ONTOLOGICALLY OR TRANSCENDENTALLY
CONSIDERED

As the cogito is the means for passing from doubt to mathematical certainty, so it is the entryway from ignorance of man's being and of his situation to an understanding of these. Descartes wrote Claude Clerselier, the metaphysician, that just as the principle of contradiction is a first principle in regard to essences, so the cogito is a first principle in relation to being; it is ontological. The doubt preceded the *cogito*, and the latter led immediately to the *sum*, which affirmed the being of the self as a thinking thing—a *res cogitans*—or so Descartes interpreted it in *Meditation* II.

What are the consequences for man of redefining himself in this fashion? But first let us ask, what is this thinking thing? Descartes's answer is to elaborate man's ontological situation. We have seen that the *res cogitans* can reflect the world, and ought to reflect it truly, or mathematically. We have also seen that mathematical thought alone can lead to no necessary conclusions about the external world. And thus it is that Descartes must discover within his own limited thought or being the evidence for a more inclusive Being and rationality that will bring him into such relationship as is possible with the world which his own mathematical thinking cannot touch except in representation or image. This evidence is the idea of an infinite Being which is also the principle of truth. Thus Descartes, as he expresses the matter, is aware of his difference from nothing; he exists, at least, whenever he pronounces the cogito. Also at the conclusion of *Meditation* VI, he comes to be aware of the radical distinction between his essential self—intellect together with its aids—and the objective world. Finally, his dependence, his imperfection, and his innate idea of infinite perfection bring him to recognition of his own finitude and dependence upon the infinite Being. His full definition of himself, then, is the thinking thing having an idea of the infinitely perfect Being (*Meditation* III, *Works* I, 166, 170). And for Descartes, this idea of infinity is, I think, the presence of Being itself to the mind.

Descartes has thus placed himself within what we may call, in order to indicate a relation of the *Meditations* to the *Regulae*, the ontological series. At the same time this ontological series is unlike the mathematical one in that the elements which compose it are incommensurable with each other (see note 18 below). For the ontological series contains the infinitely perfect Being, the finite thinking being, the finite material being, and it ends with nothing. (I should say this series "apparently" contains the finite thinking and extended substances, for Descartes's thought is significantly indecisive on this matter. It might be more correct to say that it contains man, the substance composed of soul and body. This point will be elaborated later.)

At the present, it is important to observe that the ontological series is more basic and independent in comparison with the epistemological line of thought. The latter course of thought moves from the undeniableness of the *cogito sum* through the existence of a nondeceiving deity, through the disciplined adoption of memory, imagination, and sense, and finally to the recognition of a purged and mathematical external world as the object represented to the intellect by the purged imagination. The two lines of thinking—ontological and epistemological—intersect at their point of origin, which is infinite and nondeceiving Being. This common origin is also the guarantee of their harmony. The idea of infinity, as Descartes points out in *Meditation* III (*Works* I, 166), is the beginning point of his philosophy. Later he developed more explicitly the conviction that the will of God is also the source of essence as well as of the existent world (cf. *Works* II, 226, 250f). Thus it is only in relation to the Infinite Being that the thinking being has or can determine that he has an object which he can think about. The external world, unaccessible and unknowable in itself, is accessible only as a guaranteed mathematical representation in the mind. Thus the ontological series underlies or renders the epistemological series possible. In this respect the ontological series performs a function sometimes called transcendental. As man is not God but an image of God and is specified in his very being by possession of the innate idea or representation of God, so his world is not created by him but is re-created or re-presented (via objective ideas). The world as known depends upon this function of consciousness as re-presenting truly. The ontological series is the transcendental foundation of the epistemological one. Man's being as essentially re-presenting (thinking) renders possible the shift back and forth between the world presented (or real) and the world re-presented (or known).

An extremely important consequence follows from this way of viewing the being of the self (soul) and its relation to other beings. Descartes the medieval judged both the self and matter to be substantial; Descartes the modern discovered the material world to be known as represented mathematically or lawfully to the intellect. What is the relation between these two observations?

Material and mental substances exist independently (*Works* II, 101), both have essential properties, and both may undergo modifications (*Principles* I, 51–57). Here their similarity ends. Mental substance is essentially thought; its modes are individual thoughts or representations. And the world is known only by way of such representations; the world as known is thus a modification of thought; we might call it experience. It can easily be seen, anticipating later developments, that if convictions concerning God and his certification of clear and distinct representations be dropped, the world as known takes on a curious aspect. It becomes subjective and arbitrary—unless perchance it be accepted without question as given, or unless perchance subjectivity itself should come to be seen to have a transcendental function.

Material substance is essentially extended; that is, its parts are mutually external to each other. Having this property, they then can be close to or far from each other, be quantitatively equal or unequal to each other, and be diversified by still other quantitative properties and by figure and motion. Thus the possible changes of quantity and of figure and motion are inherent in extension; their laws are its laws, and the objective of physics or mechanics is the discovery of true representations of these laws. Finally, "the laws of mechanics . . . are identical with those of nature" (*Discourse* V, *Works* I, 115). The relation of these laws to material nature is not to be conceived on the organic analogy of Aristotelian form to matter, but rather on the analogy of the mathematical description of a mechanism to the machine itself.

The only Aristotelian-like composition of form and matter which remains in Descartes's universe is the composite substance, man himself (*Works* II, 99, 102, 242). And this is just the substance which cannot be represented clearly to the intellect. Let us put aside the ridiculous and overworked hypothesis of the pineal gland mentioned in the *Passions* (and elsewhere) and consider Descartes's remarks on the composite substance which he wrote to Princess Elizabeth. He says, "It does not appear to me that the human mind is capable of conceiving quite distinctly and at the same time both the distinction between the soul and the body and also their union, since to this end the mind must conceive them both as a single thing and also conceive them together as two things, which is a contradiction (*ce qui se contrarie*)." [15] The solution to this

---

[15] Letter of June 28, 1643, *Oeuvres* III, 693f. Composite substance is mentioned briefly elsewhere (e.g., *Works* I, 244, 437; II, 99, 101, 242).

difficulty which he advanced in this same letter is that the union of mind and body is experienced in the activities of everyday life when one is not philosophizing, but it cannot be conceived clearly. Surely this is an embarrassing admission for a rationalist to have to make.

Still it is even more embarrassing to attempt clearly to describe any way in which the soul might affect or be affected by material substance. For at any point of contact between the two, the soul would have to be extended; but to acquire this property, it would have to undergo an essential change and thus would lose the distinctive being of soul. The point is that Descartes recognized that rigorous adherence to the ideal of mathematical clarity entailed the complete separation of soul from body; nevertheless, he seemed to be willing upon some occasions to compromise this ideal rather than to deny the unity of man.[16] Here in this tentatively asserted doctrine of man who is not known in a mathematical manner but who is nevertheless somehow apprehended as being a unity connecting the epistemological subject and object, we observe, I suggest, a hint of the "transcendental turn" in philosophy which was to preoccupy philosophers later in the Kantian tradition.

The ambiguities in the notion of person which we have indicated suggest that this notion must be taken over twice in Descartes's philosophy. First, the person is the soul—the essential self or mental substance which represents itself to itself and the material world to itself but is essentially distinct from that world. Second, the person is the man; as such he occupies an ambiguous status in the ontological series, being a substance composed of both soul and body. Hence the person as man is not clearly intelligible, but at the same time he is imagined to act and to be affected by the world, and thus he points to a possible—though here unexploited—solution to the transcendental problem.

---

[16] A later admirer of Descartes, Edmund Husserl, was in a somewhat similar manner to be faced with the necessity of modifying his rational ideal or else of denying, not the unity of the self, but the intelligibility of the presence of other selves. See § 36 below.

Another obscurity in this doctrine of man, one to which his activity in the world refers, is his value involvement. The ontological series and its situating of man will help to some degree in clarifying this obscurity.

The originating Being of the ontological series, God, is also the infinitely perfect Being. Indeed, Descartes, like medieval theologians, tended to identify Being and Good in God. Value, or goodness, excluded from the external world of objects, existed superlatively in the Supreme Being. Moreover, degrees of reality (as represented, for instance, to the mind by the objective function of ideas) are also degrees of perfection or value (*Meditation* III, *Works* I, 162). This point enters indispensably into the proofs of the existence of God in *Meditations* III and V, for only as a consequence of his supreme perfection can God be known to be either the adequate cause of our idea of supreme perfection or the Being who has all attributes, including existence. Good, thus, is everywhere proportional to being, and thus the ontological series is also a hierarchy of values. Is Descartes, then, in conflict with himself when he concludes that the external world, being mathematical in nature, consequently is, in the modern phrase, value-free? If the ontological series is also an order of value, and if material substance has an ontological dimension, then does not material substance have a value character?

The phrase "value-free" is ambiguous at best. It must be understood in this context to refer to the absence of known purpose and thus of value within the mechanism in relation to man. God may impose ends upon the mechanism, but these are past man's finding out (*Meditation* IV, *Works* I, 173; *Principles* I § 28). Man also may impose his ends upon it; in fact he may come to master it and to use it for the general good, in particular for the advancement of a mechanical medicine and for morals. These human uses and values, however, are not part of the object world; they come into it from the self, and the self, it must be recalled, is external to this world. Human values are merely imposed upon the object-world. However, a mechanical

world invested with human value would seem to be just as
difficult to understand clearly and distinctly as is the body in
substantial composition with a soul. Nevertheless, relying upon
the classical side of Descartes, one might still argue that human
values are not on this account merely arbitrary. For value is
everywhere correlative to being. Consequently, the uses to
which he puts objects and inventions, even the world itself, are
or ought to be a function of the kind of rational being which he
himself is—a conclusion which Descartes's Stoic moral views
included (*Passions* I § 50; also *Works* II, 138, 148). Thus the
separation between fact and value which Descartes's epistemological philosophy seeks to render legitimate and current is in
some measure balanced by the consequences of his ontology
which reunites them primarily in God and secondarily in man.
Descartes is not the thoroughgoing dualist of the later Cartesian
tradition. Does, however, the Cartesian philosophy ever offer a
cure for the sense of loss felt by some men upon their translation to an ambiguous cosmos whose objective physical character is independent of them but whose value is dependent
upon them? Has Descartes's inclusion of men upon the ontological scene compensated for the elimination of men from the
physical one?

§ 13.   THE SENSE OF THE CARTESIAN PHILOSOPHY

Attention to the two facets of the cogito has been especially
invited because it seems probable that the meaning of Cartesianism for philosophy may emerge if this curious double function can be understood and appropriately evaluated. It has
been said that the infertile side of Descartes's influence has been
the dualism of matter and mind which has so plagued
philosophers; yet the fertile aspect of this influence has been the
"Cartesian spirit"—the uncompromising pursuit of clarity and
distinctness in all phases of life and thought—a spirit kept alive
in scientific rather than in philosophic and humanistic pursuits.
I cannot agree with this judgment. The scientific enterprise
must presuppose the distinction of the knowing subject from a

deanthropomorphized object; and the exclusively scientific spirit chooses to pursue only one of the philosophic problems— the physical one—to which this dualism points. For just this reason a further consideration of the mind-body dualism may offer an important clue to an understanding of the one-sided character of modern times. Surely the modern world is Cartesian through and through in its pursuit of more and more clear and distinct ideas about a world mathematically understood and in its devotion to the achievement of intellectual and technical mastery over nature. But the ontological aspect of Descartes, representing a lingering attachment to the humanistic and classic tradition, an attachment which persists even in the face of ambiguity, ought not to be discounted. Let us consider this allegiance to the classic tradition and its significance.

For this purpose, it is needful to emphasize the seriousness which Descartes attached to the systematic doubt of *Meditation* I. He recommended that several months be given over to its study. Recall also the suggestion in this *Meditation* that nothing might be as it seemed, that life was like a dream, that one's own body might be imaginary, that other people might be machines, that humanistic learning could be illusory, that nothing exists, that God is a fable. The strange fact is that Descartes felt many of these symptoms in a very intense and personal fashion, as he indicates in a series of letters to Balzac.[17] One is inevitably led to suspect some sort of mental illness in Descartes. What might its philosophical significance be? Evidently the medieval-humanistic world in which he had been reared had offered him only disappointment. Skepticism had undermined it, and his own systematic doubt merely dealt it the finishing blow. But the new world replacing the old is a mathematical mechanism, a remote, inhuman, and valueless world. Descartes may have lacked the poignancy of Pascal's feeling for man's lostness in the new infinite universe, for man's disoriented suspension be-

---

[17] The best discussion of these letters is to be found in Ferdinand Alquié's remarkable book *La Découverte métaphysique de l'homme chez Descartes* (Paris: Presses Universitaires de France, 1950), especially Chap. 5, also *passim*.

tween the infinitely large and the infinitely small, or for man's
confused hesitation between greatness and misery. Nevertheless, is it not possible that Descartes also felt a revulsion from
the new world to which he was being led by his skeptical convictions concerning the old and by his mathematical prepossess-
sions? Did he not have something of a Pascalean sense of the
disproportion between man and the new world?

There is some reason for answering these questions in the
affirmative. Descartes is more than merely aware that the new
world of physics is not self-sufficient. The famous experiment
with the wax recounted at the end of *Meditation* II might at
first glance seem to prepare the way to mechanics by making the
distinction between primary, measurable, and object-depend-
ent qualities and the secondary or mind-dependent qualities.
Upon second glance, however, it becomes evident that its
function is to bring Descartes back from the representation of
bodies to the self which is known prior to and better than
bodies, a self which can, therefore, take the measure of perception and knowledge of bodies. He is brought back to the recognition that his own intellectual being is the basic certainty in
comparison with the known world of objects. Again it is evident
that certainty of any kind is a modification of self-certainty.
The cogito (the "I-principle") had made the same point, only
more dramatically. Here clarity and distinctness of conception
are important, but they gain their relevance only within the
ontological series of relative dependence in being.

Within the ontological series Descartes sees his own being
as marked by the trinity of will, intellect, and the idea of infinite existence. Also he sees his being as obscurely yet sub-
stantially united to a privileged body. In these essential respects, he is outside the world of objects and irreducible to
them; rather, he is obligated to submit his will by way of the intellect to the God in whose image it was created. And as for the
physical world, though it was identified with geometry, it was
specifically not identified as being in itself. In relation to man it
has being only as represented to mind. In itself it is dependent

both for its essence and for its continuous re-creation upon God (*Works* II, 226, 57). It is not even known as a being except by inference and through representation. It has value—outside the inscrutable judgments of God—only as valued by man. But this value is relative to desire, a lower faculty which ought to be severely subordinated to impersonal reason.

The whole emphasis of this ontology is to place the mechanical world in a position subordinate to man. The manifest effort is to secure the uniqueness of man by an ontological guarantee. Is this effort successful? There was reason to foresee that it would not be altogether so. I have sought to underline the ambiguous situation of man in the ontological series; he is that unintelligible thing, a composite substance. Also, although the distinct status of the self as thinking thing or soul seems to be set forth with every effort to emphasize its uniqueness, still it too is a thing, a *res*. In its substantiality, may it not be more closely akin to matter than Descartes had at first suspected? For after all, both are substance. If soul is *res cogitans*, which is it? Primarily *res*? Or primarily *cogitans*? Is it a substance which has the peculiar property of thinking? Or does thinking make *all* the difference? Perhaps Descartes intended the second and more humanistic interpretation, but such was the peculiar communication between substances effected by history that the first one became the accepted belief of an important tradition.

Although an exact science of the soul, as we have seen, is not possible in Descartes's philosophy, still the substantiality of the soul has only to undergo reinterpretation along lines already clearly set forth by the development of the exact science of material substance. Then the soul or self may be treated altogether as an object, its ambiguities removed, and represented as accessible by the methods of exact science. Then indeed the stage will be set for applying the methods of discursive thinking, observation, and experiment in the generation of a new science of man himself. Eventually this science will be concluded to be quite like physics in every essential respect. Then man will have become a physical object, distinguished to be sure by a peculiar complexity but nevertheless subject only to the fate which awaits any physical object.

§ 14.   CARTESIAN PHILOSOPHY AND ITS FATE

We have now disentangled the main themes of Descartes's thought sufficiently to exhibit their relation to the development of post-Cartesian philosophy and to indicate their management of the transcendental problem. Likewise, these themes may be related to the figures under which fate has been alluded to in this study, for the development of post-Cartesian philosophy is just that in which the complex modern character may most legibly be read. This philosophy quite explicitly anticipates the mechanically necessitated, external fate; it more hesitantly hints at the internal fate which came to characterize the Kantian-transcendental tradition.

Descartes initially thought it evident that the problem of certainty, which became the problem of identifying the relation of intellect to objects as known, could be solved by the interposition of intermediary faculties—memory, imagination, and sense—between the mathematical intellect and the mathematicizable object. But the stringent requirements of certainty and also the need to achieve generality in his results led him, by way of the cogito and the nondeceiving deity, to conclude to the radical separation of mind (including both intellect and its aids) from the external or extended object-world. The consequence, as quickly became evident, was that the transcendental problem proved to be insoluble upon the level of clear and distinct thought. As if in compensation for this disastrous disconnection of fundamental principles, Descartes also turned to another level of thought (a level which I have termed ontological). Here he manifests a grasp, although a nonintellectual one, of the unity of man and expresses this in terms of a notion of complex substance, a notion which may be interpreted as looking forward to a later type of transcendental thinking. These are the developments in the Cartesian philosophy which point to what I have termed the external and internal fate, a contrast destined to be worked out in later centuries of thought.

In spite of all its shifts and difficulties, this framework of thought brought Descartes and many another to a desired and utilizable view of man and his relation to the object-world. For, upon accepting this epistemological view, it could be argued that some of our representations of the external world could in fact be seen to possess (at second remove) the certainty of mathematics and thus to be true so long at least as memory, imagination, and sense, by means of which the world was represented, were strictly disciplined by the mathematical intellect. Likewise, in the course of the same argument, Descartes sought also to establish the being of man outside this mechanical world. Thus Descartes sought to eat his cake and have it too. He wanted for the developing science of mechanics a mechanical world disconnected from the values, the ends, the real but immeasurable qualities, and the forms with which the realism of common sense and Scholastic and pre-Copernican metaphysics had endowed it. But the resultant cosmos threatened to absorb man back into itself as merely another object amid objects. It was in any event an alien place for the living of human life. Human values had no real locus within this cosmos but were projected upon it from without and lent it, deceivingly, an insubstantial subjective hue.

Perhaps we would not be far wrong in envisaging this universe as dominated by an external fate or necessity which, like some versions of the ancient fate, is nonteleological (or whose telos, as Descartes preferred to put it, exceeds the grasp of man) but which is different from the ancient fate in being regularly predictable. The difference may be conceived in terms of the analogies which yielded the concepts used in identifying the two versions of fate. The classic version developed around arts such as spinning and weaving (see above, § 3). These arts remained in the context of artisanship and were subject to the somewhat unpredictable yet purposeful Zeus-like authority.

The Renaissance version of fate developed around the machine, powered and controlled by impersonal and external forces, seemingly independent of its inventor or of the use to which it might be put. Its necessities could be expressed by the formulae of physics. Its basic analogon is the intellect of the mathematically inclined artist, the engineer, or physicist. Its fatelike or objective character, then, is intimately related to the clarity or exactitude of its representation. This limitation of being to being-in-relation-to-intellect and this identification of objectivity with clarity of representation to intellect runs a discernible course from Descartes to contemporary times. Although Descartes's own physics scarcely survived for thirty years, the idea of the determined universe, object of exact sciences, and of its technological manipulation remains among the most powerful of contemporary convictions.

This epoch-marking concept of a lawfully determined, clearly conceivable objective world represents, however, only the rational side of the ambiguous notion of fate. The Cartesian coordinates on which the curves of nature can be mapped depict these essences clearly and distinctly; at the same time, unfortunately, these coordinates conceal whatever cannot be mapped upon them. I have tried to show that Descartes was not altogether unaware of this concealment, but that this awareness was not the most popular or influential side of his thought. Nevertheless, forgetfulness of it constituted a consignment to arationality. This irrational and forgotten side of fate could remain to disturb the peaceable flow of scientific progress. It was glimpsed from time to time in later philosophical problems and most persistently in the insoluble version of the transcendental problem.

The complex role which Descartes played in the development of philosophy may be summarized by anticipating the two main streams of influence which issue from his work. Both of these streams of influence center about the transcendental problem. The first and best known of these presents the famous mind-body problem in its unmanageable form and indicates a strong inclination to turn altogether away from such abstruse difficulties. The second gives evidence of awareness of this problem and also of an intention to turn to another level of thought and discourse—the ontological or transcendental level —in order to meet the challenge.

The first line of development, directed toward conceiving of an appropriate universe for physics, elaborates the epistemological contrast between the knowing subject and the known object. It plays with the various permutations of this dualism— realism, idealism, and the like—and on its skeptical side develops through Hume to the contemporary Anglo-American analytic schools. There is no more doubt of its high evaluation of clarity and distinctness, of precise ratiocination, and of theoretical exactness—in short, of the works of thymos—than there is of its impatient rejection of myth, poetry, and the more intuitive uses of mind (psyche).

The second line of influence issues from Descartes's interest in maintaining a line of demarcation between man and the physical world. This influence is most exercised to keep man from being absorbed into the physical or object world, and accordingly it tends to turn toward a nondiscursive use of mind (psyche) which often resembles a poetic and intuitive use, one to which is sometimes attributed the function of grounding and evaluating other uses of mind. This line of development moves through the Kantian-Copernican revolution to modern phenomenological and existential philosophy.

In brief, we may summarize by observing that Descartes destroyed the pre-Copernican metaphysics and substituted for it another within which physics could advance. Then he sought to compensate as best he could for the difficulties thrust upon the philosophy of man by taking care to exile man ontologically from the determined universe in which he plainly could not live.

Although many philosophers identify Descartes as the father of modern philosophy just because his metaphysical dualism of mental and material substances left a problem which has continued to puzzle thinkers and to dominate their philosophizing, there is yet good reason for supposing this interpretation of his significance to be one-sided. In the first place, he was not a metaphysical dualist; there are four substances in his philosophy.[18] And in the second place, he took the first steps toward the Copernican revolution in philosophy that became thematic with Kant. Descartes took these steps when he affirmed the place of the self to be clearly outside the physical and determined world and when at the same time he recognized the essential part played by the self in defining the nature and limits of the object-world. This transcendental and ontological tradition, directed toward founding the sciences within a larger framework able to accommodate both man and the sciences, is to be contrasted with the tradition of the various dualisms, monisms, and positivisms which intend the inclusion of man within an exact scientific study.

Of course Spinoza and Leibniz also attempted to integrate man back into the world by way of ontological monisms. These two, however, were philosophers' philosophers. The larger stream of history flowed with physics and the popular interpretations of physics. It moved from the Hobbesian way of integrating man into the world to the Humean one. Perhaps, that is, Hobbes had an inkling of the possibilities dormant in the materialistic variation upon Cartesianism, but it was Hume who took the consequential steps.

Meanwhile we have, I trust, made evident the close tie among several developments involved in effecting the transition into the modern world: first, the history of physics led almost inevitably to a narrowing of the ideal of rationality down to a mathematical ideal; second, this ideal led to Descartes's anti-

---

[18] It must be added that it is difficult to count the Cartesian substances, for there is no unity among them. Finite and infinite substances are totally unlike. Also the finite-composite substance—man—is not known clearly and distinctly, as are the finite-simple substances—mind and body. Perhaps it is better, then, to conclude that there are three types of substance: infinite, finite-simple, and finite-complex substances. However, out of deference to a long habit among English-speaking philosophers, I continue to speak of "Cartesian dualism" in the customary history-book sense.

anthropomorphic stand and to his new concept of the object; and third, this new nonanthropomorphic concept of the object led directly to the Cartesian dualism of subject and object that was to persist in one form or another so long as the ideal of Cartesian rationality held sway.

III

Modern Man in Renaissance Space

§ 15. LIKE COSMOS, LIKE MAN

Oscar Wilde suggests in his novel *The Picture of Dorian Gray* that a person and his portrait tend to grow to be like each other. Possibly Wilde's observation is no more than an illustration of the more general principle that we tend in some way to come to resemble our own handiwork. This principle is illustrated on a larger scale in Plato's *Timaeus*. There a cosmos is constructed and within it man is placed; his destiny is then seen as the increasing assimilation of his character to the harmonies of this cosmos. Platonists in general have continued to elaborate a philosophy within which self-knowledge and knowledge of one's good could be pursued by way of a rational study of the self and the cosmos.

Although Descartes's philosophy may in some respects have moved in this Platonic direction, a widespread choice following upon his philosophy was to pursue his epistemological inspiration further and to make use of self-knowledge only as a preliminary for continuing the deanthropomorphizing of nature. Nature thus purified offered a context within which physics and other sciences could progress. The end envisaged for this science was technological; it was to bring the world and finally man himself under control. However, the ontological basis of

Descartes's epistemology was not sufficiently disassociated from the fading theological faith of the Middle Ages. Or else it was not sufficiently cogent and persuasive in itself to stand in the face of such criticism as materialists like Hobbes and skeptics like Hume were able to direct against it. In later centuries, therefore, it was easy to reject Descartes's ontological concern for the experienced self and its kind of being, then still later to turn attention upon a quite different kind of examination of the self.

I refer to the increasingly close assimilation of man to the Renaissance cosmos, an assimilation which seemed to demand an exclusively scientific study of man. For man, conceived by Descartes as the scientist who could master and possess nature for human benefit, came finally to be conceived as an element within that same nature—a nature which could be made subject to appropriate sciences and which could be mastered and possessed by man's own technology. This transition did not occur without hesitation, confusion, and resistance. Its general direction, however, is distinct enough; it moves toward a directionless, infinite cosmos fit for the developing physics, yet a strange habitat for man. It required of man that he reconceive himself primarily as a mathematical mind, as a mirror of that universe, and more literally as a part of its mechanism than Descartes could ever have imagined. The outcome is a completely new portrait of man: a Faustian portrait.

That philosophers continue to meditate and to attempt to understand this transition is crucially important, I believe, for the achievement of this historical movement was the crossing of the last major boundary which separated medieval and humanist man from the tenant of the wholly modernized world.[1]

Here I believe it necessary to direct attention upon several phases of the development in question, phases which relate

[1] Heinrich Rombach's very perceptive reflections upon present trends in philosophy, in *Die Gegenwart der Philosophie* (Freiburg: Karl Alber, 1962), might be criticized, it seems to me, for failing to give sufficient weight to the continuing relevance of this antitranscendental movement in philosophy.

primarily to the human factor. This exceedingly complex development can scarcely be presented without use of a technique rather like caricature. However, a philosophical caricature need not distort the main traits of historical transition. Accordingly, a few bold lines can be used to set forth the relevant properties of the Renaissance-Cartesian conception of space in respect to its contrast with the older Aristotelian-Scholastic concept and in respect to its newly conceived character. The Renaissance-Cartesian concept of space and similar concepts were put to work by Hume in order to formulate the notion of a science of man and by modern empiricists to carry this project to its logical conclusion (a conclusion, incidentally, intended to render nugatory all further attempts to formulate and discuss the transcendental problem).

Most caricatures express or suggest a moral. The moral of the present philosophical caricature is that it is well to consider carefully the kind of world or cosmos into which one allows oneself to move, since one's view of man and one's view of the general character of the cosmos are likely to be functions of each other.

§ 16.   VERSUS THE ARISTOTELIAN COSMOS

The philosophy of Aristotle had expressly understood man to embody the same principles which were exhibited in the structure and working of the whole universe. Thus man actualized inherent potentialities, just as any other substance, as he moved to maturity. Hence man in his human pursuits was at home in a universe of organisms or substances in principle similar to himself. This universe was explicitly anthropomorphic. Consequently it recommended itself immediately to the Scholastic philosophers who needed to conceive of both man and the cosmos as issuing from the same personal and creative source and hence as manifesting an analogous order.

The usefulness of this philosophy, however, for the developing sciences of the Renaissance was certainly disputable. Most of the thinkers, especially Descartes, concerned with effecting the transition into the world of modern physics, although educated in Aristotelianism, could scarcely avoid reacting against it. For instance, as they clearly saw, the Aristotelian organic concept of space as developed in the *Physics* is inadequate for a science of Platonic-mathematical inspiration. There are two kinds of difficulties in the Aristotelian concept: there are internal contradictions in it, and there is little in it which could easily be made over into an instrument for solving the kind of problems which were presented to the founders of modern science.

Aristotle's doctrine of substance led him to identify space as an accident of composite substances.[2] Space is finally defined as the place of a substance, the envelope as it were which a substance occupies and which changes as the substance moves locally; thus, where there is no substance, there is no space either. This is just the Scholastic notion of place which Descartes finds to be unintelligible.[3] If we hold that space is an envelope in which objects are placed, then space (place) is finite. It is an accident of substance, and there cannot be an infinity of substances. A paradox follows concerning the place of the last sphere. Whatever moves must, of course, be in a place. A moving planet was placed upon a hollow sphere and was, therefore, understood to move in the place within which its sphere moved.[4] Aristotle, in other words, made a physical interpretation of the Platonic-Eudoxian spheres; he regarded a planet's sphere as placed within, and moved by, a series of others until the first mover, the sphere of fixed stars, was reached. This was the place and limit of the whole universe. Being the whole, the place of all places, it was not contained in any further place. Nevertheless, the sphere of fixed stars was in motion; hence it must be thought to be in some place. The *Parmenides*, it will be recalled, intimates that any whole must

[2] See Aristotle *Physics* IV. 211a; *Categories* 5a. 8–14.

[3] *Regulae* XII. Cf. *Principles* II, 10.

[4] See Thomas Kuhn, *The Copernican Revolution: Planetary Astronomy in the Development of Western Thought* (Cambridge: Harvard University Press, 1957), Chaps. 2, 3, and 4.

be considered to be part of a larger whole if it is to be understood. A final whole, therefore, is to be grasped only in a myth and, hence, will scarcely be thought without ambiguity and paradox. Aristotle's astronomy, however, is presented not as a suggestive myth but rather as a science in which paradox is out of place. These and other difficulties (such as the ones which Galileo found in the supposed Aristotelian belief that the heavier a falling body is, the faster is its fall)[5] could not be counted upon to endear his teaching to those who sought mathematical clarity.

A quite insurmountable difficulty arose from the fact that Aristotelian space is heterogeneous and nonisotropic. Its heterogeneity was made inevitable by the finiteness of this space. For if space is finite and bounded, then its class of bounding points do not have properties identical with the points bounded. Likewise, its center is a unique point, the natural locus of earth. Such a space is not homogeneous. In addition, Aristotle's concept of space was complicated by other factors which arose from its dependent relation upon the character of substances within it. For example, since sublunar substances are essentially different from superlunar ones, the place of sublunar or earthly objects is peculiar to them and their change of place is characteristic. In general, the motion of celestial bodies was thought to be circular and eternal, whereas the motion of earthly bodies was held to be linear and temporal. The places where these different kinds of motion are appropriately actualized are naturally different.[6] Here, then, is another respect in which Aristotelian space—as well as motion—are nonhomogeneous.

Even more importantly, the doctrine of the qualitatively different directions in space seemed to be least favorable for the requirements of the new science. If space is nonisotropic or qualitatively different such that the natural direction for the movement of fire is up and the natural movement of earth is

[5] Herbert Butterfield, *The Origins of Modern Science* (paperback ed.; New York: Free Press, 1962), 92.
[6] Aristotle *Physics* IV. 208b. 8–23.

down, one may well wonder why these elements are not actually in their natural places rather than merely tending to them. It is difficult, for example, to understand how a vertically placed wheel could be conceived to turn in this qualitatively differentiated space. Why do its parts not stay in the place most natural to them? A myth of the imperfection of the world was not a very satisfactory answer to this question. Even a logically satisfactory answer to the problem would not have been useful, however, since quite another sort of concept of space, one having quite different logical consequences, was needed for physics. Now, although the Aristotelian organic cosmos provided a fitting home for man, it was not a good laboratory for the development of physics. It failed to offer the concepts required for mechanics. However, a harsh judgment of Aristotle's cosmos is scarcely just; after all, he was not acquainted with the problems which his philosophy would be asked to solve eighteen hundred years after his death. Nevertheless, we can understand why Aristotelianism became the target of searching criticism.

§17.   CARTESIAN SPACE: THE TREND OF SCIENTIFIC THOUGHT

Descartes's criticism of Aristotelianism indicated quite clearly in a negative way the kind of concept which physics needed. The conclusion of his polemic against Aristotelianism was that this theory remained anthropomorphic—that is, the theory formed its myth from the ideas associated with human life and life's growth and changes and then attempted to pass these on only slightly modified and clarified to physics. It was quite natural and no doubt useful that the peasants of Homeric times should think of the universe on the plan of a temple, or that the medieval man should regard the downward direction dramatically as the way of sin and death, and the upward as morally desirable. In this manner moral directions were kept distinct and the moral structure of life was rendered concrete, imaginable, and hence persuasive. Man thus remained close to the gods. Obviously, however, the space necessary for a science of the physical world could not be defined adequately in the same mythic way. The physicist wants from the gods only a world free from the gods. Similarly he wants from his predecessors a world free from the individual human qualities of men. Such a world, as Descartes saw, would have to manifest traits akin to an impersonal, universal, and mathematical reason rather than traits akin to a somewhat poetic, intuitive, and even semidivine psyche.

Fortunately, since the classic age another concept of space had been at hand, namely the Democritean doctrine which tended to regard space as a homogeneous, isotropic, and infinite void. This doctrine was taken up again in the Renaissance and developed by such philosophers as Telesio and Gassendi. The most influential development of it is Descartes's. His residual Aristotelianism led him to substantialize the void. We have noted that the negative function of his metaphysics was to de-anthropomorphize the Scholastic world. On its positive side, his metaphysics matured in the conclusion that the objective world could be represented mathematically by the disciplined mind; moreover, these representations, when clearly and distinctly understood, were guaranteed by God to be true. In particular this metaphysics argued to the conclusion that space or extension is substantial—a plenum, geometric in essence, extended in three dimensions, diversified by figure and motion (or translation).[7]

Perhaps the most important single property of space which came to be rendered explicit by Descartes was its peculiar kind of infinity,[8] a notion which includes continuity and perhaps

[7] *Principles* II, 22. Descartes regarded the Aristotelian organically conceived definition of motion ("the actualization of what exists in potentiality in so far as it is potential") as unintelligible. See *Regulae* XII. Thus he rejected the suggestion that some definite stage of a thing's life and notion, its "maturity," is privileged or final.

[8] Descartes wrote in a letter to More (April 15, 1649), "It entails a contradiction that the world should be finite or limited, for I am unable not to conceive space beyond whatever be presupposed as the limit of the world." See *Ouevres* V, 345. But this infinity must be distinguished from the property by that name attributed to Divinity. The story of the emergence of belief in the infinity of space and its significance is told by Alexandre Koyré, *From the Closed World to the Infinite Universe* (New York: Harper and Row, Harper Torchbooks, 1958); see Chap. 5 especially.

also homogeneity and isotropism. Furthermore, space is related to bodies as substance is to mode. This concept both included the needed features of the Democritean void and at the same time moved beyond the latter by relating space essentially to the extended objects moving within it. The latter end it accomplished by neglecting all the properties of objects except their geometric ones. Objects are essentially modes of extension. Thus the laws of geometry became in principle the laws of physics.[9] The new universe was a mathematical system, and the relations among its parts (its causal relations, for example) were understood as actually existing mathematical relations. In this respect, the Renaissance physical universe was a rebirth and a development of the Democritean world view. It was a development which assumed not merely that all objective being is intelligible, but that it is mathematically intelligible. However, space and its mathematically intelligible objects are perceived and known only as represented and never directly; they are metaperceptual.

An important consequence follows from the fact that this space and the mathematically intelligible objects which it contains are perceived and known only as re-presented, never directly. This consequence is that the real or mathematical character of objects, indeed of the whole universe, is not immediately evident. This character becomes evident only to one who, having accepted the relevant metaphysical hypotheses, acquires the discipline which enables him to interpret the perceived traits of this universe as mediating or re-presenting its real or mathematical character. Just as freedom to exist within the Christian world was once held to be given to man by God through faith, so freedom to know and to control the modern universe was now assumed to be given by the mathematical intellect through discipline to the aids to the intellect. Thus the acceptability of this universe, which is a metaphysics become physics, is dependent upon the currency of a certain kind of philosophy and upon the acquisition of the correlative kind of

[9] See Descartes, *Principles* II, conclusion.

discipline. It is important, therefore, that this philosophy be carefully and persuasively developed. Descartes and later co-workers in the Humean tradition labored effectively to achieve this persuasiveness.

There are, as we have already observed, serious difficulties in Descartes's philosophy which his critics and successors did not hesitate to point out. It is difficult, as Malebranche and others indicated, to understand how motion enters into this scheme of substantialized geometry.[10] Neither is it easy for Descartes to distinguish an extended object from the extension within which it moves. As Leibniz showed, Descartes clearly failed to understand the nonspatial property of body in consequence of which it resists change of motion. Further, the difficulties in the way of understanding the relation between continuous geometrical space and physical space with its discrete objects was evident to Hume.[11] Nevertheless, that Descartes was attempting to express an essentially important notion in his metaphysical terminology seems to be clear. Substance first meant to him unity and independence in being. To define infinite extension or space as substantial is to achieve at least two objectives, both necessary for the instauration of physics. One objective is to rid space of qualitative differentiations—projections from the psyche of men who undergo their changes in the world, for these projections render space more human than geometric. The other consequence of regarding space as unitary and uniform, in short as the reflection of the mathematics entertained by the minds which studied it, is that its characteristics appear to be the same at every point. This property of spatial position may be regarded as a generalization of the Copernican denial of a privileged and central status to earth. Henceforth, there were to be no privileged points.

In losing the central, if lowly, position assigned to earth in

[10] See Norman K. Smith, *New Studies in the Philosophy of Descartes* (London: Macmillan, 1952), 197f.

[11] David Hume, *A Treatise of Human Nature* I. ii. 4. Page numbers here and elsewhere refer to the Dolphin Books edition (New York: Doubleday, 1961); hereinafter referred to as *Treatise*.

the Aristotelian cosmos, it is difficult to say whether earth lost position altogether—certainly it lost absolute position—or whether emphasis was placed upon its gaining a position of equality with the celestial substances as Galileo suggests.[12] At any rate, earth became one celestial body among others. Analogously, any point in space became homogeneous with or transformable into any other point; different directions acquired the same general properties; thus space became one infinite substance—homogeneous, isotropic, and continuous.[13] Finally, motion was conceived as change in spatial location, one and the same in kind everywhere.[14]

Perhaps by an effort of imaginative hindsight, one may see in Descartes's doctrine of substantialized space a vague grasp upon other geometrical notions which the space of physics was to develop later. For instance, his view that motion is a mode of extension may, in spite of its difficulties, not unreasonably be imagined to be a dim apprehension of the operation which today would be described as transformation between systems of coordinates. His use of the notion of substance, of a something which was understood to retain its identity throughout change, may be regarded as a metaphysical way of expressing the notion of congruence under a transformation. A homogeneous, isotropic, continuous space within which congruent transformations are possible is a space into which physical measurements can be translated. This is a space in which rigid rods preserve their rigidity as their coordinates change; it is a space fit for the needs of mechanics. Thus a condition for the existence and

---

[12] As noted by John H. Randall, Jr., in *The Career of Philosophy: From the Middle Ages to the Enlightenment* (New York: Columbia University Press, 1962), 309f.

[13] In a different context, Leibniz expresses the point even more clearly (and separately from his doctrine of substance) in his third letter to Clarke: "Without the things placed in it, *one point* of space does not differ in any respect whatsoever from *another point* of space."

[14] Motion along a curved path was reduced to uniform translation by analysis of it into two linear components. These components could also be interpreted as force vectors, a centrifugal and a tangential one, in the analysis and simplification of the forces acting upon accelerated bodies. Thus motions (velocities) and forces could be conceived to be one in kind everywhere.

measurement of physical body is definable. And thus an essentially mathematical and physical concept was born into the world from the psyche of man and his matrix of myth and inspiration. Moreover, the substantializing of the whole of extension established a close connection between space and the objects and motions within it, a connection which may be thought to foreshadow the later physics in which the property of force eventually becomes a function of the geometry of space. Some modern physicists might almost say with Descartes, *"Toute ma physique n'est que la géometrie."* My point is that Descartes's hypostatization of Euclidean space not only provided what physics then needed but may even have indicated a dim grasp of the more general ideas embodied in this idea of space. Thus it is altogether correct to emphasize the radical difference between his doctrine of space and the anthropomorphic notions which entered into the Scholastic-Aristotelian concept. It is also easy to appreciate the fascination of this powerful concept and to anticipate its influence beyond the bounds of physics.

Descartes adapted his notion of space to a conception of time, which thereupon was interpreted to be a succession of homogeneous, pointlike instants which were, in addition, unconnected. This concept of time was used on one hand to establish a conviction concerning the function and nature of God. It established God's continuous re-creation of the world (*Meditation* II; *Principles* I, 21) since without this continuous re-creation one instant of the time series would be unrelated to any other, and the persistence of any substance in duration would be unintelligible. On the other hand, time conceived in this manner could be quantified by assigning numbers to its divisions (*Principles* I, 55, 57). Time was initiated into the new universe and soon became the equitable mathematical flow which Newton, assuming it to be continuous, could divide and measure.

It is easy to suppose that the rejection of the Cartesian God would eventuate in an infinitely fragmented time. Hume awoke to this consequence.

The general trend of this philosophy of nature is evident: it is toward conceiving space, time, natural objects, motions, forces as mathematically manageable. To this end these notions had to be understood in terms of easily definable and endlessly repeated patterns. Thus space became an infinity of similar points; no directions were privileged; time became a uniform serial flow of pointlike instants; motion was uniform or accelerated translation. Then Newton expressed force in terms of resistance to change of velocity (mass). The historical developments involved were complex, but their goal is clear: to reconceive the whole of nature as mathematically manageable— to conceive of it, in other words, as if it were the projection of a discursive and mathematical mind. It will be convenient to refer to this trend as the hypothesis of uniformity. This is the hypothesis which directs the scientist to search for simply formulatable repeating patterns in the object of his study with the confidence that the discovery of such patterns will enable him to predict the behavior of the object of his study and perhaps to control it. Thus he may become the master and possessor of nature.[15]

§ 18.   THE NEUTRAL WORLD

Succeeding thinkers either altered this metaphysics or rendered the implicit mathematics more explicit. Newton moved in both these directions. For Newtonian mechanics the relation between things in space and the space itself became a more workable and a more precise notion. A thing in space may be called

[15] The question might be raised whether the ideal of mastering nature led to the mathematical vision of nature, or vice versa. Certainly, this mathematical vision itself is anticipated by Plato, but no one, I think, would interpret the idea of the Good as inviting to the mastery and control of nature. Rather, this ideal, the technological interpretation of science, is typically modern. Undoubtedly the influence of this ideal is largely responsible for the full realization of the mathematical vision of nature.

a machine. A simple machine is an object whose fundamental physical properties may be expressed in terms of transformations and congruences in Euclidean space. A complex machine, one containing rotating or accelerated parts, may be understood with the aid of the notion of force (and hence of mass). Thus Newton gave a more exact expression to the tendency to understand objects by reducing them, but only so far as experientially possible, to the character of the space wherein they moved.

In addition, Newton absolutized space. Certainly, part of what he meant by the absoluteness of space is no more than another name for its independent and substantial (or substance-dependent) character. Although he was led to this conclusion in some degree by specifically physical considerations,[16] he, not unlike Descartes, also regarded space as dependent upon the absolute or infinite Being. In the second edition of his *Principia* Newton expressed this dependence in a curious way: space was described as an organ of God's perception. Its homogeneous and isotropic character became a consequence of God's justice which considers all points equally. The absoluteness of space follows from the absoluteness of God; however, this is the absentee God who, after creating the cosmos, left it to run of its own accord. Thus theology and metaphysics were kept at a safe distance from physics, and thus physics could move on toward its theoretical and technological triumphs unimpeded by the extraneous consideration of deity.

There is one sense in which the new physical and mechanical concepts indicate a moral advance. The space which is radically separated from and indifferent to the human drama, the machine thought-model which embodies the recognition of the physical world's independence of the will and desire of men, both of these express men's growing willingness to reject submission to their own sense of omnipotence; certainly this re-

---

[16] It seemed to Newton that the first law of motion entailed his doctrine of absolute space; likewise he held that motion in this space was detectable by certain experiments, for example, a rotating bucket of water.

jection is a mark of maturity. Only the child dreams of being a god; the man dreams of being a man. But the talent for the latter dream, evidently, is unevenly distributed. Thus it is not unusual for mythical thought to convert an impressively successful science into inept poetry, or into a Frankenstein monster which takes its makers into philosophic servitude. One may see a curious psychic mechanism at work here: an inclination on the part of some metaphysicians (whether known as philosophers or scientists) to take up again a concept that has been delivered over to a science and successfully used and then to reify it or to project into it all the feelings and qualities that their mythical thought can invest in it. Possibly they fail to distinguish between myth and its function and the sciences and their function. One might express the inclination which they exemplify as a kind of psychic rule: Whatever occupies the forefront of attention tends to preoccupy the whole, at least in the sense that the prime object of consideration tends to become the receptacle for the sense of reality. This persuasion is a species of unconscious metonymy. The effect of the successful function of the concept of space in physics lent it a sense of reality. The concept was, then, taken as real (i.e., as exhaustively true of its object), and its success in physics was attributed to its exact correspondence to reality.

Now, a further common consequence of accepting a concept in this manner is that it comes to be taken for granted. As taken for granted, it is accepted as an obvious fact; no longer is it the matter for wonder, nor the object of change, nor even the topic of examination. It becomes a part of the routine and customary furnishings of the mind. The consequences of the operation of this rule for human life and thought are momentous. One consequence results from the common human tendency to assimilate the convictions that men entertain about their own nature to the dominant concept of the cosmos (and vice versa). Thus when exiled from the Aristotelian world, men tended to think of themselves as natural inhabitants of its contemporary alternative, the new mechanical cosmos. Consequently, men undertook to look upon themselves as unexceptional objects within a universe which was adequately characterized by the hypothesis of uniformity. Men tended to think of themselves as objects altogether like other objects. Evidently, it is quite possible that concepts or models which come to be reified and accepted in an unquestioning manner become stumbling blocks that inhibit the insights which might reveal new possibilities; initially these concepts, however, were products of insight and inspiration. Thus inventions and discoveries which enlarge the empire of mind often become its prison.

Elaborating upon the metaphysical aspects of the Cartesian extended substance, a kind of doctrine was developed by Hobbes and others which allowed only a one-sided and mechanical interpretation of the human and dramatic universe. Thus the so-called neutral universe became the most persuasive option. It was neutral in the sense that it excluded all considerations which bear upon human destiny and upon the myths and doctrines through which such matters are communicated. This is the universe developed from the reified machine analogy. This reification is accomplished by building up habits of regarding the physical and geometrical properties of any object as exhaustive of its whole nature. Now, values are never parts of a machine. The use of this analogy required, therefore, that men learn to value the universe from which all value was excluded. But a universe without value is a universe without intrinsic relation to man, a universe in which man is present only accidentally, if at all. Thus men had to learn to think of themselves as living somehow in a universe in which man as he experiences himself is unessential. Such a universe could no longer function, as did the Platonic world of the *Timaeus*, or the Aristotelian, or the medieval Christian worlds, as a key to self-knowledge and as a means for orienting human endeavor toward appropriate activity. Rather it is without humanly relevant meaning; it is the world-without-man. The hypothesis of uniformity was extended to include human values, even man himself. In other words, these philosophers took the step beyond the Cartesian ontology which, as was suggested in the preceding chapter, Descartes himself had dimly foreseen and Pascal had feared.

The very considerable light shed by this mathematico-mechanical thought-model upon the workings of nature was reflected back upon man with strange consequences; to many philosophers it seemed impossible to think of the whole human being in such restricted terms. If, indeed, the person could be said to exist in this world, then he must have exclusively mechanical properties. Hence, for a La Mettrie he is "man the machine." Specifically, La Mettrie regarded man as a sort of clock, but he saw nothing unique in the fact that this particular kind of clock could tell the time. This tradition is continuous to Bertrand Russell, who has vividly portrayed this option in the well-known essay "A Free Man's Worship." [17] Now, if this limitation appears to do too great violence to the person as he has been traditionally understood, then he must be allowed some nonnatural (i.e., nonmechanical) property, which either effectively alienates him from this world or renders him unknowable. Alfred North Whitehead has beautifully expressed the situation facing men who paradoxically find themselves in this nonhuman world.[18] This is just the situation which goes far toward explaining the revolutionary character of nineteenth-century Romantic thought about human nature and the even more radical revolts of contemporary times. Perhaps Nietzsche's characterization of this predicament in terms of the death of God is overly dramatic. The predicament may be more soberly expressed in a few propositions: (1) the real universe is the universe described by mechanics; (2) propositions or questions concerning value have no meaning in this universe (i.e., values are merely subjective); (3) propositions affirming the value of this universe accordingly have no meaning; (4) human beings are objects in this universe and accordingly are

[17] In *Mysticism and Logic* (New York: W. W. Norton, 1929).
[18] See *Science and the Modern World* (New York: Macmillan, 1926), Chaps. 4 and 5.

devoid of meaning. (One is moved to wonder, in consequence of this development, whether man may have some strange antipathy to man, so that even the cosmos itself came to be conceived and used as a weapon of self-destruction.)

In any event, an impasse is reached. The impersonal study of the uniform and the nonpersonal, the attitude appropriate to the physicist, seemed to be reaching out to include the personal as well. The possibility suggested itself of working changes either in the concept of the nonpersonal universe or else in the understanding of man in order to bring the two back into mutual accord. Under the influence of the successes of mechanics, and opposed only by a weakened conception of the critical function of philosophy, the latter option appeared to many thinkers to be the more promising. It was not difficult to suppose that the traditional understanding of man was, like the Aristotelian concept of space, the lingering shadow of an outworn anthropomorphism—a ghost in the machine. Perhaps the most strenuous resolution to eliminate the threat of alienation by exorcising the ghost—that is, by fitting the concept of man to the exigencies of a mathematically and logically conceived nature—was expressed by Spinoza in book III of the *Ethics*. His intention to study man as if he were studying lines, planes, and solids is a classic statement. It is also an extreme statement, made without appreciation of the not-exclusively-logical necessities of experienced nature. The more influential efforts in this direction were made by the philosophers who recognized explicitly that regularities or experiential "necessities" in events were of a nonformal kind.

That knowledge of fact of whatever sort was nondemonstrative and nonlogical, probabilistic at most, was a guiding insight of Hume. He developed this conviction by attacking the theory of causality which had been derived from the Cartesian mathematical view of nature, the view which credited the theological assurance that the clearly perceived relations among natural objects and events were relations of a mathematical and logical kind. In fairness it must be recalled that Descartes himself did not confuse mathematical with physical necessity; for just this reason he felt driven to find a Divine assurance that the world was a rational (i.e., mathematical) structure and that mathematical thought, using the properly disciplined aids to the intellect, could represent it truly. Hume, however, discarded all theological assurances. Also he showed that logical and mathematical propositions are not verified in the way in which propositions about nature are verified; hence he concluded to their radical distinction. Eventually he reduced the nonmathematical relation called "causality" to an association of ideas or to a belief infused with feeling. Thus he seemed to attack the Cartesian mathematico-metaphysics of nature at its roots but without, however, impugning the use of mathematics as a handy and even indispensable device in the scientific study of nature. The scientist is still enjoined to continue the Cartesian search for simply formulatable, repeating patterns in the object of his study. The thing now desired was an understanding of man which would allow the application of these insights to the scientific study of the human object.

§ 19.   THE HUMEAN SCIENCE OF HUMAN NATURE

Although Hobbes had favorably assayed the new mechanical ideas as applied to the human being, none grasped more clearly than Hume the possibility of studying man from a characteristically modern and scientific standpoint.[19] His *Treatise of Human Nature*, "an attempt to introduce the experimental method of reasoning into moral subjects," expressly envisages an adaptation of Newtonian rules in philosophy to the study

[19] I do not mean to suggest that this project was Hume's only or greatest contribution to philosophy, but it certainly is one of his important philosophical themes. Neither is it asserted that he was the first to think of a science of human nature; in fact, Sir William Petty has already grasped this possibility in his *Political Arithmetic* (1690), and Locke foreshadowed the same. Neither do I deny humanistic philosophy in Hume's writings; in fact, Charles W. Hendel does discover such a philosophy in his *Studies in the Philosophy of David Hume* (New York: Bobbs-Merrill, 1963). The present concern, however, is confined to Hume as the ancestor of positivism, behaviorism, and similar philosophies and philosophic trends.

of man. Hume not only resolved to remain strictly within the limits of human experience; he is implicitly confined within the limits of the officially recognized experience of his time. Therefore he eschews the theological infinite. He likewise eschews any appeal to essences or to "occult entities" of mind or nature and confines his speculations to objects of sense by generalizing upon observations within strict empirical limits. "For to me it seems evident, that the essence of the mind being equally unknown to us with that of external bodies, it must be equally impossible to form any notion of its powers and qualities otherwise than from careful and exact experiments, and observations of its particular effects."[20] This resolve issued naturally from his so-called antimetaphysically oriented bias, which has rightfully earned for him the position as metaphysician for positivism.[21]

Hume recognized, however, more clearly than some of his successors that the scientific method cannot be applied to man without adaptation. For instance, experimentation with a human being is difficult, and in some respects impossible, since the very process of collecting data about or from him tends to change him (*Treatise*, p. xv). On the other hand, the study of man is unique in that the student is his own topic of study (*ibid.*, p. xiii). A man can investigate himself, for data relevant to him is accessible through introspection. The differences between man and the objects of other sciences are not radical enough, Hume thought, to prevent his being accepted unequivocally as the topic of scientific investigation. One declaration of this conviction is expressed in terms of kinds of evidence: "When we consider how aptly *natural* and *moral* evidence cement together, and form one chain of argument betwixt them, we shall make no scruple to allow, that they are of the

[20] *Treatise* I. iv. 7, p. 246. For Hume's explicit acceptance of the Newtonian world and its determinism, see *ibid* II. iii. 1, pp. 361f.

[21] Whether Hume succeeded in excluding metaphysics from his own philosophy is a question. Cf. Charles Hartshorne, "Hume's Metaphysics and its Present-Day Influence," *New Scholasticism*, XXXV (April, 1961), 152–71.

same nature, and derived from the same principles."[22] The pursuit of knowledge of man by exact scientific methods promises to be most rewarding, for the human being and his powers of knowing are deeply and basically involved in any science. "There is no question of importance, whose decision is not comprised in the science of man; and there is none, which can be decided with any certainty, before we become acquainted with that science. In pretending, therefore, to explain the principles of human nature, we in effect propose a complete system of the sciences, built on a foundation almost entirely new, and the only one upon which they can stand with any security" (*ibid.*, p. xiii). In other words, one aspect of Hume's claim is that scientific philosophy can include adequately the whole of human data. The other aspect of his claim is that the natural sciences cannot be complete and well founded unless they do include the human being as part of their study, indeed as the foundational part.

The very important first step toward elaborating the science of human nature required Hume to eliminate certain convictions concerning man which may, with a touch of irony, be called anthropomorphic. Hume turns his principles, which he considers to be simple and obvious, to this task of destruction. We shall not discuss all these principles, but it will be appropriate to mention here three of the most important of them. The first principle in the science of human nature maintains the origin of all experience in elementary sensory constituents, impressions, and hence the dependence of all ideas upon these. From this principle follows the empirical rule that the meaning of any idea can be determined only by the discovery of the impressions from which it is derived.[23]

---

[22] *Treatise* II. iii. 1, p. 367.

[23] *Ibid.* I. iii. 1, p. 66. See also Hume's *Enquiry Concerning Human Understanding* (New York: Liberal Arts Press, 1955), Sec. II. Of course, the decisive impressions are those of sense. But there are also imaginative impressions (imagination can supply the idea of an unsensed shade of color) and impressions of reflection. The principle of the association of impressions and ideas, Hume's mental "law of gravity," will be remarked upon below.

Another essential and frequently stated principle (one which may be termed the principle of atomism) is this: "Every idea that is distinguishable is separable by the imagination and . . . every idea that is separable by the imagination may be conceived to be separately existent." [24] One might presume that this principle, together with the first, would provide a hard problem for the philosopher to solve. This problem, in fact, is Hume's version of that problem which we have called transcendental. In order to manage it, the third principle, the association of ideas, will not be sufficient, and Hume will be forced to call upon belief, reinforced by arational feeling and "nature"; only thus could he hope somehow to relate the otherwise unrelated impressional data of experience. Our interest in Hume's management of this problem will be limited mainly to its involvement in his treatment of the notion of self.

The empirical fate of the belief in the Cartesian substantial self was sealed when Hume reasoned to the meaninglessness of any idea of substance conceived both as the subject (or substrate) of inherence and yet as distinct from its inhering qualities. For our impressions are impressions only of qualities. Thus, according to the empirical rule, the concept of substance as substrate is meaningless; it is derived from no impression of sense; hence it has no referent. Hume takes special pains to point out that the immaterial soul substance, supposed to exist separately and by itself, corresponds to no impressions and therefore is a meaningless notion.[25]

These metaphysical or meta-impressional claims disposed of, Hume undertakes to deal with the alleged experience of the personal and persistent self. This too is easily dismissed, for were a permanent self to exist, then its idea would be derived from some distinguishable impression. But, says Hume, "I never

[24] *Treatise* I. ii. 5, p. 50 and *passim*.

[25] *Ibid.* iv. 5, pp. 211f. Hume is, after all, merely expressing the immediate consequence of Descartes's own view that substance cannot be known. *Principles* I § 52. Hume, however, might allow the concept of substance as a persisting collection of qualities having a kind of family resemblance. Cf. *Treatise* I. iv. 5, p. 221.

catch *myself* at any time without a perception, and never can observe anything but the perception" (*ibid.* I. iv. 6, p. 228). Introspection uncovers no impression of a simple, self-identical, and persistent entity. Hence no such entity should be presumed to exist.

This conclusion is important. Hume may be interpreted as extending to the theory of self a generalization already applied to space. This conclusion, in other words, illustrates the tendency to accept ideas which are valued by reason of their success in achieving an envisaged goal in one area of experience as probably valid in another. The success of physics became the incipient prediction of similar science of man. Hume had only to place man in space, so to speak, so that the (temporal) flow of his life and the properties of an impersonally conceived and uniform space could be conceived in some significant sense to be analogous. Through this "spatialization" of the self he could expect to achieve the advantage similar to that which Descartes had achieved through the mathematicization of Scholastic-Aristotelian space—namely the elimination of metaphysical elements which, from the point of view of the new method and its goal, could only be regarded as "occult." Hume, however, goes further than Descartes. His assumption that whatever is discretely conceivable is discrete in fact will prevent his discovering any logical or logiclike connection among the atomic events into which his life history is divisible. Descartes had in effect, as has been noted, taken the first steps in this direction by maintaining that the time series is spacelike and discrete in itself and becomes continuous only by the re-creative act of God. Perhaps it may be imagined that the self, existing in time, would similarly be discrete unless unified by God. Naturally, then, upon rejection of God as a metaphysical *passe par tout*, the self as well as time fall apart and remain discrete like points in space.[26]

[26] Perhaps Hume could have developed a theory of the self as the teleological unity of a persisting collection of qualities, but in fact he did not do so. In any event, his definition of identity could scarcely have been applied without alteration to such a unity.

Physical space, as we have remarked, was conceived to be homogeneous and isotropic, having an unlimited number of points, all without privilege. Similarly the events of the flow of psychic life now came to be conceived as a series of perceptions, no one of which was privileged or endowed with any special identity or unique quality or exceptional permanence. The equivalued points of space, the "mathematical flow" of time, are mirrored in the impersonal sequence of conscious point-events. This concept of an impersonal flow of pointlike conscious events eliminates a metaphysical obstacle and seems to mark an important step toward getting man within the context of the observable and the measurable. A "Copernican" science of man quite similar to the new science of physics and astronomy could then be envisaged, for, as Hume observed, "there is no known circumstance that enters into the connection and production of the actions of matter that is not to be found in all the actions of mind." [27] Thus the human being is assimilated into the Newtonian world-without-man, and one of the purposes of the Cartesian ontology—to maintain man distinct from and external to the Copernican physical world—is frustrated.[28] Hume thus showed the way to subsume man himself under the hypothesis of uniformity. Now, the flow of percepts may have the properties attributed to a series of impressions or ideas, but these are certainly not the generally accepted properties of personal identity. Hume saw this and therefore felt it imperative to raise the question: What is that which has for so long been thought to be the self?

Hume's introspective search for himself discovered nothing more than a habitual "transition of the mind" from one percept to another one resembling it. Failure to analyze this situation, Hume believed, had produced the fiction of the unitary self. For no real, separate, and persistent identity was discoverable

---

[27] *Treatise* II. iii. 1, p. 366.

[28] I do not and need not specify whether the space to which the self is here reduced is the space of geometry or the space of physics. Hume himself failed to draw a clear distinction between these two; cf. *ibid.* I. i, iii, and iv; also *Enquiry* XXX. iii.

by observation and analysis within the homogeneous psychic flow.[29] Hume concluded that only inattention to differences among percepts and memories and to their natural separateness led to belief in personal identity.

In fact, a loose attention of this kind allows of associations expressed in several sorts of presumed or conventional identity or "family resemblance." [30] For example, unnoticed changes in quantity lead to our pronouncing an object to be materially self-identical. Likewise, very gradual change permits the judgment of identity in a changing object. Again, cooperation of various parts toward a common end, continued reciprocal relations of cause and effect, or changes which occur in customary and hence unnoticed ways, all lead to the judgment of identity. In particular, the sort of identity called personal is similar to the fiction of identity attributed to a slowly changing animal body; likewise, it is analogous to the unity in a republic whose mutually cooperating parts give rise to other persons who continue to maintain it. Memory is the faculty which reveals to the mind the resemblance of its perceptions and their (probable) cause-effect relations; memory—or rather the natural vagueness of memory—thus renders the transition among more or less resembling ideas. So-called personal identity is a certain kind of resemblance among ideas which facilitates the mind's transition among them. And it can be observed to be nothing else than this. Any supposed real or rationally justifiable connection among the impressional elements of mental life or of personal identity can, then, be nothing more than illusion. In this manner Hume accounts for the presence in us of the fiction of personal continuity and identity. It evidently follows that the scientist must leave such fictions strictly to one side and limit his attention and his descriptions exclusively to what is observed. Thus, as Descartes had purged external nature of certain

[29] We are reminded of Descartes's difficulty in distinguishing separate objects within the extension of which objects were said to be modes.

[30] Hume held that association in the science of human nature was analogous to gravitation in physics. *Treatise* I. iv. 1, p. 12.

traditional human qualities which had been projected upon it, so Hume purged internal nature of similar qualities.

The further profitable empirical study of human nature may now be directed in two ways. The first is toward the study of the types and functions of trains of perceptions. This is a physical and anatomical study of the causes of original perception into which Hume does not wish to enter. The other is the study of secondary or reflective ideas and the passions, to whose analytical and descriptive examination Hume decides to devote himself. Our limited purpose does not require our consideration of these analyses.

§ 20.   ON HUME'S SUCCESS AND FAILURE

A common initial reaction to Hume's philosophy is to suspect that the skeptical instrument has cut too deeply even for the skeptic's purposes. Such appears to have been Hume's own occasional reaction. The conclusions that the only tie among atomic impressions is custom and belief and that his own identity is a fiction led him to a sort of philosophical delirium from which only nature herself, by the agency of the practical concerns of dining, conversation, and playing games, could deliver him.[31] Has Hume's philosophy in fact eliminated the object of the projected science of human nature? He admitted that belief in the unity and reality of the person are persistent and undeniable beliefs. Yet on the basis of his philosophy, there seems to be nothing left of the person except a series of discrete impressions which seem to bear a family resemblance to each other. Further, considering the discrete nature of time, as Hume viewed it, and the independence of impressions as related among themselves, one can scarcely say that there remains even so much as a *series* of impressions. As it might be expressed, Humean man tends to disappear into space.

In addition, impressions in Hume's system of thought play quite the same part as substances in continental metaphysical

[31] *Ibid.* 7, p. 243. Nature may also be said to operate through psychological functions which issue in beliefs and customs, for example, the belief in nature.

systems, for impressions can be considered as separate and may exist separately. In fact "every distinct part of a perception is a distinct substance." [32] Hence a difficulty parallel to the transcendental problem as encountered by Descartes—the problem of understanding the unity of material and immaterial substances—is discovered by Hume in his effort to relate any two impressions. The old problem of the communication between substances persists in altered form. Furthermore, as we shall see, Hume explicitly recognizes the problem to be insoluble in his philosophy. But I think he may be interpreted to mean that such difficulties are irrelevant to his project for establishing a science of man.

Hume means that metaphysical hypotheses and their difficulties may safely be ignored. It may have seemed to be unfortunate that a skepticism whose purpose was to eliminate metaphysics had also eliminated the philosophical basis for the sciences. But this loss, upon Hume's interpretation, was none too serious; it was nothing which faith and feeling, under the firm guidance of eighteenth-century common sense, could not replace. Nature herself forces reflection into practical situations where "abstruse" problems must be sidestepped. The sciences, then, may safely pass over transcendental problems and paradoxes while they pursue their limited and definite objectives. Hume's skepticism, that is, was directed against the philosophic basis of the sciences but did not question established scientific practice and belief.

Taking his cue from everyday practical situations, Hume remarks, "We might hope to establish a system or set of opinions which if not true (for that, perhaps, is too much to be hoped for) might at least stand the test of critical examination." [33] The truth of which he despaired I take to be a rationally or philosophically grounded truth. I take the examination proposed to be a logico-empirical examination. The science of human behavior, like the science of physical behavior, is pos-

[32] *Ibid.* 5, p. 221; cf. *ibid.* 6, pp. 234f.
[33] *Ibid.* 7, p. 246.

sible for Hume in the sense that its rules are based upon custom and belief, which in their turn have been built up by the operation of such basic principles as the laws of association responding to experience. The object of this science will be the data of scientifically disciplined observation. Even though this basis seemed to some philosophers—to Kant, for example—to be insufficiently examined and to alienate man from the certitude concerning his own nature, it has continued to be quite acceptable to many philosophers and scientists. Human nature in the sense of conventionally identified entities engaged in observable and describable behavior remains in his system. Questions about human being, subjectivity, temporality, unity through change, or freedom and its conditions are abstruse questions which may safely be forgotten by men who confine their interests to scientific matters.

This is the philosophy that not merely takes the sciences seriously, but that takes them as the only acceptable philosophy. Past philosophies it regards as "chimerical systems" and looks forward to a new era of slow, patient, but cooperative and rewarding scientific effort. In this era of enlightenment all human problems will certainly be solved by the instruments of science. At last the human being had been got into the laboratory! The Baron d'Holbach, who based his reflections on Newton and was influenced by Hume, was only moving further in the same direction when he remarked in his *Système de la nature* (1770), "Man is purely physical being . . . . Moral man is man acting by causes which our prejudices prevent our understanding." He, like Hume, concluded to a kind of physical science of man of an associationist type in which "amour de soi" functioned analogously to gravitation. In later times positivism and other "isms" raise convictions of this kind to the position of unquestioned dogma. A contemporary psychologist begins his book with the sentence, "Everything can be the object of scientific study—even science itself." [34] He allows no

[34] K. B. Madsen, *Theories of Motivation: A Comparative Study of Modern Theories of Motivation*, trans. Mr. and Mrs. Arne Hyldkrog (2nd ed.; Cleveland: H. Allen, 1961).

suggestion that it may be worthwhile to question or to investigate belief in the self-founding and self-explanatory character of a science except within the assumptions of present-day radical empiricism. There are, however, very grave difficulties in this program which developed within the Humean tradition. In this section our concern with these difficulties will be limited to the form which they take in his own writings.

There are two problems within Hume's system which call for our notice. To one of these he has himself specifically called attention in the course of his discussion of the self. This is the question of how distinct and separable perceptions can form a whole of any sort. He expresses the problem in terms of two necessary but inconsistent principles, to both of which he is committed: "that all our distinct perceptions are distinct existences and that the mind never perceives any real connection among distinct existences." [35] Hume sees no resolution to this conflict of principle. Once committed to the finality of analysis into atomic parts, the scientist cannot expect to find a whole among those parts. The only wholeness or relation among parts which he can discover is put there by his own act. That he is convinced of the presence of a union or relation (e.g., a causal relation) among analytic elements is in every instance the product of custom and belief. But the nature of the belief, which convinces him that certain of his percepts form stable and recurring wholes, is enigmatic. It surpasses scientific understanding and can be attributed only to a nonrational sentiment or feeling. But one may also observe that, by means of such feelings, "nature herself strongly inclines us to certain beliefs, persuading us irresistibly to associate together those beliefs which are resembling or contiguous." [36] All syntheses of ideas are produced by acts of mental association. So far as logic is concerned, they might always have been different.

[35] *Treatise*, appendix, 560. However embarrassing these principles may have proved for the formulation of a satisfactory theory of the self, Hume certainly could not have given them up since they provided an essential step in his refutation of the contemporary theories of causality.

[36] *Ibid.* I. iii. 7, 8, 14.

Only an inexplicable feeling, somehow aroused by nature, leads us to expect regularities in our experience of the world and of ourselves.

In order to include in his philosophy all that seemed to him to demand inclusion, Hume was thus forced to compromise with the ideal of rationality which he had inherited. Feeling, although not impression, becomes a sort of evidence, the only evidence which can be adduced in favor of the belief that there are regularities, continuities, relations among discrete impressions. Here is the explicit admission that the transcendental problem concerning the relation among the elements accepted as basic by his philosophy could not be given an intelligible solution. That which may have established and explained this relation (i.e., feeling) is concluded by Hume to be arational. At its foundation this philosophy is incoherent.

The self, then, is nothing more than a customary unity whose basis is discovered in a firm though arational belief. It has been remarked that Hume left his home, locked the door, and threw the key away, but he at least had the honesty to look in the window and see that he was not there. However, his feat should not be cavalierly dismissed. The situation had to be such that Hume himself could look into the same window and observe the absence of the identical self; likewise, he had to find it worth while to do so. Did nature prompt him to place his belief in these syntheses and to accept these values?

What is this nature to which appeal is so often and so crucially made? It is the nature that prompts us to breathe and feel, and likewise to pass judgments—even to judge in rather specific ways.[37] But this nature is never defined. Hume himself remarks upon the vagueness of the notion. Still, nature is that which somehow forms those convictions which are of too great importance to be entrusted to reasoning and philosophy.[38] This is the nature which inclines us irresistibly to certain beliefs. There is a suspicion that this confidence in nature

[37] *Ibid.* iv. 1, p. 168.
[38] *Ibid.* 2, p. 172.

represents a compromise with the empirical ideal and even suggests a disguised toying with Platonic recollection. Perhaps, however, it may be better identified with the web of convention with which every Britisher of his day was so familiar that he never considered questioning it. This was the air he breathed, nature herself. We recall that nature prompted Hume to engage in conversation (in the eighteenth-century style) and to play games! Such was the nature or custom which solved metaphysical puzzles for Hume and allowed him to envisage an end to philosophical difficulties and to foresee the beginning of a science of human nature. In view of the customary character of the nature upon which Hume had to rely so heavily, we can only conclude that his philosophy was a world constructed within another world. This second and more basic world, however, was not susceptible to analysis by his techniques, yet its presence—like a kind of fate—forced itself upon his attention and was acknowledged in terms of belief and arational feeling. Belief and arational feeling thus perform the founding and unifying role exercised in some other philosophies by a doctrine of the transcendental.

Now, certainly not every set of conventions could have been used by Hume to formulate the beginnings of a science of human nature. Fortunately for his philosophy, his was a sophisticated and scientifically maturing culture. It had prepared for him the notion of a homogeneous space containing masses which differed among themselves in limited and mathematically predictable ways. Furthermore, it was by no means unfavorable to the suggestion of extending these concepts to include human nature. Thus his world afforded him the luxury of leaving aside the attempt to define the world and the self and of accepting current notions as the starting point for observing man with some expectation of precision and communicability. If man is treated as a natural thing, a scientific object (although in some respects an exceptional thing), then much that is important can be learned about him. On the other hand, this context of sense impressions and observation controlled by the customary association and ideals of a scientific society limits possible discoveries to matters already implicit within this context. A philosophy seeking above all to fortify and preserve such a context invites the reification of the status quo. This acceptance of the current scientific universe as final limits change to "progress" within that one universe. This limitation is also a rejection of the function of philosophy to interpret the transition over boundaries; rather, it is a doctrinal avoidance of unfamiliar boundaries. Eventually this kind of philosophy will seek a means to exclude in principle all inquiry which might call the status quo into question.

The historical transition, then, which reaches clear expression in Hume's philosophy culminates in the view of man as an object-being. In one sense, no one would be disposed to dispute this view; a man occupies a definite space and time and like any object, if he falls from the Tower of Pisa, he obeys the Newtonian laws of motion. But in addition this transition also led to an increasingly severe restriction of the convictions concerning man to just this object-view. He is identified as primarily or exclusively an object in a cosmos of basically similar physical objects. And every effort is made to give official status to these opinions. Man thus grew up to be a machine.[39]

§ 21.   THE BRAVE NEW HUMEAN WORLD

Hume may not inappropriately be regarded as the artist who added the final essential touch to the portrait of modern man

[39] The typical contemporary defense of this thesis is no longer metaphysical but pragmatic. It is argued that "Man is a machine" is equivalent to "Everything a man can do a machine can do." The latter proposition is understood to mean that if the input into human activity and its output can be exactly (that is, mathematically) formulated, then a machine can be constructed which will use the same input to produce the same output. Then it is concluded that a man and a machine are operationally equivalent. And indeed, many human operations can be simulated in this manner: for example, machines can figure; they can play chess (badly); they can prove theorems; and so forth. No doubt all the operations of thymos will eventually be mechanized. The negative side of this polemic holds that other traditionally human characteristics such as existing, being conscious, being charitable, having insights, and others which cannot be exactly formulated are not intelligible at all. By such adroit definitions, it is easy to conclude either that man is unintelligible or that he is a machine.

in the modern cosmos. This is the man who is freed of everything that Hume and his successors would call sophistry and illusion. Accordingly, the portrait is painted in a style which cultivates the mathematical ideal of clarity and distinctness, the spatialization of the self, the devaluation of psyche, the objectification of man and the world, the technological interpretation of science, and the scientizing and institutionalizing of philosophy. These ideals and aims become ever more explicitly and clearly expressed and ever more efficiently applied as this tradition developed.

The Cartesian decision to thin man's relation to himself, to others, and to the world down to clearly definable "rational" relations was destined to be carried to its extreme within this tradition. Henceforth it is obvious that the world is the collection of objects studied by the sciences. Now, we have already observed the tendency of self and world to acquire the same or analogous characteristics. This inclination was noted in both the Platonic and Aristotelian philosophies. For instance, we considered the ethical utilization of this tendency in Plato's *Timaeus* (see above, § 4). Mention has also been made of the Christian belief that self and world are respectively the image and trace of the same creative Being. And now we find that the Humean evolution of thought repeats this same tendency of self and world to come to resemble each other. What are the consequences of this latter assimilation?

The Humean world is the spatialized world of physics. Thus the space to which the self is accommodated is not that which is receptive or susceptible to being space-forming, as was the Platonic receptacle; rather, it is a space envisaged by thymos. The Humean world presupposes the givenness of the geometric extension intuited by Descartes and defined by Newton. Furthermore, Hume rightly saw that this space, though measurable, contained within itself no natural unit; its unit is said to be arbitrary. Hence the identity of the self, conceived on analogy with this space, was likewise arbitrary; yet its behavior was conceived to be measurable and predictable once the appropriate science of it was discovered. In addition, every phase of life—poetry, religion, art—tended in this tradition to become manifestly the expression of minds fascinated by geometry. Recall, for example, the formal gardens of Versailles—"Nature methodized"—or Comte's project of organizing the whole of society along mathematical lines.

It is imaginable that a stranger to the Humean tradition could be brought to despair upon being persuaded that the self is an object in the object-world; or that it is a spacelike combination of mental atoms whose unique identity is illusory; or that it is a collocation of sensations like all other items composing the so-called physical world; or that it is a grammatical fiction. To view the self thus might seem to him to reduce it to nothingness. The Humean world very easily appears to be a world without man. The stranger to this world must murmur, with Pascal, *"le silence de ces espaces infinis m'effraye."*

Why is it that the Humeans themselves do not react in the same despairing manner to this self which seems to fade away into space? Perhaps the Humean is saved from this despair because he has managed to shift his sense of identity to something other than the punctate self which his philosophy discovered. The locus of his sense of identity is not far to seek. Consider that positivistically inclined Humean philosophers place the highest value upon scientific knowledge; consider also that they identify themselves as those who correctly evaluate the sciences. They are the impersonal minds who know the truth about the self of the classic and medieval traditions. Thus a kind of emotional dualism is established—on one side the world which includes the self and the values of ancient belief, on the other side the positivists or scientific philosophers who know the truth about the former.[40] Thus a sense of identity,

[40] By "positivism" I mean naturalism influenced by Hume; I use the term broadly to include the scientific socialism developed by Comte, who identified Hume as his most significant predecessor, and by his successors up to and including Marx and Engels, as well as the scientific humanism developed by the logical positivists and other kinds of analytic philosophers who look to Hume as their intellectual Abraham. Of course Hume's influence is far wider than this: I do not pretend to indicate its full sweep. However, see Gerald Feinberg, *The Prometheus Project* (Garden City, N.Y.: Doubleday, 1968).

even of superiority, is set up to take the place of the older self or soul.

History too is brought into line with this development; it is read as a continuous struggle of the irrational and reactionary forces of religion, myth, and metaphysics against the forces of logic, science, and technological progress. This new identity and these flattering convictions are reinforced by organized association with others of like mind and unified by the exclusion of dissidents.

When the fact became generally evident—which philosophers like Descartes and Bacon had already foreseen—that science did not contribute merely to understanding but that its practical applications opened up great new sources of power and wealth, institutions facilitating its growth were developed. The relevant point is that the Humean philosophic tradition concluded that its own fate was bound up with this trend. In particular, positivist philosophers, who become anxious unless closely associated with scientists, sought a rapprochement with scientific and technical institutions.[41] Hence they went to work to establish their tradition, either by integrating the whole of society within their general scientific and progressive ideology —the tack taken by philosophers like Comte or Karl Marx—or else by integrating themselves within the modern scientific and technological organization—the route followed by many Anglo-American philosophers.

These philosophers could have taken their motto from Seneca: "If you wish to subject everything to yourself, subject yourself to reason." The modern use of reason and experimentation seemed to open the way to complete domination of the *anagke,* or fate, in which Whitehead has seen the ancestor of the concept of natural law. With the definition of the object as

[41] It is of interest to recall in passing that this kind of institutionalism is also deeply affected by the perfectionism of the Enlightenment—the doctrine that all men are equally naturally good—and hence by the correlative conviction that evils come into the world through defective institutions, and finally by the corollary that men can be perfected by changing their institutions. Here, however, we shall not be able to attend further to the systematic connections among scientism, perfectionism, and millennial thinking.

mathematical in essence and of man as an object which can reason mathematically, only scientific and technological questions remained upon their intellectual horizon. Here transition into the modern world was, in principle at least, complete. Within this horizon (the mirror and natural habitat of thymos), it seemed easy to discipline psyche and to repress those of its impulses and intimations not adapted to the status quo. More to the point, the acceptable intimations of psyche were frequently interpreted as subliminal problem-solving operations which popped into consciousness when the appropriate stimulus was present. Thus psyche was reduced to thymos. Symbolic of this world, conceived under the hypothesis of uniformity, is a set of Cartesian coordinates on which the curves of both nature and man can be represented without remainder.

The philosophers who accepted the intellectual discipline of this world and consented to being molded in its image quickly became *ancillae scientiae*. Since they accepted as axiomatic that all that is, is knowable and that all knowledge is scientific knowledge, the more rigorous of their number also concluded that the sole office of philosophy consisted of the analytical clarification of scientific and methodological concepts. The less rigorous allowed themselves to extrapolate from the sciences in order to advance understanding of the sciences, of their utilization, or of their relation to society. Always philosophers of this kind tend to defend the bounds of sense already laid down by a scientific culture rather than to seek out a context within which these bounds could be questioned critically.

The philosophers who charged themselves with carrying out the positivist programs have achieved their purposes with remarkable success. They have not only constantly perfected their doctrine, but they have also succeeded either in dominating social and political institutions or else in being admitted within them as a new profession.[42] They assumed the position of

---

[42] G. J. Warnock, however, observes that philosophy has been accepted upon the professional scene with a certain anxiety. He concludes that this anxiety arises from the fact that it has come only quite lately upon this scene. See his *English Philosophy Since 1900* (paperback; New York: Oxford University Press, 1966), 110f.

leadership in Anglo-American philosophy and bear much of the responsibility for its present state. Nevertheless, the philosophies which are not science-centered have not been altogether eliminated.

Despite the temptation, not always resisted, of linking positive philosophy in some causal way with the more unfortunate and self-contradictory characteristics of our technological age, the wholehearted enthusiasm with which this technologically allied philosophy is held and communicated has not diminished. And undeniably certain traits of our kind of civilization do give one to wonder whether the light of science may not have been forced from its orbit. If so, will the Furies mentioned by Heraclitus put it back within bounds? Is the technology which was designed to control nature and man out of control itself? Is technology a Greek gift? Or are the philosophies now interpreting the sciences insufficiently Greek? In any event, no principle has been discovered for assigning to any specific type of philosophy its proportionate guilt for social disaster. Positivists are not concerned with this guilt and seem least of all to feel it. When doubt concerning their programs or viewpoints is expressed, it is usually countered with the argument that the technological process has not yet been carried far enough or applied in sufficient detail. The appeal is constantly and insistently made to the millennium. These scientific philosophers remain doggedly devoted either to the task of furthering the technological rationalization of society or of serving science itself by clarifying concepts which the sciences use or promise to need.

For instance, positivists analyze the behavioristic study of human beings, but they do not examine the behavioristic context of study from a point of view outside this context. But a nonpositivist philosopher might ask: If a group of men are measured by the use of precisely the same technique, will not the individuality of each escape this scientific study? And how will judgment be passed upon the effect of this omission unless the individuality thus omitted be already understood? Does the program requiring an impersonal study of the personal not demand a distortion at its very inception? Are man and his world subsumable under the hypothesis of uniformity as objects that can, without further question, be made the topics of a (mathematical) science? Indeed, it is not altogether clear whether we have in Hume's skeptical foundation for the science of man the beginning of the bright new world of a scientific society or the initiation of the burial of the individual and the destruction of the world. Without a more inclusive context within which the positivistic one could be situated and by whose standards its adequacy and completeness might be judged such questions can scarcely be settled rationally. But the positivists believe their context to be all-inclusive. Hence such questions, which lie outside their context, cannot be raised intelligibly by positivists.

A critic of the Humean programs might understandably find Henri Bergson's analysis of Punch and Judy to be a most suggestive comparison. Punch and Judy are comic just because they are both puppets and people. Their comic character originates in the insight which opens up a rapid transition between the mechanical and the human contexts. The scientific philosophers, however, miss this comedy since they either dismiss the second context or seriously predict the recognition of its precise identity with the first.

Criticism of this tradition might be carried beyond pointing to its blindness to the insights of comedy. It might point to the difficulty of accounting for any insight at all. For when knowledge is no longer seen as a way to virtue but rather as the way to power over nature, and when man himself becomes understood as an object within nature, then man falls prey to his own exploitative knowledge. He tends to become an element in the social and industrial mechanism. Furthermore, his knowledge becomes a natural object or a process somehow within nature. Then true propositions seem to be derived from the data just as the input into a computer determines the output. Within this epistemological determinism, the distinction between true and false becomes paradoxical. In addition, if knowledge gives us power over nature, and if knowledge is a natural object or process, then knowledge must somehow yield power over knowledge. Following this inference, not a few philosophers have indeed concluded that knowledge is altogether subjective and its axioms arbitrary.[43] In this manner the naturalizing of man and of knowledge have turned the tables upon Cartesian certainty and perhaps upon the scientific spirit as well.

The limited purposes of this book now entail a decision. Having designated the drift of Humean themes in philosophy, we must forego further explicit criticism of Humeanism and further study of its history. The great importance of this kind of philosophy, however, must continually be borne in mind. Indeed, its continuing relevance can hardly be stressed too heavily. I need only add that the success of its programs points to a shift in the stress-center of European philosophy.

Frequently empiricism is regarded as the prime contender against rationalism, and Hume's system is set down as a phase in empiricism. Then Kant's significance is said to lie in his recognition of the insufficiency of either of these two one-sided ways of coming to terms with experience and in his moderation and reconciliation of these extremes. This interpretation of the history of philosophy may be true up to a point, but it fails to do justice to the kind and extent of Hume's significance.

The present interpretation regards the sort of philosophy that Hume advocated as one of the two storm centers around which the modern era revolves. This interpretation sets forth as the central intellectual issue the question whether to seek understanding solely through the sciences and their methods, or whether to locate the sciences within some larger universe upon which they would in some manner depend and from which they—along with other activities—would derive their meaning. In other words, the issue is whether the hypothesis of uniformity is to be expanded without limit to include all

[43] I have attempted to analyze and criticize certain supposed quantities generated, as it seemed to me, arbitrarily. See my article "Operational Definitions and Theory of Measurement" (and criticisms of the same by P. W. Bridgman, S. Ceccato, and V. Somenze) in *Methodos*, 1953, pp. 233–49.

that is—on the assumption that it specifies an adequate meta-physics—or whether this hypothesis will be examined within a more inclusive context, one that is open to other kinds of being. A subordinate but scarcely less weighty question concerns the human being: Can he or can he not be exhaustively studied by the sciences and their techniques? Or as otherwise expressed: Is man homogeneous with the spatiomaterial world which his sciences discover around him? Or is there a basic and irreducible difference between him and nonhuman objects? The response to this problem is in turn intimately linked to the question whether men are to pursue their collective and institutionalized desires by technologically altering the world to suit these desires, or whether each man is to pursue his own good (e.g., harmony with his fate) by seeking to produce some sort of change within himself. These issues eventually become clear after Hume, for then the alternatives were either to accept his kind of system—or at least his objective—together with an exalted evaluation of the sciences and of their institutionalism, or else to take his doctrine as the *reductio ad absurdum* of this trend in philosophy. Which of these is the way of wisdom?

Within either the older or more recent Humeanism there is no doubt about the answer to this question. A contemporary representative of this philosophy, B. F. Skinner, has very adequately summed up the whole outlook in a sentence not intended to be ironic: "Science supplies its own wisdom."[44] The Kantian tradition remains, however, to make the revolutionary suggestion that the wisdom of science is a Faustian wisdom and that the price paid for it is exorbitant: loss of the individual self. The philosopher incarcerated in the narrow confines of this wisdom must continually protect himself, I think, against wondering what being might lie masked and forgotten behind the Cartesian coordinates which stand symbolically for the whole spirit and aim of this Humean and positivist endeavor.

[44] *Science and Human Behavior* (New York: Macmillan, 1953), 6. Skinner also recognizes and accepts the anti-individualistic character of this philosophy; see *ibid.*, 448.

IV

Kant on Nature and
Human Nature

§ 22. KANT'S TASKS

After the Renaissance a new method and a new metaphysics
(greatly to the advantage of physics) took the place of the
classical religious and humanistic philosophy. We have seen
how successful this new metaphysics and its method were in
seeming to open up an era of progress in all fields. Problems
seemed to disappear upon the touch of science or of scientific
philosophy like mists after sunrise. Nevertheless, not all were
converted to the positivistic religion of science, and some were
disenchanted. Again an old story was repeated: A disaffection
developed during the eighteenth century with the regular Newtonian world and its precarious values. The great Lisbon earth-
quake, occurring about the middle of the century, was felt—
Voltaire saw to it—as a shock to the established order of the
Enlightenment. Less than a decade before Kant completed the
Critique of Pure Reason, Goethe expressed the climate of feeling in *The Sorrows of Werther* (1774), whose hero moves from
naive optimism through despair and through loss of identity
and of meaning to suicide. A multitude of suicides followed
upon its publication. Poets began to feel and to express the disproportion between man and the neutral universe. Less than a
decade after the publication of the great *Critique* the Bastille

113

fell and with it, the old order; Frenchmen turned to killing Frenchmen for the good of humanity with what some historians have regarded as the first phase of Romantic enthusiasm. Kant's philosophy must be viewed within this changing context.

Kant was sensitive to the inadequacies of Enlightenment scientific philosophy of his time, especially to its complete failure to recognize and comprehend the uniqueness of the human being. Hence he determined to understand the moral law within man as well as the physical law without, even if this understanding were to require a denial of reason in order to make room for faith. His primary concern was to recapture a unified view of the whole man and of his place in the Copernican cosmos. It was evident that this wider view to which he aspired would require a new point of perspection, a new vision of the arché of philosophy. Like Descartes, he turned to the estranged element of the world—man himself—to discover this arché. But the direction in which he first turned was determined by the chaotic state in which he found the basis of scientific knowledge.

We have seen that the nature of man and his union with the rest of nature had been regarded by rationalistic philosophers through a set of metaphysical premises whose theological character had seemed sufficient to guarantee their validity. Although this metaphysics had been questioned and partly discarded by empiricist philosophers, its place had been taken by only an inadequate view of human knowledge. Briefly, according to the Lockean copy-theory of truth, sensations (which are already knowledge, being simple ideas) are compounded into complex ideas that copy the external physical reality and thus yield knowledge of this reality. But since this correspondence could never be tested by direct confrontation and comparison with reality, the theory inevitably led to the Humean skepticism.

In order to avoid this skeptical outcome, Kant sought to effect a transition into a new type of philosophical context. The time was ripe for a critical philosophy.

Schelling remarked in his Berlin Lectures that "the criticism of a concept questions the possibility of its object." We have already observed that examination of the Cartesian extended physical object betrayed its inaccessibility through the pineal gland, and that examination of the Humean world of customary associations yielding beliefs about a world of persistent objects and "selves" demonstrated it to be incoherent, at best caught within a narrow circularity. Although Kant developed such criticisms in a new manner, his criticisms were determined as much by thorough respect for Newtonian science as by his classical and humanistic convictions. He retained confidence in the power of man to know himself in a manner not derivative from empirical introspection, a belief which he expressed in terms of the power of reason to perceive its own nature and limits and to comprehend its infinite aspirations within the finitude of its rational powers. In addition, he retained a devotion to the general ideal of mathematical clarity and distinctness as the guide to progress of the sciences within the Cartesian-Newtonian world. His philosophical problem was to discover a view within which the claims of these beliefs and ideals would not be contradictory.[1] His way was prepared by the genial recognition of the contrast between transcendental knowledge and empirical knowledge. In these terms he rethought the whole of the foundations of the Cartesian-Newtonian world in its relation to the knowing subject. He then undertook to extend his thought appropriately to include the whole human-being and his noncognitive experience, so far as this inclusion seemed to be rationally possible.

[1] See *Prolegomena*, trans. P. Carus (Chicago: Open Court, 1933), § 60. Also cf. *Critique of Judgment*, trans. J. C. Meredith (Oxford: Oxford University Press, 1952), 13: "That it is possible for us at least to think without contradiction of both these jurisdictions (freedom and nature), and their appropriate faculties, as coexisting in the same Subject, was shown by the *Critique of Pure Reason*."

Kant aspired to show the way across the boundary, if I may so express it, between the Humean skepticism and scientism to a renewed rational and humanistic tradition. This crossing is a movement from a narrowly conceived reason, completely in the service of problems occurring within the well-established Cartesian-Newtonian world, to reason understood as the "whole higher faculty of knowledge." [2] It takes as its task not only the understanding of the physical universe but also the acquiring of insight into human-being and the world of its possible experience, its limits, its ideals, and its goals. Thus, in sum, Kant sought to effect the transition from inherited incoherence and skepticism, as he saw it, into an autonomous physical-human world.

Nevertheless, such was the prestige enjoyed by the Newtonian world, which Kant took for granted, that it contained everything which could properly be regarded as the object of knowledge. Kant, however, like Descartes, recognized that men also possessed infinite ideas, but unlike Descartes, he was unable to rest assured that the primary infinite idea, the idea of God, was placed in man by the Creator Himself as testimony to His handiwork. Thus Kant could not appeal to this idea as the basis for a proof of the existence of God and for an indication of the source of truth. Rather, his critical analysis of the human mind pointed to the finiteness of all man's cognitive powers. In consequence, the objects of these cognitive powers should also be finite and experienceable. Thus the objects studied by the traditional special metaphysics—i.e., the cosmos as a whole, the human soul, and God—not being within the Newtonian world, could not be genuine objects of knowledge. Kant therefore felt it necessary to provide a discipline for the uncritical or infinite use of the reason which might otherwise tend "to tear down all those boundary-fences and to seize pos-

[2] *Critique of Pure Reason*, trans. N. K. Smith (London: Macmillan; New York: St. Martin's Press, 1958), A835, B863; Bxxii f (A and B refer, here as elsewhere, to the standard pagination of the first two German editions). Hereinafter the book is cited as *Pure Reason*. Occasionally, my translation will vary from Smith's; when it does so, the German will be given.

session of an entirely new ground (*Boden*) which owns to no demarcation line" (*Pure Reason* A296, B351). Following upon this destruction of rational metaphysics, Kant expected to discover room for disciplined and defensible beliefs about the human soul, its place in the cosmos, and its fate.

A problem still remained in understanding why men had always aspired to knowledge beyond the boundary lines of the human. Was there some disproportionate and contradictory element within human reason and nature itself which drove it to continual cognitive self-frustration? We know that Kant solved this problem by a reinterpretation of man's nisus after the infinite and of his drive for the complete perfection of knowledge. He reinterpreted the rational ideas which once had seemed to offer a grasp upon the unconditioned condition of the whole universe, an insight into the whole of his own fate, and an understanding of the essence of God, as being properly regulative rather than constitutive in function. Unreified, and correctly understood, these regulative ideas express cognitive values, as it were, and serve rightly to direct the investigator in the making of sciences and in the conduct of human life. Ends and values are thus translated to the human mind and presumably legitimated as part of the mind's natural structure. The cosmological, psychological, and theological ideas, then, specify the character of the tasks which men ought to pursue. So understood, these regulative ideas redirect energies back upon the man and his experience rather than allowing them to be dispersed in infinite speculation. Cognitive values and standards thus have their ground within human subjectivity. Kantian reason is more inclusive and more powerful than empiricist reason, less inclusive and less pretentious than Rationalist reason. By understanding it in this newly delimited sense, Kant expected to manage the unruly but inevitable drives to infinity by redirecting them largely toward scientific endeavor.

Even so, the whole of the value problem is not solved by this interpretation, and Kant's overall task is to see his way completely through the antinomy of freedom and determinism and thus to comprehend how all human values are possible or rationally defensible within a world of rigorously ordered and determined fact. That is to say, his task is to come to see how doctrines in philosophy derived both from the mechanistic analogy and from the artistic analogy are coherent and possible within the same intellectual framework. If he can demonstrate the coherence of scientific knowledge together with views and problems involving choice, moral insight, and aesthetic feeling within an inclusive universe of human reason, then perhaps he can show in particular that human freedom is independent of the mechanical world. Finally, he will attempt to show that human-being can effect changes in the mechanistic world for which man alone is responsible. The consequence might then be the elimination of the sense of alienation which from time to time motivated the elaboration of materialistic or idealistic metaphysical systems and their conflicts, or else seemed to recommend the abdication of philosophy.

Did Kant's revolution enable him to achieve these very considerable aims? Our special concern here is to determine Kant's revolutionary transcendental standpoint and whether or not it successfully moved beyond the inadequacies which were associated with the Renaissance ideal of complete clarity and mathematical exactitude in the knowing of a world and man cut to the uniform pattern of the scientifically intelligible. Thus we ask: Did Kant effect a complete transition into a new Copernican world where the sciences are preserved in union with a just and comprehensive view of the human being and his fate? I want to show how Kant's response to this question, though revolutionary, was not complete. He reached only a foreshortened view of the nature of the objects which men experience. Correlatively there appears a certain incoherence and even an arbitrariness in his philosophy of man. The inadequacies in his view of the world and of man were typical of those aspects of the eighteenth-century thought that led to the Romantic rebellion.

It must be added that the task of considering these matters is rendered difficult by the fact that many of those who have written in English on Kant have been deeply influenced, at least in important facets of their thought, by the Humean tradition. Accordingly, their writing on Kant is often permeated by a sort of naiveté that is the consequence of the failure to understand, or to take seriously, the transcendental direction of Kant's thinking. Their interpretations, being dominated by the scientific model, tend to be psychologistic or subjectivistic. Consequently, it is dangerous to rely heavily upon their interpretations.

§ 23. KANT'S EPISTEMOLOGICAL PROBLEM

The difficulty with much of the epistemology preceding Kant was that the knower had been uncritically considered to be possessed of passive though sensitive organs acted upon mechanically by external objects. The apparent desirable consequence of this view was the continuity of relations between sensation, object, and concept; however, opinion was divided on whether sensation was obscure idea or whether idea was faded sensation. In either case this continuity of linkage seemed to offer the basis for developing an assurance that perception and empirical knowledge were truly related to their referent, the physical object.

As both the rationalist and empirical views were subjected to sharper criticism, however, this view came to be exhibited as a concession to metaphysical determinism which, as associated with the doctrine of representative perception, effectively placed the external world beyond reach and invited an easy transition from Cartesian dualism to Humean skepticism. For whether sensations are identified as obscure idea awaiting only the disciplined inspection by the intellect in order to become knowledge, or whether sensations are the completely formed atoms of knowledge awaiting only their correct compounding by the mind in order to become true copies of objects, in either instance knowledge is essentially already made and given to the knower (*Pure Reason* A271, B327). Knowledge upon both views is prefabricated. Both views solved the epistemological problem by assuming it to have been already solved. Both assume that knowledge itself is something given, even though in somewhat imperfect form. Is the mind (psyche) just this sort of wax tablet which so exactly takes the impress of knowledge from a nature already prepared to give it?

One of the important departures in Kant's philosophy was its divergence from the conviction that sense and concept are continuous. Kant held intuition and concept to be two quite different yet mutually dependent and reciprocally limiting components of knowledge. His arguments in favor of the separation of intuition and understanding are nowhere systematically presented in the first *Critique*. Several of them are offered as criticisms of Leibniz's philosophy in the "Note to the Amphiboly of Concepts of Reflection." There he observes, for example, that two objects which are conceptually indistinguishable—such as two drops of water which have identical properties and hence, upon Leibnizian principles, ought to be a single individual—are in fact two different phenomena. Since their differences are not conceptual, Kant concluded they must be intuitional.[3] In addition, a great part of the first *Critique* is directed toward showing that intuition and thought differ in extent and are mutually limiting, though in different ways (e.g., *Pure Reason* A287f, B343f; A254f, B310f).

On the other hand, this distinction between sensibility and understanding could not have been accepted by either rationalists or empiricists, for it would have left the rationalists' concepts without access to reality, and it would have provided a sensibility which was less passively related to a world more ambiguously external than the empiricists could tolerate.

---

[3] See *ibid.* A272, B328. Similar arguments are advanced in *Prolegomena* § 13. Similarly, it might be added, two definite figures, such as a circle and a square, do not differ *qua* spatial, except that one is here and the other is there. But the hereness and thereness are not conceptual differences; hence, the Kantian conclusion will be, they must be intuitional.

Since Kant made and accepted this distinction, he had to rethink his convictions about the natural world, the self, its experience, and its relation to nature.

Kant's rethinking of these problems must be contrasted with Hume's thought. Hume's philosophy locates the rationale of the sciences and of man within a larger context of custom, belief, and feeling. However, his analytic and reductive methods do not allow him to examine this context philosophically. His philosophy is like a world within a world. Kant's philosophy takes as its task the completion of Hume's kind of philosophy by submitting the larger world of custom, belief, and feeling to critical examination. These spatial metaphors, suggesting that Hume's doctrine lies within a larger context, should not be taken literally. Hume's philosophy is, of course, in no sense contained in Kant's as if derivative from the latter by some sort of restriction. Rather, the sciences and beliefs about man which entered Hume's thought from outside, as it were, and are accepted upon the recommendation of custom and strong feeling, come to be included within Kant's psychic household as to the manner born. But Kant's psychic household is dominated by a reason able to achieve a certain insight into rational nature, its principles, and its standards. Thus Kantian reason is different in kind from the scientific reason allowed in the Humean tradition. Humean reason can be directed upon the self only to the extent that it can discover impressions in and of the self through introspection; Humean self-knowledge is formed strictly on the model of scientific knowledge of an object. Kantian reason is more inclusive in that it questions the possibility and sufficiency of scientific self-knowledge and seeks to justify its results by a measure other than by scientists' customs and contemporary belief.

Kant's reason, the power of judging, is able to comprehend this same power. It expresses its more important conclusions in synthetic a priori propositions. The epistemological question was initially understood to turn on the problem of how we can

make or know such universal judgments about existing things
or nature when we admit that knowledge begins in experience
and that we experience only particular events.[4] How can we
justify our belief that laws of nature will hold true in experience
prior to having had that experience? This is the problem of
induction which Hume had found to be insoluble except in
terms of irrational belief and feeling. Kant forged a concept of
"possible experience" which expresses how disparate particulars
of sense may be understood to be interrelated and unified. Thus
the solution to the problem of induction lies in comprehending
"possible experience."[5]

My purpose here will not be to offer another review of
Kant's thoughts on these topics nor a commentary on his sen-
tences. My purpose is to expound, in his own terms when useful, the sense of his doctrine sufficiently to illuminate the
transcendental turn which enabled him to include scientific
knowledge within a larger rational domain. Thereupon, the
nature of the Copernican revolution in philosophy should
become perspicuous. We may then ask whether or how Kantian
man and nature are able to live together after his revolution.

§ 24.   ON THE POSSIBILITY OF COGNITION

Kant, for the most part, pursued the epistemological and the
transcendental phases of his philosophy simultaneously. The
epistemological phase consisted in identifying instances of
knowing (e.g., the induction of a law in physics), analyzing
these instances into their components, and reducing these components to their essential elements—conceptual and perceptual,
formal and material. The transcendental or metaphysical phase
consisted in the determination of those characteristics of rational being which render possible the synthesis of these elements

---

[4] Kant defines nature as "the existence of things so far as it is determined
according to universal laws," *Prolegomena* § 14. Kant's task may be understood
as the task of discovering the rationale of this definition.

[5] *Pure Reason* A94, B126f; B185; A158, B197.

back into knowledge.[6] Our present purposes entail no need for examining the minutiae of Kant's treatment of these two processes. It will be sufficient to specify the way he understood the receptive-active cognitive powers of human-being in forming his possible experience and their role in opening onto a universe of physical objects. The type of cognitive contact which a man can make with an object will thus be delineated.

Two elements in man's cognitive makeup call for brief comments.[7] One is the active power which he has in common with other beings (Kant often speaks of *any* rational being). The second is that which limits man's cognitive power to just the human world, his passive or receptive power of intuition. The possibility of man's intuition, his sensibility, is the touchstone of finite human-being. An infinite power of intuition would have made him a god.

This receptive sensibility is the representative in Kant's thought of psyche. It is significant that for Kant psyche is much attenuated. No longer is it poetically dreaming, nor is it receptive of inspirations, nor of Platonic recollections, nor of intuitions given by God. To this philosopher of the Enlightenment only the waking and natural function of intuition remained. Intuition functions only aesthetically in rendering sensing possible.

In order to understand Kant on this point, it is essential to avoid the error of supposing sensibility to be identical with sense organs. The supposition that a man receives sensa through sense organs is a psychological hypothesis which must be based upon prior convictions concerning the kind of being man is.

---

[6] "Metaphysical" suffers from an ambiguity. Kant uses the term to refer to totalities, to beings which are said to be beyond-the-physical, such as God, the soul, the cosmos. It is also used, for example, by H. J. Paton in *Kant's Metaphysics of Experience* (New York: Macmillan, 1936), to refer to the transcendental doctrine; "ontological" is probably a better term for this sense.

[7] The reader may interject that a non-Humean account of Kant's transcendental aesthetic and analytic requires more justification and clarification than is offered here. I agree. My apology is drawn from the need to make the most useful emphasis. Not everything can be accomplished in one book.

Hume was willing to accept convictions about man's being from local British belief. Kant, however, is not concerned with psychology, nor does he accept local convictions at their face value. Rather, he takes it as his task to determine the a priori conditions characterizing human beings. As Heidegger has pointed out, we do not receive sensations because we have sense organs; we can have sense organs because we are already sensitive beings.[8]

Kant analyzed our sensitive being into two functional parts. The first is the given sensory elements in perception which are usually interpreted as entering man from "outside" the self. This "outside," however, is not given; rather, it is a metaphor formed upon the basis of the way in which sensing is received. The way in which the sensing is received is determined by the given formal element constitutive of sensibility. With an eye to Newtonian physics, Kant concluded that these formal elements were space and time.

The space and time which are forms or determinations of the sensibility, permitting the reception of intuitions in a certain way, are not yet, however, physical nor even Euclidean beings. Space and time in the sense of forms are rather the dispositions to organize intuitions in a certain manner, a manner describable by mathematical and physical concepts. Rather than being identified as a psychological organ or dismissed as subjective "spectacles," the sensibility should be compared with the Platonic notion of the receptacle (*Timaeus* 48D *sq.*), the foster mother of all worldly beings. The receptacle is receptive of that which becomes definite and localized things. The receptacle, however, is not a perfect mirror of being and leaves its own indefinite trace in that which it receives. The Kantian receptacle leaves more specific traces; in fact, the Kantian foster

[8] Martin Heidegger, *Kant and the Problem of Metaphysics*, trans. J. S. Churchill (Bloomington: Indiana University Press, 1962), 31f. Heidegger, *What Is a Thing?* trans. W. B. Barton, Jr., and Vera Deutsch (Chicago: Henry Regnery, 1967), 143.

mother of physical being has very definite Newtonian prejudices.

This analysis of receptivity into two components, material and formal, is not merely a gesture toward Aristotelianism. It expressed Kant's recognition of the difficulty of distinguishing in a clear-cut and objective manner between the receptivity and the activity of mind at the level of perception. The doctrine of the imagination expressed the same recognition but in another context and for another purpose.

Kant's account of spontaneity constitutes his version of thymos. This version should be understood to go beyond Descartes's view of reason by incorporating within the cognitive faculty the power, which Descartes had rooted in God, of applying concepts beyond themselves and of critically understanding this application. For, according to the form of Cartesianism which influenced Kant, one's own created reason was constituted by one's self-recognition as the knowing subject (the cogito or the "I-principle") together with the principle of contradiction, which was held to be the basic principle of abstract thought (e.g., of mathematics). But the principle of sufficient reason, guiding the use of abstract thought in its reference to other things, was understood by rationalists to require the guarantee of a nondeceiving deity. Kant, however, included the principle of sufficient reason in human reason; it became in his philosophy the highest principle of all synthetic propositions (*Pure Reason* A158, B197). The Transcendental Deduction, the Schematism, and the Principles form respectively the argument, the observations, and the conclusions which justify nontheologically the application of concepts to experience. As we shall emphasize subsequently, possible experience is thus automatically narrowed down to that which is determinable by these principles.

The logical categories, schematized or oriented to experience by the rules constitutive of time or the internal sense, are united by means of the transcendental imagination with spatiotemporally localized intuitions. Spontaneity is thus joined with receptivity by the power of imagination into a unity such that "I think" can be prefaced to any item of experience, any proposition, or any unity of meaning. For example, in speaking such a word as "temporality," the syllables are each received and apprehended. When "—po—" is being uttered, the imagination retains "tem—" and anticipates "—rality." When the utterance is complete, the meaning of the whole is recognized; that is, it is subsumed under a concept (e.g., succession in experience) and can finally be subsumed under the appropriate category or categories.

These syntheses, performed by my one cognitive power, take their place in my unified experience. The emphasis on their unity and on the basis of all knowledge in the transcendental unity of apperception (Kant's I-principle) is another testimony to his recognition of the subtle interlocking of the receptive and the active powers of mind.

Kant showed that the properties of human experience and knowledge entail a definite metaphysical character of human-being such that this being has cognitive access to objects. To attribute this unifying and ordering function primarily to human-being (to transcendental subjectivity) is the Kantian transcendental turn in philosophy.

§ 25.   KANT'S THEORY OF PHENOMENAL OBJECTS

In considering the traits of existing things, the objects of knowledge, we note that these objects are neither reality in itself nor an illusion produced by the imposition of our forms of knowing upon a passive given sensory material, but they are objectively experienceable and knowable. Kant's concept of the phenomenal object presents this insight. Unless this concept proves to be understandable and adequate, the Kantian effort to establish a sound doctrine of nature as the object of the sciences—yet a nature which is the setting within which a man can somehow live and act—will have to be modified or perhaps abandoned.

According to the Transcendental Aesthetic, intuitions are given in sensibility. Then upon this basis the phenomenal object is synthesized. If we reject the subjectivistic view of Kant, which holds that objects as known are arbitrary interpretations of sensa (sense organ stimulations), how shall we conceive of the restriction placed upon our liberty in constructing and knowing the world? Triangularity and circularity are equally figures constructible within the pure intuition. But it is not equally possible that a given sensed object should be interpretable in all respects either as a circle or as a triangle. This limitation placed on possible experience when it is interpreting actual experience raises a question. What is it that necessitates my judgment to admit that a presented figure is a triangle? Intuitions considered alone certainly do not compel my judgment. Color, tactile qualities, other qualia no more entail triangularity than circularity. Conversely, a given mathematical form lays no restrictions upon the sensory qualities which may be associated with it on any occasion. Finally, the concept of circular functions is what it is quite irrespective of any instantiation. It is difficult to avoid the conclusion that these sensory intuitions, pure intuitions, and concepts are distinct factors of knowledge of objects and must indeed be synthesized if a physical object is to be perceived and known.

We have seen that Kant's analysis points to the imagination as the synthesizing agent. Yet if we accept the conclusion that the imagination is the synthesizing agent, we are forced back upon the problem of identifying that factor which prevents the imagination from tyrannizing over its data and interpreting or synthesizing them arbitrarily, without limitation. If the given intuitions have nothing at all inherent within them which might determine their identity objectively, then a given set of intuitions would seem to represent a circle no less easily than a triangle. In other words, the transcendental conditions of experience understood in the sense of empirical knowledge of an objective event are also the transcendental conditions of experience understood in the sense of mere consciousness (e.g., dreaming). These conditions alone, then, provide the necessary but not the sufficient means for distinguishing between truth and dreaming. But an implicit axiom which Kant always holds is that we do live in a sane world where truth is radically distinct from dreaming.

Kant remarks, "Knowledge consists in the determinate relation of given representations to the object" (*Pure Reason* B137). Evidently he means to say that a representation (*Vorstellung*), if true, must correspond with the object to which it refers. But what of this object? How is *it* known to be objective? This standard object which measures the truth of representations does not immediately identify itself or its relations to other represented objects. Kant's distinctions between pure and empirical intuitions and between intuition and concept eliminate any immediate access to the object of knowledge, and they equally eliminate any access mediated by a causal sequence such as some empiricists had imagined to exist. All knowledge consists in representations, and representations are syntheses of intuitional and conceptual elements. If knowledge of an object is measured by a standard object, then we must insist that this standard object be known and, consequently, that it be a representation. It, too, is a synthesis of intuitional and conceptual elements. What, then, is inherent in a representation which determines one interpretation of it to be more objective than another?

Kant answers, "The difference between truth and dreaming is not ascertained by the nature of representations, which are referred to objects (for they are the same in both cases), but by their connection according to those rules, which determine the *coherence* of the representations in the concept of an object, and by ascertaining whether they can subsist together in *one* experience or not." [9] Kant is saying, it seems to me, that not in

---

[9] *Prolegomena* § 13, Remark iii. Italics mine.

virtue of the sensory character of intuitions (which may be the same in dreaming as in waking) but in virtue of their structure (a structure expressed in rules yet also apprehended and recognized in perception) are they known to refer to objects. Structure or form here is not to be understood merely as referring to the organization of intuitions which constitute a single object, for the structure of a representation (*Vorstellung*) may also be the object of a dream or a deception. Rather, the present reference to structure is intended to mean that the object in question belongs to a coherent organization which constitutes my whole unified experience, or better yet, the whole of experience without reference to a particular subject.[10] My interpretation of intuitions as representing a certain object is said to represent objectively and truly in virtue of the coherence of these representations with others (*den Zusammenhang der Vorstellungen*). The necessary elements constitutive of this coherence are the categories; thus Kant can write, "Appearances, so far as they are thought as objects according to the unity of the categories, are called phenomena" (*Pure Reason* A248).

This coherent structure is, as we have seen, determined according to rules which are based upon and express the unity of consciousness and its transcendental conditions. Even so, when these rules are applied in the interpretation of a single object or to a limited span of intuitions, or for an isolated subject, they may be incorrectly used. Error is possible; the ellipse may be mistaken for a circle. But the hypothesis that a given set of intuitions does represent a circle may be shown to be incorrect by noting that it does not cohere with several other hypotheses which are coherent with each other and with the remainder of my experience or with the experience of others. As Kant expresses the same matter, "In order to escape from

[10] See *ibid.* § 20, where the judgment about perceptions related in a particular state of consciousness, and valid only for that state, are distinguished from judgments relating perceptions in consciousness generally (*in einem Bewusstsein überhaupt*). In the latter case the judgment becomes an item in the systematic whole of interdependent judgments and its status in this whole of knowledge is independent of any particular state of consciousness. See also the *Pure Reason* A219–20, and *Prolegomena* § 48.

these false appearances [i.e., dreaming and error], one has to follow the rule that *whatever is connected according to empirical laws with a perception, is real*" (*Pure Reason* A376). When a hypothesis about the identity of an object has been shown to cohere with other objects (similarly identified) so that they all belong in "one experience," then we may say that the phenomenal object has been truly identified. My (our) one experience, it is to be understood, extends over a considerable time. Objects in it persist; they are involved in cause and effect relationships in past and future time as well as in relationship with coexisting objects.[11]

One of Kant's remarks sums up the whole matter. "Knowledge is [essentially] a whole in which representations stand compared and connected" (*Pure Reason* A97; cf. A210). Objectivity, then, is defined in terms of coherence with the whole of experience. A representation of an object which is thus coherent with the remainder of experience is a phenomenal object.

The situation in which we have knowledge of nature, or of "the existence of things" so far as determined according to laws, may be summarized in this fashion. Representations (i.e., intuitions having objective structure) are what we know. A representation is objectively true when it corresponds with a phenomenal object. An object is phenomenal when it, too, has objective (intuitive–conceptualizable) structure and when, in addition, it coheres with and is determined within the whole of experience. This is to say that the experience of existing objects has the same structure or is developed out of the same conditions as the objects of experience. Obviously in this philosophy we never achieve a knowledge of noumenal reality, for the object of knowledge is (experienceable) nature; neverthe-

---

[11] Coherence of objects, in other words, is to be defined primarily in terms of the three categories of relation: substance, causality, and community. These categorial ways in which the understanding—the faculty of rules—operates are expressed as principles in the Analogies of Experience, principles which determine the relations of objects among themselves. A nonobjective object (e.g., a dreamed object) is one which does not belong within this rule-determined whole. See *Pure Reason* A200, B245.

less, we certainly can distinguish between illusion and phenomena.[12]

Although we can distinguish illusion from what Kant calls phenomena, this definition of phenomena by reference to empirical law seems to narrow excessively the field of phenomena. For what, precisely, does Kant mean by empirical law? Does he not refer only to the laws of physics as known in his day? And does he not also tend to eliminate the phenomena as experienced when its empirical law is not known or is irrelevant? More pointedly, does he not also remove the value dimension of experience from phenomena? Kant's phenomenal object, it is easy to persuade oneself, is rather thin in comparison with the phenomena as experienced. Thus there is ample room for doubt that Kant has succeeded in providing a doctrine of a nature or world in which men may live and act. We must, nevertheless, endeavor to see his doctrine of the phenomenal object in relation to the function which it was to perform.

If, therefore, we revert back to the definition of nature as "the existence of things as it is determined according to universal laws," perhaps it will be agreed that Kant's term "existence of things" refers to the coherently interconnected whole of specifically Newtonian phenomena. When an appearance can be shown to belong within this coherent whole, then it becomes a genuine phenomenal object or an objectively exist-

[12] I distinguish here and elsewhere in this chapter between nature or the world of phenomenal objects or substances ordered by empirical law and the unexperienceable noumenal reality which is of a different genus (e.g., God, the moral law, *ibid.* A259). Also I distinguish between phenomenal objects or objects of experience and "those same things as things in themselves" (Bxxvii). The latter might be in experience in a certain respect, but they are never wholly in experience but only in themselves (A42, B59). They, however, may function in their capacity as fully determined as limits toward which our knowledge may ideally be directed. This second sense of the thing in itself is Kant's guard against what has sometimes been called the fallacy of misplaced concreteness; whereas the first distinction is metaphysical. It must be admitted that Kant was not always consistent in his use of this terminology. But it does not follow that he was confused about it. Cf. George Schrader, "The Thing in Itself in Kant's Philosophy," *Review of Metaphysics*, March, 1949, pp. 30–44. Reprinted in Robert P. Wolff (ed.), *Kant: A Collection of Critical Essays* (New York: Doubleday, Anchor Books, 1967), 172–88.

ing thing (*Pure Reason* A542, B570). It can become, then, an object of physics or of a science like physics. Otherwise it is a *mere* appearance, and though it may be discussed as the subject of a judgment of perception, we cannot be certain of its objectivity. It may, therefore, be a dream or a deception.

Now, this doctrine effectively disposes of the subjectivistic view of Kant (the spectacle analogy). The forms of space and time are not to be arbitrarily imposed upon sensa. Phenomenal objects themselves limit and determine our interpretations of intuitions. The same doctrine also enables us to avoid the opposite epistemological extreme, the realistic belief that the object in itself determines our interpretation of intuitions. For we could not even become aware of an object in itself unless the interpretative activity of the mind is called into play. But then the object in itself becomes interpreted in respect to our perceptual perspective and is no longer in itself; rather it is in the sphere of experienceable objects.

Knowledge, then, is the perceptual and theoretical transform of objects in those limited respects in which objects, as Newtonian phenomena, are accessible or fall within the horizon defined by transcendental conditions of cognition.

Kant's enduring gift to philosophy is the insight that the phenomena which we come to know objectively are the result of a cooperative interplay between the intuitable and rationalizable object and the rational maker who, strangely, can reach toward the object, as it were, outside his subjectivity. And yet such a maker will readily admit that "outside" can have no literal or empirical meaning in respect to subjectivity, and in any event a *meta*-physical object, an object in itself, cannot be "reached" nor even "reached toward." Nevertheless, such terms can be understood transcendentally; they are then referred to that original making, the initiation of a unified world, which is the interplay of the human cognitive power with that which is not it but yet is not inaccessible to it. And this is the interplay from which everything that we can know or experience is derivative, including such relations as "outside" and "inside" and such activities as "interplay." With Kant, in short, we reach the stage in philosophy where knowledge of this inception of our world—its possibility—can be critically pursued. With Kant the transcendental needs and orientation of philosophy become self-aware.

§ 26. THE NATURE OF TRANSCENDENTAL KNOWLEDGE

The general characterization of transcendental knowledge can be accomplished by stressing the nonobjective character of this knowledge, its priority over objective knowledge, its peculiar relation to the subject, and its function in providing a basis or ground for inductive empirical knowledge and for a more adequate doctrine of man. The general sense of the term "transcendental" is clear enough; this is the sense which may describe, for example, the discussion of a science or a discipline which transcends the methods used by that science or discipline. Thus, when a professor on a university faculty asserts that physics has great humanistic value, his statement cannot be tested by the methods and criteria of physics. For the statement refers to the whole of physics and must, therefore, belong to a context of thought which includes physics as one of its elements. We may then say that that statement is transcendental, at least as respects physics. In this generic sense, Kant's investigation of knowledge was transcendental with respect to all scientific and mathematical knowledge.[13]

Kant's investigation and its stated results are also transcendental in a more specifically philosophical sense.[14] For he was not merely concerned to characterize scientific knowledge. He was especially concerned to determine the character of human-being, in consequence of which he can come to have experience

[13] Today this point might be made by describing transcendental speech as metalinguistic. But this grammatical description of the language used provides no new understanding of the topic which Kant was endeavoring to grasp.

[14] In Kant's words, transcendental knowledge concerns "the a priori possibility of knowledge or its a priori employment." See *Pure Reason* A56, B81; again, transcendental logic concerns the nonempirical "origin of the modes in which we know objects" (A55, B81).

or knowledge of objects. Kant's interest was transcendental with respect to the whole of human experience.

Empiricists had assumed that human-being is somehow possessed of whatever may be required to experience objects in a Cartesian-Newtonian world—the world which they presumed men to inhabit—and to come to know them. Kant did not merely accept this assumption; he regarded it as a problem and investigated these requirements. The determination of what we must have or be in order that an object or a determined sequence of objects or events be experienced and known to us is precisely Kant's transcendental problem (*Pure Reason* A11, B25). It merits repeating that the question concerning the psychological or physiological organs and operations by means of which these conditions become effective is an entirely secondary and dependent question. Let us, then, recognize that Kant is making a transcendental investigation into the conditions of experiencing and knowing, and let us attempt to follow his lead in determining just what kind of knowledge this knowledge about knowing may be.

I think it evident that the knowledge which he is seeking is a very special sort; accordingly, we must distinguish it with great care from other sorts of knowing. Kant repeatedly makes it evident, for instance, that the imagination which unites the receptive power of intuition with the active power of conceiving is the *transcendental* imagination (e.g., *Pure Reason* A115f, B151f). Imagination in this sense is that which renders our unified experience possible. As such, this imagination cannot itself be an occasion of experience; being a condition of experience, it is not an experienceable and analyzable object (e.g., an organ or psychological faculty); hence it is not the object of any science (e.g., of physiology or psychology). What, then, can this transcendental element or function be if it is not a psychological faculty, or an image, or a statement, or an object? Since it is none of these, this transcendental imagination cannot be defined by way of contrast with some other object or class of objects. Moreover, if it is not objectively definable, then neither can it be subjective or identical with an empirical subject, for such a subject is always correlative to a knowable object, indeed is recognized by contrast with the objective—a point made quite clear by Descartes (and see *Pure Reason* A274f and B422a). Evidently, then, as Kant recognized, this transcendental element is nonobjective and is prior to knowledge of both object and subject. Then also, if it is known, knowledge of it must be a rather special sort of knowledge; certainly it is not scientific or mathematical knowledge.

The "object" of transcendental knowledge is, in Kant's view, that which we must possess in order to grasp a knowing subject as subject. Thus it is that which enables a distinction between subject and object to be made. It refers to the conditions which something must meet in order that it be able to know objects. It is thus prior to the knowing subject's scientific understanding of objects and of himself.[15] For instance, a man is spatializing or space-forming prior to sensing himself in a place or to bumping against objects in space. He must be space-forming in order to perform these operations. We may say, then, that his psyche is such that it enables him to live under these conditions. As we could say, a violinist "knows" how to play the violin, meaning that he possesses the habits and sensitivity enabling him to make violin music, so we say that all men possess transcendental "knowledge," meaning that they are originally endowed with that sensitivity enabling them to meet objects in terms of far and near, early and late, and the like. Kant's endeavor is to analyze and to conceptualize this (prepropositional) transcendental knowledge, its basic forms,

[15] Up to a point, this interpretation is consonant with Heidegger's. Heidegger, of course, quite clearly expresses the transcendental character of Kant's undertaking, but he goes on further to identify the imagination as the common root of the two stems (sense and understanding) from which knowledge grows (cf. *ibid.* A15, B29). See Heidegger's *Kant and the Problem of Metaphysics* § 27. The present interpretation does not need to determine the origin of sense and understanding and hence neither affirms nor denies Heidegger's identification of their source with the imagination.

its kinds, and its modalities. The result of his investigation is transcendental knowledge in a second and philosophic (propositional) sense.

It will be well to make two of these points, the priority of the transcendental and its function in separating the subject from the object, in still other ways.

Consider what would be the consequence if the unity of consciousness, the unity of the possible perceiver-knower, were to cease. Then the unity of the perception or of the experience of knowing would *ipso facto* be destroyed; however, the interruption of the existence or character of the object perceived or experienced need not compromise the unity of the subject. Thus the unity of the knowing subject is presupposed by the unity of the experienced object. This unity of the subject, which transcends the unity of the object, can also be apperceived. But the empirical apperception of the self is intermittent. The self's continued identity, then, presupposes a further unity of apperception. This transcendental unity, the "I think . . . ," can always precede any synthesis of intuitions presently apprehended in space or time, in the memory or reproduction of their permanence in succession, and finally in the recognition of the constant species of unity which they exemplify. In short, if an object is knowable, then it is in principle within my unified conscious experience, which is to say that it is knowable a priori to be both intuitable and subject to the definite kinds of intellectual patterning or synthesis which already belongs always to the structure of the transcendental unity of apperception.

Conversely, the transcendental conditions of experience also maintain the separation of the experience of the subject from the object experienced. For the functioning presence of these prior conditions defines the transcendental subject; and the effect of this presence is exhibited in the empirical self or in the object as unified and known. The experiencing or empirical subject is, as it were, between the transcendental conditions as such and the experienced or conditioned objects. The mind

(*Gemüth*) is the means through which transcendental conditions organize objects and the world of objects which we can come to know in a manner that is expressive of the intelligible character of objects as well as of the intelligent structure of mind.

Again, the matter is worth repeating: that "in" which subject and object both are, which also enables the distinction between them to be made, would seem to be neither empirical subject nor object but rather transcendental in relation to both. So much at least is the outcome of Kant's ontology of the experiencing subject. This ontology has dual consequences: It provides a ground or rationale for empirical and inductive knowledge; secondly, it opens the way to a nonobjective doctrine of man. In both these respects Kant opened a way to the solution of philosophic problems which Hume and the Humeans had relinquished.

Thus, in the first instance, Kant's ontology enabled him to give an account of the unities and uniformities in experience without appeal either to psychological laws (e.g., association) which need to be induced from that same experience, or to pragmatically defended customs or definitions whose further defense would likewise beg the question, or to the theological postulate concerning a nondeceiving deity somehow known to act in uniform ways. For if we accept Kant's determination of man *qua* knower, then we may conclude that our perception and theoretic knowledge of objects is the transform of objects in just those possible aspects in which the transcendental conditions that Kant found to be in and through us are effective in rendering objects accessible to us. Since objects experienced and experience of objects must always conform to the same conditions, our knowledge of objects may be extended beyond those objects actually experienced to others which are experienceable. The hypothesis of uniformity and its use in grounding inductions to empirical laws of phenomena from the experience of a few instances is thus justified and Humean skepticism in this regard is annulled. Transcendental knowledge assures us that the gap between man and nature in respect to cognition is bridged. To this extent Kant provided a solution to his version of the transcendental problem.

Probably most readers must continually remind themselves, just as Kant did, that the conditions for experiencing objects or the conditions which objects meet when they are experience-able are themselves neither experienced objects nor experi-enceable. These conditions are not things which are determined by these same conditions. Thus the second part of the Kantian ontology takes note of the fact that the knowing subject bears a peculiar relation to these nonobjective, a priori conditions of objects. For this subject, being immediately determined by the transcendental conditions, is distinct from an object in at least one crucial respect: precisely in its power of mediating experiential and cognitive contact with an object (or with itself as object). This power of making cognitive contact with an object is not the consequence of a peculiar locus in space and time nor of any categorializable factor; such loci and factors are rather the cognitive contact already made. The power of making such contact is just the being which the knowing sub-ject is; thus this transcendental subject is the medium between abstract transcendental conditions and empirical objects. Kant, investigating this mediating being, is making an ontological investigation. This knowledge of being is the transcendental knowledge which must be sharply distinguished from that which it limits and renders possible—namely, experience and knowledge of objects, or experience and empirical knowledge of the self (*Pure Reason* A735, B763).

It is quite difficult to imagine how some of Kant's commen-tators could have thought his transcendental investigation to have been a sort of confused psychology. What kind of psy-chological investigation could be supposed to yield knowledge of its own possibility? It is equally difficult to divine what those critics mean who conclude Kant's philosophy to be a doctrine of a "man-made world." What infantile fantasy is such a making supposed to be? If anything is made, it is a view of the possibility of interacting perceptually and conceptually with the objective world. Or a man may be said to *make* contact with the world, and thus in a sense he makes what it is from his point of access to it. But this "production" came into being with a man's birth. Kant is seeking to analyze and to conceptualize what makes a man to be in a human world.

Something rather more like the distinctive character of transcendental knowledge may be brought home by an attempt to design an experiment for testing that "being $= X$," which is supposed to mediate the transcendental conditions that we are discussing. Perhaps an environment could be designed which would be favorable for learning mathematics and physics. Then someone may reason: If the being $= X$ makes progress toward learning mathematics and physics in this environment, then he will possess the human cognitive power and will, therefore, be human. However, it must be noted that failure to make this progress is not conclusive proof that the being $= X$ is not human. More importantly, it is to be observed that this learning-experience is not the outcome of an experiment in the proper sense of the term. The being $= X$ is not, in fact, designed to embody the given conditions nor can this being be altered in this respect in order to observe possible correlative changes in its behavior; we merely altered the character of the environment in order to elicit evidence of the conditions possibly already present in the being $= X$. Most significant, however, is this fact: that these conditions were discovered in the first place by a reflexive analysis of our own knowledge and of beings which we had already recognized to be human cognitive subjects. The grasp upon this human power must be a priori, and the "experiment" of testing for it is only deceptively similar to building apparatus and experimenting with the objects of a science. The deceptiveness of this "experiment" lies in the ease with which we either overlook our elementary human powers altogether or else presume them to be effects or combinations of the objects which those same powers have enabled us to experience. To examine this presumption is to launch on a critical and transcendental investigation into the inception and foundation of our world.

I believe, now, that Kant's main point may be summarized in a sentence: Any being conditioned by the sort of transcendental imagination which he described, one which limits and determines imaginative functioning in the manner analyzed in the section on the transcendental schemata (*Pure Reason* A137 *sq.*, B176 *sq.*), will experience and will, accordingly, be able to know his experience just as human cognitive subjects actually do experience and know. The emphasis here falls on the term "know." Kant's primary interest is in our mode of access to the Newtonian universe. It is this which we experience and know.

A very important limitation upon the possible acceptability of Kant's philosophy follows from his initial and uncritical acceptance of a view of knowledge associated with the Enlightenment. The character of this limitation is best seen in relation to the general drift of his transcendental reasoning. We may abbreviate his reasoning thus: If a being does possess and can use the transcendental conditions which Kant describes, then that being can come to experience and to know in the human manner. Since we are plausibly assumed to acquire and possess some knowledge, two further questions become relevant. First, how is the knowledge which we possess to be described? Second, how is this knowledge to be analyzed in order to isolate and conceptualize its conditions? Kant directed his critical attention upon the second rather than upon the first question. Guided and limited by the Cartesian ideal of clarity, he thought it obvious that mathematics and physics were knowledge and that other kinds of knowledge would resemble these types in all essential respects. He naturally concluded, therefore, that the transcendental conditions for this knowledge—the two forms of intuition and the twelve categories, unified in the transcendental imagination—were the necessary conditions for *all* human experience.

In this acceptance, Kant was the child of his times, sharing both in its insights and in its blindnesses. For since he accepted the assumption that mathematics and physics are knowledge in an archetypal sense, his analysis of this knowledge and its objects naturally led to the discovery of conditions for just this kind of knowledge and thence to the conclusion which expressed this assumption explicitly—that "knowledge," not the product of these conditions, is not genuine but sophistic. Likewise, objects of experience which do not meet these conditions are not genuine objects but illusions. Indeed, this latter conclusion follows immediately from Kant's usual equation of experience with empirical knowledge (*Pure Reason* B147). The value-laden objects of living experience are, then, somehow not genuine objects, for all real objects are phenomenal. Real objects are physical substances interacting according to empirical laws in uniform space and time. In spite of the rich new possibilities for philosophy opened up by Kant's search for the arché in the direction of the transcendental, the fact that he limited phenomena to phenomena-for-physics showed that his thought was still determined by the Cartesian ideal of rational clarity.

We are returned to a previously recognized difficulty—the difficulty of living a human life in a neutral universe. Kant's revolution, as so far considered, has placed man's cognitive relation to the world upon a new basis, but only his cognitive relation. Before, however, considering Kant's struggle with other aspects of the whole transcendental problem, it will be useful to locate his revolution within the history of thought.

§27. THE KANTIAN-COPERNICAN REVOLUTION
      AND ITS AVOIDANCE

Specifying the transcendental character of knowledge about the origin of the phenomenal object and about the subject's mediation of the conditions of phenomenal reality brings the discussion to the point where the significance and accomplishment of the Copernican revolution in respect to cognition can be viewed in a historical perspective. The Copernican revolution in philosophy is the turn to transcendental thinking in the search for solutions to such problems as these: What sort of thing is an object? What sort of being must a man be in order to experience and to know objects and their laws? What is the character of the intersection of the object-world with human subjectivity? In executing the turn to transcendental thinking about such problems, the Kantian revolution, prepared by Plato, completes the Cartesian one.

Plato's analysis of sense experience had led him to the conviction that the recurrent and permanent properties perceivable in experience were inexplicable apart from the transcendent-immanent forms or ideas in which perceived objects and true opinion about those objects participated. Evidently participation of the self and of the mind in ideas is different from participation of objects in them. Thus Plato points to a kind of psychic participation or recollective knowledge which anticipates experience. This nonobjective and precognitive knowledge finds a place in Plato's philosophy partly in his attempt to solve the problem of participation by use of transcendental notions such as being, good, and similar ones (*Sophist*), and partly in his account of the receptacle (*Timaeus* 40D *sq.*), which provides a situation for objects.

The Cartesian philosophy began with the cogito; that is, it elaborated an understanding of the existence and nature of the self in independence of knowledge of the world of objects external to the self. The human-being's initial and primary certitude refers only to itself. This certitude provides a sort of negative definition of objects: Objects are that which the self certainly is not. This negative definition may be viewed as a summary of Descartes's anti-anthropomorphic polemic and as the beginning of his anthropocentrism.

The positive doctrine of objective being and knowledge of the same is a development out of Descartes's view of the ontological dependence of human-being upon the perfect and infinite Being and out of his presupposition of the superior cognitive value of mathematical ideas. The objective reference of the latter ideas is mediated by a theological critique of memory, imagination, and sense—intermediaries between the self and the external world—by means of which the mathematical essences of objects can be concluded to be represented truly to the self by clear and distinct ideas. Such knowledge has an "as-if" status. The route to certainty lies through insight into the nondeceptive nature of God. Thus God is the transitional being who renders it possible for man to acquire an access to the objective world and to be assured of the truth of his representations of this world. The negative doctrine of objects or their nonmental character becomes positive when it is shown, with the help of theology, that the criterion of truth can be applied through the mediation of the disciplined aids to the intellect in the acquisition of knowledge of objects. Thus something like the principle of sufficient reason is derived.

Here, then, the way seemed to be opened to positive knowledge of the object-world external to the mind within a context in which human-being is not reduced to object-being. For Descartes could argue, as against the possible absorption of the human-being into the physical world of the Renaissance, that, strictly speaking, man was not and could never have been within the physical world. He was ontologically excluded from it. The risk, however, of assigning to the self this nonobjective status was that the ontological dualism could easily be altered to produce other contexts less favorable to man. Moreover, the logical defects of his dualism kept an insoluble form of the transcendental problem alive as a motive for turning to other such contexts.

Thus Descartes's beginning with the cogito or self-certainty, which was independent of knowledge of objects, only to arrive at knowledge of objects in a subsequent and dependent stage of thought, is the first step in the Copernican revolution in philosophy. It is easy to see that Kant took the second and more self-critical step.

Although the movement of Kant's thought is quite different from both Plato's and Descartes's, the essential features of the three are sufficiently similar to warrant considering them to be partners in a philosophic venture. Kant saw no less clearly than Descartes that the object of physics could not be conceived anthropomorphically. He did not, however, turn to theology in order to discover a means for passing beyond the negative definition of the object—as nonanthropomorphic—to positive knowledge of its mathematical and mechanical character. He turned rather to an analysis of the cognitive experience and to its limitations in order to discover the necessary conditions under which physical objects can be experienced and coherently represented as they are in fact. Also like Descartes, he found the first principle of knowledge about the human cognitive power to lie in the cogito, the unity of consciousness. Again, he did not need to follow Descartes's subsequent recourse to theology nor Plato's reference to an all-inclusive and superrational being, for he discovered within the self the transitional being which would mediate the conditions of experience. Human thought limiting and limited by receptivity provided a sufficient account of the a priori conditions of experience. Man becomes the bearer of the transcendental. And thus for Kant, man's psyche naturally and constantly performs the mediating function which Descartes could understand only with the help of theology and Plato only through a kind of unspecified recollective insight. The principle of sufficient reason has thus come to be intrinsic to reason.

Kant's famous metaphysical absorption of the Copernican configuration into philosophy should probably be understood in a Keplerian sense. For Kant the horizon of the objective world has two foci: the ideally determined thing in itself (a focus occupied by no experienceable thing) and the transcendental self with its receptive-spontaneous powers. The laws which determine experienceable objects in their orbits around these foci are the four sets of categorial principles. All experienceable objects are in these orbits, including (in a modified sense (see § 29), the empirical self. To make the illustration fit, it must especially be remembered that the two foci are not merely unique points. They have transcendental functions;

hence they are different in kind from other points of the figure. This metaphor is the appropriate Kantian one and should replace the popular but misleading spectacle analogy.

This view of the relation between man, the subject, and the objective world—the object of the sciences—should be contrasted with that offered by the Humean positivists. For these latter philosophers may be regarded as returning man to the Copernican-physical universe. According to their opinion the purified positive knowledge of objects is final and self-sufficient in that it requires neither a theological guarantee nor a determining relation to conditions of cognitive subjectivity. It requires, for the positivists, only verification by officially accepted methods of logico-empirical procedure. According to their opinion, any view which is not the issue of a science or mathematics can be nothing other than sophistry or illusion. Thus, if anything performs the transcendental function for their philosophy, it is the scientific opinion that has been blessed by official recognition (compare Hume's custom, belief, and feeling). Hence they deny that there is any knowledge about so-called nonobjective and conditioning elements of human experience. Are these philosophers merely displaying a semantic prejudice? Or do they fail to understand the problem and fail to see the transcendentally functioning conditions which contain its answer? Or are they correct, and is Kant peddling a pipe dream?

A beginner in philosophy might attempt to counter the positivists' antitranscendental stand by observing that the empirical criterion of truth is neither a formal proposition, and thus true by definition, nor can it be verified (without committing *petitio principii*) by use of the empirical methods adopted by positivism. He will probably find, however, that the logical positivist has armed himself in advance against this objection, for the beginner will be informed that the procedural rules of scientific method are not the sort of thing which are either verifiable or nonverifiable. They are, rather, like definitions which may technically be called arbitrary; yet they receive an accolade or defense not on formal grounds, but from the fact that they work predictably and are accepted by those members of the scientific community who enjoy the highest authority.

I think it not difficult to see that this line of defense suffers from the same defect which Kant found in Hume's rejection of the causal principle. Hume had concluded the relation of causality to be in fact only a custom bred by association, a confident expectation that B would follow upon A just as it always had. In effect, as Kant points out in the discussion of the Second Analogy of Experience, Hume cannot distinguish between an object dependent upon his personal viewing, having only a subjective order (one which is altogether a function of the subject and his perspective) and an object having an objective order (one whose serial character is independent of the viewer). Kant also makes a psychological point: He argues that the experience of objects in objective succession, such as a ship moving downstream, is required if one is ever to call association into operation in the first place and to build up habits or customs in viewing things. Custom, even arbitrarily accepted definitions and the habits of the most respected of scientists, can be developed only within a regular world. Structures of such customs and psychological habits constitute a kind of dependent world within a world. In other words, the development of habits or customs and their gradual changes presuppose that life goes on in an already existing physical and objective environment where we can and do distinguish the sophistic from the objective, the illusory from the real. This latter, the real world, becomes the noncustomary and objective basis for the customary. Hume's philosophy, in other words, assumes such a world of orderly, interacting, and uniform physical objects to be given. His is a world within a natural world, but unlike a philosophic Copernican, he takes this second world for granted. No less do later positivists take for granted both the scientist and his powers and the persistent and regular object which he studies. Positivists turn away from questioning this world, man, and the relations between them and attempt instead to become the scientist's assistant. They avoid the Copernican revolution in philosophy.

In a word, Kant is concerned to understand the necessary conditions under which there can be an objective world and knowledge of it. The Humean tradition, on the other hand, is concerned with understanding and using the sufficient conditions for acquiring knowledge of such a world—the scientific method itself. There is this additional difference, however: The Humean tradition tends to ignore or to deny the cogency of the Kantian problem and method.

Although customs are dependent upon relations to objects whose regular behavior transcends custom, it does not follow that objects as known transcend all relation to the knower. Such a transcendent object would be the famous thing in itself. And being in itself—not in relation to a subject, not within the orbit of his experience—would be quite off the knower's horizon. For Kant, the experiencing subject is the medium for the transcendental conditions which experience must meet if it is to fall within the human horizon and be known or be experienced. Finally, this defining relation of objects to a subject is not a relation to the everyday personal and empirical self. Since any man possibly embodies these impersonal subjective conditions, any man can become the disciplined subject without whose impersonal view there could be no impersonalized object. To be a physical object is to be cognitively related to such a subject.

Thus, in summary, Kant has moved from common and scientific knowledge, which was understood to be subject to analysis, back to the impersonal transcendental knower—its *sine qua non*—with the insight that the physical world—the object of knowledge—is located within the purview defined by the knowing subject's transcendental powers. This is the direction of thought initiated by Descartes when he placed the knower outside of the known object-world. Kant took the next step by discovering the possibility of the object-world within transcendental subjectivity. This is just the direction of thought which both the naturalistic metaphysics of a Hobbes and the empirical and behavioristic doctrines of the Humeans have chosen to avoid. They remain altogether within the Copernican-physical world. These two, then, the Humean and the Kantian, the Britisher and the European, designate the two foci around which modern thinkers have arranged their uneasy tensions.

It will now be desirable to inquire concerning the relation of this transcendental cognitive self to the human being as he functions in other relations and in other contexts. Does Kant succeed in complementing his account of the impersonal viewer's knowledge of the depersonalized world with an account of the concrete individual's involvement in the world in which he lives and acts?

§ 28.   KANT'S DOCTRINE OF THE SELF

In considering the relation of the self to the natural or phenomenal world, our emphasis, like Kant's, must now be placed upon the not exclusively cognitive but more inclusive sense of the self. However, no matter what doctrine of this more concrete self is developed, it must remain consistent with the metaphysics of nature as elaborated thus far. The problem arises from the fact that the self is empirical or natural, at least in part; but its ethical involvement suggests that it also exceeds this sphere. Thus our question is not merely whether the self can live with nature after the Kantian revolution. Rather ours is also the prior question whether the self can live with the self. Is self coherent with self in all its Kantian senses?

Two of the central conclusions of Kant's metaphysics are the doctrine of existing things (phenomenal objects) and the distinction between these and noumenal reality. Phenomenal reality was established by the former doctrine as "in" (*Pure Reason* A373) or dependent in certain ways upon the cognitive mind. One might have expected this conclusion to be developed along with a doctrine of the self which would be no less rational than the world it contains or conditions but which would also possess specifically human properties of its own, the object of a genuine self-knowledge. Thus Kant's first conclusion, developing the account of phenomenal objects, established physics upon a firm basis and seemingly placed the external world at man's disposal as a knowable and dependable scene wherein to live his life and as a reliable instrument for accomplishing his purposes. The second conclusion, distinguishing phenomena from noumena, might have been thought to offer a basis for this other discipline which would organize knowledge of human nature and its world of values. Just as natural phenomena are the objects of physics, so one may at first expect noumena to become the objects studied by an appropriate science of man's human nature and good.

Kant's purged epistemology, however, takes back what his metaphysics of experience might have seemed to promise. For Kant, like others of his time, never questioned the conviction that mathematics and mathematical knowledge of nature were knowledge in a unique and superior sense. Just as Descartes had been dominated by certain inherited theological ideas, so Kant's thought was determined by the leading scientific ideas of his day. Moreover, his own epistemological defense of these ideas ruled out of court the possibility of acquiring knowledge, in the proper sense, of a nonempirical yet real self. In fact, the distinction between phenomena and noumena became the conceptual instrument for destroying the supposed sciences of the infinite which belonged to the traditional special metaphysics. Among these destroyed sciences was rational psychology, whose object, the real and immortal self, is just as unknowable as any other noumenon.

Nevertheless, Kant never doubted but that he lived in a sane world. And a sane world is one where rationally defensible standards of value apply to human motivations, achievements, and feelings. It behooved him, therefore, to discover the rationale of such a world. The difficulty lay in developing a doctrine of the self which would be coherent with his purged epistemology.

The difficulty of his task is manifested by the multifold guises in which the self enters the *Critique of Pure Reason*. For instance, the self possesses a phenomenal and objective aspect quite like any other space-occupying object (*Pure Reason* A546, B574). This self may be called body; it is an object of the sciences of physics and physiology. There is, in other words, room for a behavioristic study of man in the Kantian economy.

In addition, Kant points out that one is aware of oneself as affecting the inner sense and as appearing to oneself in every act of attention. This is the empirical self which must be understood in the same manner as any other temporally unified object (*Pure Reason* B153f).

Likewise, there is the pure self of apperception; this is the transcendentally synthesizing self of whom we can only say *that* it is or exists, not *what* it is (*Pure Reason* B157). But the sense in which this apperceived self is said to exist is unusual. The existence affirmed of it is not categorial existence, for this latter is a function of the synthetically active self organizing its experience, whereas "self" in the present sense is intended to refer to the self which is thus active. Kant holds that there is no determining intuition of this self (B157a). The categories, therefore, bear no determined relation to it. Nevertheless, Kant does remark that the "I think" of pure apperception expresses an "indeterminate empirical intuition" which is not definable categorially, but which gives occasion for an intellectual representation of the real self—or so I interpret the difficult note on page 422 of the second (B) edition of the *Critique*.[16] Possibly Kant is referring to something between the empirical self, object of inner intuition, and the unknowable noumenal self. Possibly he is anticipating the judgment of reflection which is analyzed and discussed in the *Critique of Judgment*. The self regarded as the subject of such a judgment would not have a specific predicate; rather its predicate would be felt. Still it would not be felt in an arbitrary manner; it would be felt under certain

[16] Paul Ricoeur regards this version of the Kantian self as approaching the Husserlian notion of the transcendental ego; see his "Kant and Husserl," in *Husserlian Studies in Phenomenology*, trans. Edward G. Ballard and Lester Embree (Evanston: Northwestern University Press, 1967), 185f; and see below § 34.

transcendental conditions as determinable (though not determinate). It might be represented intellectually by the moral theorist, or it might be apprehended poetically or inspirationally by the artist or moral hero.

Kant, however, does not explicitly develop the suggestions contained in the note to which allusion was just made (*Pure Reason* 422a). Nor does he develop the note's possible connection with the doctrine of the second and third critiques. He devotes most of his attention, rather, to elaborating what may be believed or what must be postulated concerning the noumenal self. Accordingly, our attention will be turned mainly upon the noumenal self. An appropriate transition to this topic may be made by way of some remarks upon the empirical self, for this is the self which may be presumed to achieve or to fail to achieve moral worth.

§ 29. THE EMPIRICAL SELF IN THE PHYSICAL WORLD

The soul, as the drift of the discussion of the first three paralogisms indicates, can be known only empirically. This empirical study is psychology. But of what sort is this study? Is it a science? No doubt what was just termed the "bodily self" (§ 28) is known empirically, but surely it is impossible to suppose that the soul is a phenomenal object empirically knowable. As the Transcendental Aesthetic established, empirical objects are intuitable in space and time; the soul or self, however, is not in space and cannot be intuited where it is not. "The representation of myself, as the thinking subject, belongs to the inner sense only, while the representations which mark extended beings belong also to outer sense" (*Pure Reason* A371; cf. *Prolegomena* § 49). It follows that geometry is not applicable to psychological data. Thus one of the essential characteristics of phenomenal reality is irrelevant to internal data.

More specifically, the category of substance cannot be applied to data relating to empirical self-knowledge in the same fashion as it is applied to data having the full spatio-temporal reference. "Though both [soul and body] are but phenomena,

yet the phenomena of the external sense have something permanent, which suggests a substratum of transitory determinations, and consequently a synthetical concept, namely, that of
space, and of a phenomenon in space; while time, the only form
of our internal intuition, has nothing permanent, and makes us
to know the change of determinations only, but not the determinable object" (*Pure Reason* A381; cf. A350). It follows, then,
that the study of psychology is provided with no fully determinable and substantial object like the physical sciences. Just
what, then, does it study? One is forced to conclude that the
empirical ego is only semiempirical and hence only quasi-
knowable. In any event, the soul is not a substantial physical
object and does not endure like such an object.

Perhaps, again, these observations imply merely that as the
knowing relation is a unique relation, so the knowing creature
is something by way of a unique being which can never in its
entirety be made the object of a science analogous to physics.
Unlike the Humean tradition, at least in its behavioristic phase,
Kant remained faithful to this article of common belief. But
now, admission of even the semiphenomenal character of the
experience of the self leads one again by an easy step to expect the elaboration of special studies of this unique being and
his particular kind of self-experience. It might be thought that
Kant could have made extensive use of what I have called the
semiempirical or semiphenomenal experience of the self for the
elaboration of such studies as ethics, aesthetics, and the like.
He does not do so, however, but continues to think of the phenomena of physics as the only phenomena in the proper sense.[17]
Consequently, he felt himself forced to provide a basis for ethics and aesthetics by developing only admissible beliefs and
postulates concerning the noumenal self, that aspect of man's

[17] The sense of reverence or respect (*Achtung*), which plays so important a
part in Kant's ethics, may be taken as an exception in that it offers a kind of
experience of moral law. But the status of reverence is not altogether clear. At
least it does not embody ethical law in just the same sense in which the
experience of balls rolling down an inclined plane embody objective physical
law. If reverence is to be called a "value object," it cannot be analogous to a
phenomenal object, as the next section will show.

being which escapes the mechanism of nature and is entirely nonphenomenal. What, then, is the nature of this self, object of these beliefs? What relation binds it to the empirical self?

§ 30.   THE NOUMENAL SELF IN THE INTELLIGIBLE WORLD

Although the *Critique of Pure Reason* and the *Prolegomena* cannot be expected to establish a complete doctrine of the nature of man, nevertheless, as part of their function of delimiting the sphere of human knowledge, they determine the boundary between phenomena and noumena. Since the knower himself is in some sense also noumenal, the boundary within him between the noumenal and phenomenal will naturally be laid down with particular care. This care is all the more necessary since man's noncognitive functions may be expected to be related to noncognizable aspects of his being. To some extent the two studies remain analogous. It is, however, difficult to determine the sense in which the study of the noumenal self and its freedom possesses a genuinely transcendental dimension. Transcendental conditions mediated by certain faculties determine the possibility of cognitive access to the phenomenal world. Moral, aesthetic, and other values, however, being nonphenomenal, are not thus transcendentally conditioned. They are *meta* physical (here metaphysical means *meta*-phenomenal, beyond the phenomenal). No faculties structured by schemata mediate the reference of moral and aesthetic categories to "value objects." Thus Kant cannot carry through his transcendental thinking in a manner exactly parallel to that exemplified in the Aesthetic and Analytic of the first *Critique*. He develops, rather, the role of regulative ideas and engages in a kind of transcendental thinking, only to determine the requirements and limitations that human life in a sane world— albeit within a mechanical world—imposes upon belief and feeling. He develops a doctrine of access by transcendentally conditioned will and feeling to nonphenomenal "value objects," some of which obligate the real self.

It must be emphasized that value objects or ends cannot be

related to the will or to moral sensibilities in the same way that phenomenal objects are related to the cognitive power. For the phenomenal object must determine the cognitive power; only thus will knowledge of the object be the issue. However, the valued object cannot determine the will, for then freedom—the very identity of the rational will—would be lost. Just such an error was committed by the philosophers who attempted to discover in an end (e.g., a state of happiness) the element determining the good will and the source of virtue.[18]

If, therefore, we are to continue to describe the moral life in terms of means and ends, then the only end which would not deprive the will of freedom will have to be identified in the free will itself.[19] But this free will has no content; it is not a definite object or organ which some transcendental structure brings within range of possible human contact. Rather, it is that transcendental structure itself.

Kant pursues through four overlapping stages the complex notion of a free and obligated self who can be effective in the phenomenal world. In the development of the difficult, perhaps antinomial, concept of the free self, this self is, first, independent of the phenomenal world yet causally effective in it.[20] The free self is causally effective in a rational sense, and finally, it is causally effective in a rational but merely ideal sense. Much is at stake in the elaboration of this doctrine. If the study of human freedom and its works can be established as a nonphenomenal and hence nonscientific yet genuine study, then the other humanistic pursuits ought to be salvageable. For at least once in modern history, perhaps, the tension between

[18] *Pure Reason* 218 *sq.* Cf. J. R. Silber, "The Copernican Revolution in Ethics: The Good Reexamined," *Kant-Studien*, Band 51 (1959); reprinted in Wolff, *Kant*, 266–90.

[19] *Critique of Practical Reason and Other Writings in Moral Philosophy*, trans. L. W. Beck (Chicago: University of Chicago Press, 1949), 193. Hereinafter this translation of the second *Critique* will be cited as *Practical Reason. The Foundations of the Metaphysics of Morals*, also in this translation, will be abbreviated as *Foundations*.

[20] Cf. *Pure Reason* A522–59, B560–87; *Prolegomena* § 53; *Practical Reason*, 121f; *Foundations*, 102.

the two kinds of knowledge—human and natural—could have been eased.

Kant first engages his problem in these terms: "Admitting that in the whole series of events there is nothing but natural necessity, is it yet possible to regard one and the same event as being in one aspect merely an effect of (phenomenal) nature and in another aspect an effect due to freedom, or is there between these two kinds of causality a direct contradiction?" (*Pure Reason* A543, B571). Here Kant is asking whether, in order to complete the account of the rational animal, we shall have to accept a set of complementary theories—one for man as animal or phenomenal, another for man as rational and free—or whether we shall accept a single theory containing a contradiction between freedom and necessity. He first seemed to aim at developing two logically independent theories, since never for a moment did he deny the reality of freedom and the moral responsibility of rational beings within the human world any more than he denied the necessary order within nature. The moral law within is no less compelling in its own way than the natural law without. And since, for Kant, reason is quite definite, it was not difficult—as the second part of *The Foundations of the Metaphysics of Morals* demonstrates—for him to determine its requirements by analysis.

Clearly a new sort of transcendental thinking is at work in this attempt to discover through reasoning guided by tradition or by common experience—in any event by the conviction of sanity—the nonphenomenal conditions for human action in the phenomenal world. Is this new kind of thinking adequate to solving the ethical transcendental problem? Kant might hope to demonstrate in this manner that moral transcendental conditions are not impossibly relevant to experience. He could demonstrate this possibility if he could show that freedom and phenomenal necessity are nonoverlapping, hence noncontradictory, concepts. Reason, however, will be expected to do more than merely demonstrate that the demands of morality and the possibility of freedom are independent of natural phenomena.

Some natural phenomena must be shown to be possibly dependent in at least some sense upon the rational will. For if freedom
and nature are altogether independent, then man's actual
achievement of moral value would not be intelligible. If the
real self is completely different from the empirical self and
world, then his moral living within that world and his instru-
mental use of it become insoluble enigmas. An adequate doctrine concerning their relation must show that freedom can
productively affect the phenomenal world if the actor is to be
responsible for his phenomenal acts. We must, therefore, answer the question: How can a man make practical use of
phenomena? How can values be conceived to determine
facts?

Kant's strategy is to maintain that the free and rational self
is exempt from physical (or alien) law, but that it can act in
terms of its own rational law. This strategy requires him to
clarify and to justify three beliefs concerning man's noumenal
character. These beliefs are: (1) that freedom must be conceived independently of phenomena; (2) that rational human
freedom conceived in this manner does not contradict the
mechanism of the phenomenal world; (3) that, additionally, in
its positive aspect, freedom can effect changes within the phenomenal world. Now, the first two of these propositions may be
rendered acceptable, as we have seen, if the real and free self
is identified with the noumenal self. The difficulty lies in ascertaining whether the third of these propositions is or is not in
conflict with one or both of the other two.

In order to clarify the meaning of the third of these propositions, Kant undertakes to find an intermediary faculty that can
bridge the gap between nature and fredom. This mediating
faculty, he concludes, is the will. He holds that will is subject to,
but not coerced by, sensuous inclinations since there "is in man
a power of self-determination, independently of any coercion
through sensuous impulses" (*Pure Reason* A534, B562). The
will, thus, is said to possess a dual character; it is empirical so
far as it is an appearance (though it is a semi-appearance, being

phenomenal only in respect to time), and to this extent it is determined naturally. Also, it is intelligible. As Kant expresses it, "Reason does not here follow the order of things as they present themselves in appearance, but frames to itself with perfect spontaneity an order of its own according to an idea, to which it adapts the empirical conditions." Ordinarily we think an act is intelligible or meaningful when it is well adapted to an envisaged end. Kant uses this term "end" in the same sense. The "order of its own" which reason frames is the order of ends or values. These are the values which, by means of an act of the will, can be brought into relationship with human conduct and thus lift conduct out of the mechanical order and render it intelligible. Among these ends the morally preeminent one is, of course, freedom itself.

The intelligibility of an act of the will, whether moral or not, follows from its determination by a concept (e.g., a concept of a law). For concepts of the mind are not phenomena of nature. When a purposive concept dominates the will and when the same will gives rise to a phenomenal course of events, then the will is both free of phenomenal (alien) causality and is the source of changes in nature. Thus Kant defines a free act of the will as a decision made in accord with a concept.[21] In addition, when the concept concerns the possible moral value of an action, it is not only free, it is obligatory or categorically enjoined upon the moral being. By virtue of his rational will, we may say that man is categorically "determined" to be human, that is to seek to act freely. This relationship of the will to rationally or to freely willed ends is never the relation of natural causation which holds among phenomena, but the relation of obligation which holds between a rule of conduct (a concept) and possible human action.

This dual-charactered will is the moral pineal gland through which Kant believed freedom and the intelligible world could come into determinative contact with the phenomenal world. He says as much in so many words: "Freedom ought not, there-

[21] See *Foundations*, 72, 85.

fore, to be conceived only negatively as independence of empirical conditions. The faculty of reason, so regarded, would cease to be a cause of appearances. It must also be described in positive terms, as the power of originating a series of events" (*Pure Reason* A553, B581; cf. *Practical Reason*, 72).

In this fashion Kant meets the antinomy which states that man is either altogether free of the empirical world or altogether determined by it. He seeks to maintain that both of these alternatives are true under suitable restrictions. Man as phenomenal can be known to be causally determined; nevertheless, as rational (noumenal) man may be believed to act freely and to intitiate sequences of events for which he is responsible (*Pure Reason* A661, B679). But it also follows that we cannot *know* ourselves to be both moral and empirical. We cannot in principle know that our will is completely undetermined by empirical inclinations and desires. Moreover, we cannot discover a schematic structure of the will which shows that moral law (the law of rational being) necessarily applies to any sort of value objects, for example, to our experienced motives. Strictly speaking, therefore, we cannot know that our motives are moral even if they are. We must, nevertheless, act as if the conceived self were the real self. More light, however, urgently needs to be shed upon the means by which the real but unknowable self of belief is related to the empirical self and its activity with the result that the former can initiate events in the latter.

The paradoxical color of this doctrine is somewhat dimmed when one recalls that the intelligible self, not being phenomenal, is not in time and is not subject to the conditions of succession in time. There is no before and no after in the intelligible realm (*Pure Reason* A551, B979). Hence, when we speak of reason initiating a series of events, we cannot be using the notion of *beginning*, which refers to a first moment of time, in its literal sense. How then shall this beginning be conceived? If we are looking for a phenomenal point of contact between the atemporal and unknowable, though intelligible, self and the phenomenal self, we shall merely run counter to all the confusions which dogged the Cartesian dualism. We had better think of reason as a faculty through which an empirical series of effects receives not an initial physical impulse but rather a rational direction. Beginning, then, refers to an ideal or intelligible beginning which, being conceptual, is also atemporal. It does not refer to an efficient cause or to a beginning movement which initiates a new series of movements in time.

The real will, or the will of any rational being, subject to the laws of freedom, can be understood to be related to changes in the phenomenal world only if it be regarded as their rationale or as the forevision of the end which the empirical will intends or ought to intend. This is a reasonable interpretation of Kant's meaning, the interpretation which he himself followed up. Expressions indicating that the real will "effects changes" in nature and alters empirical conditions are unfortunate in that they suggest the expenditure of energy in the empirical world (*Pure Reason* A556, B584). But only the empirical will can be effective in the empirical world. Such expressions will have to be understood in a suitably metaphorical sense.

The present interpretation of the real will is confronted by still another difficulty, however, that is not easily dismissed. Kant accepted the view that the real will of the noumenal self is free and rational. Since it is free—free of the physical and phenomenal world—it is also atemporal. If, however, it is atemporal, how is moral progress possible? For the progress through which character is matured must occur in time. There seems to be no alternative but to admit that the real self cannot be said to make moral progress. Perhaps, then, we are to understand that the real or noumenal self is complete and perfect and that it stands in relation to the empirical self as the model of the end to be achieved. The life and moral growth of the empirical self and character is a gradual movement toward embodying the real or intelligible self empirically. Moral progress, thus, is to be attributed only to the empirical self; life is an effort to become empirically and actually what we are ideally and noumenally. This view certainly represents a swing toward

Stoical patterns in ethical thought, as Kant recognized.[22] He observes that this intelligible or ideal man cannot be said to exist, for we cannot have experience of it. It is not empirically, but only noumenally, real. Nevertheless, it provides an indispensable archetype and regulative idea to conduct. "Virtue, and therewith human wisdom in its complete purity, are ideas. The wise man (of the Stoics) is, however, an ideal; that is, a man existing in thought only, but in complete conformity with the idea of wisdom. As the idea gives the rule, so the ideal in such a case serves as the archetype for the complete determination of the copy" (*Pure Reason* A569, B597). Two characteristics of this rational self, now the ideal moral archetype, call for comment: The first is its essential remoteness from realization; the second is its unchangeableness.

The remoteness of this ideal presents the ethical version of dissatisfaction with the actual self and the yearning for infinity or for unending progress toward an unattainable goal, which is later to be associated with Romanticism. "Only endless progress from lower to higher stages of moral perfection is possible to a rational but finite being" (*Practical Reason*, 212; and cf. 164, 180). The yearning for infinite knowledge was in considerable part turned back into scientific channels by interpreting these yearnings, the impulse to metaphysics, as properly regulative in function. The endless effort after unattainable moral purity, however, seems to be appropriate to man, and no less appropriate is the creation of beautiful objects having infinite meanings. It is important, however, to recognize that the infinite moral goal is unattainable in fact. The empirical self and the real self never can become the same. No less important is it to recognize that the aesthetic infinite goal, prompted by the human impulse to transcend human limitations, however natural it may be, cannot but be frustrated. There remains a disproportion between man's infinite impulses and his finite possibility.

---

[22] A swing, moreover, justified in the light of the defense of the idea of purpose developed in the *Critique of Judgment*.

The unchangeableness of the moral archetype suggests another kind of disproportion. It is not harmonious with Kant's conviction that the moral law can be given no specific content. The definiteness and unchangeableness of this vision of the noumenal self, expressed as the ideal wise man of the Stoics and forever held up to man as the proper goal of human behavior, has the effect of limiting free acts to those which are means for moving toward this fixed goal. Is human freedom indeed limited in just this way? Moreover, have men no choice with respect to the self which they are to seek to realize? Have they no responsibility for the end which they ought to pursue? This limitation suggests the arbitrary; it surely is not proportionate to the pretention to rational autonomy, nor is it proportionate to the abstractness of the moral law. No doubt the Stoic man of Stoic freedom and virtue was elaborated by inherited reason, but whether this ideal reflects insight into the total possibility of human-being may reasonably be doubted. Perhaps it presents a conventional type which the culture or some malign demon has devised for our imitation. Perhaps it is merely a seductive mask concealing the real self. Without some intuitive access to the noumenal human-being which would take the measure of competing ideal men, it is difficult to see why the Kantian Stoic should be judged the winner.

We conclude that Kant's effort to continue his transcendental thinking about the noumenal-empirical dimension of man's nature does not lead him to a unique solution of the ethical problem; a basic lack of coherence remains. The transition between the noumenal and empirical selves has not been adequately effected. The last word has not been said on the antinomy of teleology and mechanism.

§ 31.   THE ROMANTIC FATE OF KANTIAN MAN

Along with the effort made in this chapter to characterize the nature of Kant's transcendental thinking and the sense in which it constituted a notable transition in philosophy, three criticisms of the results of this thinking have been made. These criticisms constitute an answer to the question whether Kant succeeded in making a complete transition to a world where the physical universe is conceived in union with a just and comprehensive view of the human-being and his fate. These criticisms also point the way to the Romantic developments within this tradition.

The first criticism dwelt upon Kant's failure to carry his philosophical technique through more explicitly with respect to phenomena as they are experienced in everyday living.[23] Kant discovered in the *Critique of Judgment* a kind of transcendental ground for belief in the subjective feeling that the world is good for knowing, that the universe is the fitting home for the rational being. However, he indisputably had to conclude that nothing can be known in the phenomenal object to correspond with this feeling of value, for he had already identified the phenomenon as experienced with the phenomenal object of physics. He had chosen the physical object as the standard object. In consequence, he could not take advantage of all the possibilities offered by his approach in philosophy to rectify the disproportion between man and the typically modern or physical view of the universe. That he would, then, encounter difficulties in attempting to understand man's place in and relation to this physical universe was hardly accidental.

The second and third criticisms elaborated some of the difficulties within Kant's philosophy in understanding the relation of the self to this physical universe. Clearly Kant's overall intention was to conceive of the natural universe as falling within a larger context defined by way of its relation to man's whole founding subjective nature. Such may be understood to be the meaning of the "primacy of the practical." The

---

[23] It may be objected that I have laid too much emphasis upon this failure, for in fact Kant did discuss objects of ordinary experience in *Pure Reason* (although not without ambiguity). Also he wrote in the *Prolegomena* of "the fruitful *bathos*, the bottom land, of experience" (appendix, note 1), to which, no doubt, propositions of perception refer. My point, however, is that he failed to develop this point thematically and to utilize it in elaborating his view of the relation of man to the world; see below.

difficulty in executing this intention lay in satisfying the rational demand for grasping the whole as a coherent unity. Specifically, Kant's treatment of the problem concerning the relation of man's feeling and acting nature to the natural and phenomenal world runs a gamut of paradoxes. Our last two criticisms issue from these.

One of these criticisms arose in the attempt to understand the will which mediates between the real and empirical selves, for on the real side the will is free and on the empirical side it is determined. Can a man conceive an end completely undetermined by (empirical) inclination? Even if he can conceive such an end, can this concept be known to incline his empirical or phenomenally determined will? There is little surprise that Kant should refer to this dual-natured will as "an inscrutable faculty" (*Practical Reason*, 157).

Further, the contrast between the real and the empirical self indicates that the real self must be atemporal. At once the notion of moral progress becomes most difficult to understand. Hence a third criticism arises from Kant's effort to moderate the tension between these two aspects of the will by understanding the end, the real self, in terms of the Stoic archetype— an ideally free man—which is approached infinitely by the empirical self; however, this end can never be known to be attained. Does not this end present a rather specific and even culturally characteristic content—a definite value object—as the object willed? In so presenting moral value, Kant compromises the will's freedom and denies responsibility for the choice of self. Without claiming some definitive and revelatory insight into the human being itself, it is difficult to believe Kant could maintain this ideal. He, however, rejects claims to this kind of insight. Thus the third criticism of Kant points to the narrow and arbitrary character of the self which he held out as the ideal. Kant could not bring himself to question the moral authority of this classic ideal any more than he could question the scientific authority of the Newtonian view of phenomena.

Kant's solution to the transcendental problem of the unity of man presents us with a semiempirical self united to an unknowable noumenal self, which nevertheless limits men to a very definite moral ideal, by way of a dual-charactered will whose nature, especially on its noumenal side, is not clearly defined. Something very like an ontological dualism persists into Kant's philosophy of the self in the terms of a contrast between freedom and mechanism. Not only, then, is the self not really at home in the phenomenal world, but it is not even at home with the phenomenal self. Is there, finally, on the Kantian theory any alternative to the Cartesian exclusion of man from the physical universe or to the Humean absorption of man completely within it?

History has recorded the disastrous attempts to reduce either of these kinds of study—humanistic and scientific—to the other. Kant heroically strove to include both within an overall rational view which would still recognize the profound differences that separate them. Consequently, he recognized that the principles which explicate nature are different in kind from those which serve to explicate man. The consequence seems also to be that the transcendental problem remains incompletely solved. The intelligible self is unknowable. The verbal play alone suggests a predicament. Perhaps his difficulty is the failure to find somewhere a direct insight into his own moral nature or some intuitive access to it. In this respect it is surprising that moral decisions or poetic inspirations are not given the status of immediacy; being free, they originate within the self and are, as it were, gifts of psyche directly to itself. But Kant denied this status to anything except the given in sensibility, and that only as functioning cognitively. Also he explicitly denied the possibility of having intellectual intuitions; however, he never subjected this denial to clarification and detailed criticism, a project to be undertaken by his idealistic successors.

Could it be, then, that the human situation is absurd, that the understanding of man contradicts knowledge of his world? The less desperate alternative is to suppose that the persuasive force of the Cartesian ideal of rational-mathematical clarity compelled Kant arbitrarily to limit the sphere of phenomena to the Newtonian world of physical objects, and, consequently, to suppose that he was forced into the dilemmatic position either of accepting an exclusively natural and empirical theory of the self—the Humean alternative—or of admitting that the self is in some senses nonphenomenal. He chose to attempt to live with the humane second alternative despite its paradoxical implications. Perhaps, had he developed the distinction between natural phenomena (belonging to physics) and phenomena as experienced by men engaged in the pursuits of living, he would have encountered fewer difficulties in understanding the relation of man to his world, and he might have worked his way through to a more thoroughgoing transcendental view of the whole of human experience. As it was, he took some of the most difficult steps in this direction, if not all of them. Romantic philosophers and literary men attempted to continue the movement in this same direction.

Of course the complex and many-sided post-Kantian development in philosophy cannot be adequately considered in the few pages now at our disposal.[24] It will be useful, however, to mention a few salient features of this development which will help to render intelligible its peculiar fate and also its effect upon contemporary transcendental philosophy.

In the first place it is important to note that on one side the Romantic period was a rebellion against the Cartesian intellectualist tradition as it had lingered on into Kantianism. In this sense the Romantic period developed into an irrationalism; it continued to be determined, but negatively determined, by the Cartesian version of the rational ideal. It violently did not believe that all problems could be solved and all mysteries unveiled by the persistent use of mathematical rationality, Lockean common sense, or Newtonian experimentalism. Many of its typical characteristics derive from this rejection of the

---

[24] I have treated some of its aspects at greater length in my article "On the Nature of Romanticism," *Tulane Studies in Philosophy*, III (1954), 61–95.

scientism, orderliness, and progressiveness of the eighteenth century.

On its positive side, the rebellion turns about the ego. We have observed that Kant's teachings concerning the ego left much to be desired. On the other hand his distinction between the empirical self which is conscious and the real self which cannot be directly experienced suggested other dimensions of the self, other selves as yet scarcely dreamed. Indeed it suggested the presence of a whole forgotten life behind the superficial clarity of the Cartesian cross.

The self for enlightened Humeanism was the empirical personality, reasonable, disciplined, uncomplex. The Humeans could scarcely deny that persons sometimes exhibited irrational or unsocial impulses, but they regarded these impulses as subject to being disciplined and thus to being redirected or repressed. For the Romantics, however, the self had a depth dimension; it had infinite yearnings, irrational impulses, manifold expressions. All of these elements or expressions of the real self were to be respected, rescued, integrated into a more varied and complex self than the previous century had known. Quite understandably, a tension developed between people of firm faith in progress toward a scientific society and these bearded rebels with their dangerous inclination to explore unapproved, possibly illicit, impulses.

Romantic philosophers, seeking a more effective rescue of the whole self than Kant had effected, developed a doctrine which held the self to be primordial, complex, and active. Its primordiality is exemplified in its active and creative character. Romantic philosophers may be said to have collapsed the two foci of the Kantian-Copernican figure into one. The transcendental self tended to absorb the thing itself, only to give birth to the latter in a new guise. Thus the Romantic self is unlimited by the objective world. Rather the world is in some sense an issue out of the self. As Schelling remarked, "Nature is visible mind and mind is invisible nature."

The complexity of the self is instanced in the dark and

unruly elements of the personality and also in the diverse roles which the Romantic genius tended to play. Yet this diversity is characterized by a drive toward unity. The self is an organism in need of health. It must respect all its feelings, inclinations, and all the roles it can play, even the evil ones, as parts of itself and especially as indispensable indications of the nature and requirements of its lesser known aspects. Its destiny is the rescue of its own depths. A fundamental theme of Romanticism is the salvation of the whole person.

Activity is the means by which the organic self moves to achieve unity with itself and with the world. But this activity is the activity of an organism; it is to be conceived as a growth and a maturation, a gradual unfolding of unknown and unsuspected potentialities. There is no reason to expect it to be terminated, unless in the passivity of death. Thus the activity of the self is an infinite growth toward an ideal unity unspecified by previous customs and recognized values.

These four elements, the rejection of the Enlightenment, the recollection of a self which is metaphysically primordial, complex, and creative without limit, are the prominent components of the Romantic *Zeitgeist*. They characterize the new life which this period strove to attain. But this new life was not to be reached by an impersonal acceptance of postulates nor even by a common discipline to which anyone might submit. It was to be attained only by the reception of a new insight which was granted to some but not to all. Schelling, for instance, apologized for the unintelligibility of his philosophy on the ground that it was accessible only to the initiated. Shelley makes a similar appeal to an arational intuition or feeling. The movement requires of its adherents something like a *rite de passage*. It is a doctrine of secular conversion.

Romanticism, however, makes a characteristic usage of the pattern of conversion.[25] For one thing, Romanticism with its

[25] M. Peckham, "The Unity of European Romanticism," *Comparative Literature*, I (1944), 147–72; Richard P. Adams, "Emerson and the Organic Metaphor," *PMLA*, LXIX (1954), 117–30; also his "Romanticism and the American Renaissance," *American Literature*, XXIII (1952), 419–32.

natural interest in the primitive finds a spontaneous satisfaction in this ritual pattern of the ancient mysteries. For here is found a way of thought which is primarily dramatic, a bond with the world which is poetic rather than rational and scientific. It is a return to a more primitive way of thinking which, it would seem, is a matter of considerable moment in that it centers attention upon the archaic, "inner," and "deep" layers of the human psyche and the transition to and among them. It calls for a reconsideration of this arational aspect of human nature and its relation to the capacities for rational and clear thought.

In addition, Romanticism uses the conversion pattern as a means to its own end. This usage may best be expressed by observing that the Romantic conversion is expected to culminate in a feeling, or rather in a new relationship between feeling regarded as belonging to an obscure, neglected, but perhaps more significant part of the self (the psyche) and clear conscious thought. This culmination is recorded in a crucial instance as the emotional self-awareness which Schelling called intellectual intuition. Coleridge, also following Schelling and, more remotely, Kant, called it imagination. We may regard the Romantic conversion as a turn to psyche and its poetic inspirations shorn so far as possible of the habits and controls of eighteenth-century rationality.

Some conceptions of fate and its irony are indissolubly connected with the conversion pattern. For the Romantics, fate clearly becomes, as it were, internalized; it becomes entirely an issue out of man's subjectivity, perhaps out of his individual feeling. It is not by accident that Melville's Moby Dick, the great white whale, is an ambiguous symbol. The whale becomes what it is because of the view which Captain Ahab takes of it, although this view becomes explicit and conscious only gradually and partially. This attitude is typical. What a man is at any moment of his life is the adjustment which he has effected between his conscious self and the unconscious to which he has access through feeling. But this unconscious is part of himself; it is within. "Working out one's fate," then, is conceived sometimes as coming to dominate the unruly element within, or sometimes as conforming to its dictates. At any rate fate is conceived to be internal and is "worked out" by being rendered explicit and conscious. The stage and the drama of man's life have come for Romantic philosophers to be found within the man himself; the measure of a man—his fate—is somehow within him.

Among many Romantics the expression of no matter what impulse, so long as it was one's own, came to be regarded almost as an obligation. The Byronic personality conceived its greatness to arise from its being dominated by the volcanic emotions which well up within the soul and which are discharged through poetry—only to well up again in another form. Thus fate is conceived subjectively; coming to terms with one's fate is coming to terms with elements already a part of the self. This same internality of fate is evidenced in the pursuit of diversity so characteristic of Romanticism. For if fate is internal to the person, then no doubt it varies from individual to individual. Consequently, conforming to external mores may well be only an avoidance of fate; whereas a free expression of one's idiosyncrasies and individuality would seem to be the more courageous move of acceptance of one's self which is one's fate. Consequently, Romantic life is subsumed under the hypothesis of variety. Romanticism is something new under the sun.

Yet it is also something paradoxical. For if the self is so varied and if fate is something within this variety, just which element is it? How is the harmony of the self and its fate to be understood? We are able to discover, however, no persistent identity but only a multitude of personalities within some of the more Romantic individuals: Byron will be remembered, for instance, as Manfred, as Mazeppa, as Lara, as the Prisoner of Chillon, as Childe Harold, as Don Juan, to name a few only. But under this rich variety there runs a note of melancholy. Consider the question which must have plagued Byron: Which of these, if any, is Byron himself? By what measure of himself is he to be guided? The Kantian and Stoic archetype of the wise man (and others like it) being relinquished, the free rein given by Romantics to all expressions of self led directly to the existential problem of authenticity.

The consequences of internalizing fate, then, was the removal or obscuring of just that factor which might have been the means for selecting from among the possible answers to the question concerning the authentic self. The Kantian notion of limits, the conviction of the finitude of man, had been rejected or ignored by typical Romantic philosophers and poets. The consequence was an infinite expansion and loss of a *point d'apui*. The Romantics illustrate, even in their rebellion against the cosmos of the Enlightenment, their homelessness and their alienation in a universe unlike themselves.

If the problem of the Romantic philosophers was to effect an intelligible transition into a universe where the self owns to a richer and more complex identity and where experience possesses a greater fullness and poetic depth, then the movement must be said to have failed. It provided no lasting and triumphant synthesis of thought. Its achievement lay elsewhere. Romantic poets recovered something of the richness of man's original relation to the world, the relation which had been so attenuated by Renaissance men and later rationalists and empiricists. In addition, the darker side of human life, the "work of the negative," as Hegel termed it—tragedy, frustration, anxiety, loss—were given their due. This new data was not branded as merely subjective, immeasurable, unmanageable, hence to be rejected. Rather it was accepted as no less human and significant than that which could be clearly and impersonally conceived and related—e.g. a la Descartes—to the intellect.

Thus Romanticism left its lasting mark not so much in the direction of new intellectual constructs as in the way of the discovery of new or forgotten elements of experience. It enlarged the domain of the phenomenal which Kant had so restricted. Hence to judge that Romanticism was altogether frittered out in indecisiveness is not just. But the consequence of its receptiveness to a greater depth and variety of experience meant that it embraced the source of its own change; the seeds of its destruction and its rebirth lay concealed within it. Søren Kierkegaard, who received his education during the waning days of Romanticism, became its most perceptive critic. Also he had listened to Schelling's Berlin Lectures in 1841 and carried away more than a further distaste for Hegel, who seemed to him to fail in respect for the individual. He also carried away some tincture of Schelling's late "positive philosophy" [26] in the conviction that a fruitful opposition to the fixation of life in the abstract categories of Hegelian logic could only be effected through the discovery of something which these categories could not include. This extracategorial something would have to be the direct and immediate experience of individual human existence. This existence is conceived by Kierkegaard not in the traditional sense of the term as actuality, but rather it refers to the involvement of the individual human self with something or someone other than himself. Moreover, this involvement is understood as a movement beyond the self which is at any particular moment; at the same time this orientation is not vaguely directed toward variety or unlimited self-assertion. Although he defined the self somewhat Romantically as the synthesis of finite and infinite, he also added that this synthesis attained definiteness, equilibrium, and authenticity only when it was related to the power which constituted it.[27]

Of course, for Kierkegaard, the religious writer, this creative power was the Christian God and relation to it was the relation of faith. However, these theological ideas were susceptible of philosophical formulation and eventually received it. Before such a formulation could be profitably undertaken, however, a method was needed for opening a more disciplined view out upon the new domain of human experience. This method, and with it a renewed impetus, was offered by phenomenology.

---

[26] See Emil L. Fackenheim, "Schelling's Conception of Positive Philosophy," *Review of Metaphysics*, VII (1954), 563–82.

[27] Søren Kierkegaard, *Sickness unto Death*, trans. Walter Lowrie (Princeton: Princeton University Press, 1941), Pt. 1.

V

Objectivity and Rationality in Husserl's Philosophy

§ 32. HUSSERL'S BEGINNING

Any movement of thought may be called transcendental if it seeks to turn reflection upon the incoherent aspects of an event, a theory, a tradition and to resolve the puzzle by including it within a larger horizon. Such a transcendental turn becomes philosophic when this larger horizon explores the possibility of the event, the theory, or the tradition in question. Thus Kant showed mathematics and physics to be possible. Romantic philosophers strove to effect a transition into a world where aesthetic and certain other kinds of experience could be seen to be possible. Then Edmund Husserl undertook to show that all experience, especially including the initial and primitive experience of the world, could and should be transcendentally and philosophically understood.

Husserl's phenomenology completes the transition into twentieth-century thought. His training as a mathematician and as a psychologist bred in him an initial sympathy with Cartesian and positive ideals.[1] His breadth of training led him to express

[1] Husserl received his Ph.D. in mathematics in 1883 from the University of Vienna and served for a time as assistant to Professor Weierstrass at the University of Berlin. He then studied psychology and philosophy under Brentano at the University of Vienna.

the ideal of Western intellectualism more explicitly and more generally than it had ever been expressed before. This is the ideal which he termed "presuppositionlessness." Then in addition, following upon Romantic philosophy, he envisaged the inclusion of the totality of phenomena within a horizon founded upon doctrines of the transcendental ego and transcendental intersubjectivity. We shall see, however, that he encountered difficulties in this undertaking. Finally, he was led to modify the strict requirements of the rational ideal in a manner which opens the way to quite recent philosophical developments.

Husserl had to reckon not only with a complex philosophical filiation but also with more mundane and threatening historical movements of the late nineteenth and twentieth centuries. His philosophical difficulties together with the troubles of the times led him to a reevaluation of the ideal of reason which had been his guide. He developed, I believe, a lively sense of the irony of historical fate and grew aware of his era as the time of reason becoming a time of unreason. Was it possible that reason had misunderstood itself?

It is most relevant to recall that Husserl himself suffered from a meticulously cultivated prejudice, one deriving from the official conviction that his race was less than human and ought to be enslaved or annihilated. Husserl was forced, during his last years, to live virtually incommunicado, and his books and manuscripts were saved from the destructive rage of Hitler's followers only by the daring exertions of Father Van Breda of the University of Louvain. It is well in this context, I believe, to ask ourselves how these Nazis are to be viewed. Did they exhibit bad form by breaking the gentleman's agreement to devote their energies to the advancement of science and technology? Were they evil men who trespassed against the moral codes? Or were they more instruments of an avenging fury, man turned against himself? Martin Heidegger, Husserl's estranged friend and coworker, suggested the last interpretation when he remarked during the early 1930's that the significance of National Socialism lay in its exhibiting the encounter of man with technology. In any event, history rudely forced the rational calm of Husserl's university study.

But we anticipate. Upon returning to consider Husserl's initial training in mathematics and science, it might be inferred that his lifelong devotion to the ideal of clarity and rigor was merely an affirmation of his acceptance of conventional standards of accuracy in reasoning and measuring. However, the meaning of the rational ideal to his independent and original mind was far from any such routine declaration. Husserl interpreted the ideal as referring to the clear perception and rigorously accurate description of both basic (given) and derived aspects of the whole of human experience. He maintained that his expression of the ideal identified it, rather, with the Greek ideal of epistēmē which demanded a radical beginning and complete clarity in all subsequent developments. Thus it requires the utmost of both psyche, which apprehends or receives the given, as well as of thymos, which elaborates and uses this given. It especially calls for criticism of all presuppositions, presuppositions being beliefs which are not given but are taken over because they are convenient or customary. Thus his ideal demands "presuppositionlessness."

Husserl distinguished between the ideal of mathematical exactitude, the Cartesian ideal appropriate to a science such as mathematical physics, and the ideal of rigor which is appropriate to a nonmathematical science or to philosophy. Under guidance by this intellectualist ideal of the accessibility of all being to the human mind, Husserl intended to escape prejudice or the slavery to an official view of the world. It seemed to him that this escape would be possible only if the philosophic life were begun anew by way of a return to phenomena, to the "things themselves" just as they are presented to a receptive and unprejudiced perception. Thus rationality for Husserl means a clear view of all that is; it is not limited in advance by a mathematical or other official preconception of what must be presented.

Husserl remains Kantian to a certain degree, for he understood his ideal in its reference primarily to perception. It is the perceived world about which he desires to be clear. This is first the world of passively received phenomena. The arché of philosophy appeared initially to be the phenomena as they are presented. It is not easy, however, to identify phenomena purely as presented. Certainly Kant's philosophy had turned to phenomena, but it had done so by way of reason. Kant discovered in eighteenth-century reason the standards, principles, and limitations of that which properly could be called knowledge; naturally the phenomena that he discovered were only those objective phenomena that the reason of his day could measure and understand. But Husserl's philosophy seeks to return more directly to phenomena and to discover within phenomena themselves the standards, principles, and limitations of that which is properly to be regarded as phenomenal. What he discovered was not reassuring either to the naturalistic or objectivistic philosophies or to the psychologistic philosophies of his day.

In the present study we shall not linger over Husserl's polemics in opposition to objectivism (including positivism) and to psychologism. Suffice it to say that objectivism might be defined as the conviction of the metaphysical ultimacy of the object as studied by the physical sciences. Psychologism, on the other hand, grants this privilege to the objects of psychology.[2] The failure, according to Husserl's judgment, of both psychologically and objectively oriented philosophies arose from the fact that the philosophers who elaborated these doctrines had failed to return to the beginning but had started their philosophizing with a sophisticated and specialized method and its data. They began with the presuppositions of a favored science

[2] The polemic against both "isms" is carried forward in "Philosophy as Rigorous Science," in Husserl, *Phenomenology and the Crisis of Philosophy*, trans. Q. Lauer (New York: Harper, 1965), 71–147. Husserl, *Logische Untersuchungen* (3 vols.; 2nd ed.; Halle: Niemeyer, 1913–21), hereinafter referred to as *Logische*, attends especially to psychologism; objectivism is a theme of *Die Krisis der Europäischen Wissenschaften und die Transcendentale Phänomenologie*, ed. Walter Biemel (The Hague: Nijhoff, 1954), hereinafter cited as *Crisis*.

but did not trouble to consider the relationship of the favored science, its data, or its method to the peculiar problems and needs of philosophy.

Husserl's first major task was the devising of a method (the "reduction") for becoming aware of specialist presuppositions as well as of the gratuitous beliefs and common presuppositions of everyday life; only after reaching this awareness could he expect to return to the phenomena as they are given. In order to enter sympathetically into Husserl's philosophy one must be willing to assume provisionally that the mind can discipline itself to be merely receptive and can, therefore, return to uninterpreted phenomena; at least it can return to phenomena which are not actively interpreted. However, Husserl's doctrine of passive genesis suggests that he entertained some reservations about this possibility, as § 34 will indicate. (It must also be remembered that he continually questioned the meaning of the reduction.) Then his positive program required him to show how the natural world of the sciences and of modern everyday life was derived from the purified phenomenal world. This latter task designates something like his own version of the transcendental problem. We may call it the problem of objectivity.

Husserl begins by asking how the cognitive subject can possibly get outside itself to gain access to the object. How can it happen that the playing rules of consciousness are the same as the playing rules of objects? [3] This is his form of the Cartesian problem.

Husserl's solution for the problem shows that "the mind is in

[3] See "Philosophy as Rigorous Science." Other of Husserl's books pertinent to this problem and to the development sketched in this section are the following: *The Idea of Phenomenology*, trans. W. P. Alston and G. Nakhnikian (The Hague: Nijhoff, 1964); *Ideas: General Introduction to Pure Phenomenology*, trans. W. R. Boyce-Gibson (New York: Macmillan, 1931), hereinafter cited as *Ideas* I (this latter is the translation of the first volume, the only volume published during Husserl's lifetime, of the projected three-volume introduction to phenomenology); *Phänomenologische Untersuschungen zur Konstitution*, in *Husserliana*, ed. W. Biemel (11 vols.; The Hague: Nijhoff, 1952), the second volume of Husserl's introduction, hereinafter cited as *Ideas* II; and *Cartesian Meditations*, trans. Dorion Cairns (The Hague: Nijhoff, 1960).

a sense all things," but in a sense unsuspected by Aristotle, the author of that phrase. The reader may already be acquainted with Husserl's route to his transcendental idealism. If so, he may for present purposes refresh his memory with the following statement: The reductions lead the philosopher back to pure consciousness within which all phenomena have their being; the essence of consciousness is intentionality; intentions are factorable into noesis (e.g., an act of perceiving) and noema (e.g., a perception); among the properties of noemata is certainty, the protodoxa, which is the essential property of object-noemata; thus object-noemata are within the sphere of consciousness—although they are naturally assumed to be external to consciousness; consequently, the sphere of conscious being includes all that is; thus the natural world (object-world) is not separate from subjectivity; and thus, finally, the playing rules of consciousness apply within the natural world.

§ 33. FROM THE TRANSCENDENTAL FOUNDATION TOWARD
        OBJECTIVE REALITY

The notion of real or objective existence had been suspended in the regressive movement back to pure phenomena. However, reality claims are constantly being made in the everyday and technical worlds. Are these claims merely subjective? What is the basis and extent of their validity? In the interest of satisfying his ideal and of making his phenomenological insights applicable back again to the real and existent world, Husserl devised in the last section of *Ideas* a theory intended to settle reality claims. This theory concerns evidence and its interpretation. It is called for by "the problems of reason" or the general problem of justifying judgmental claims to objective reality.

Briefly the theory is developed in the following way: The thing-noema, a unified X, is like a subject related to its predicates, its predicates being the intended properties. A full perceptual noema is a meaning-intending-a-real-being. A problem is presented so soon as one recognizes that even when the specified perceptual conditions are met, one may still raise the question, as Husserl himself does (*Ideas* I § 135), whether the object-meaning determined by the predicate properties specifies a real being (*ibid.* § 133). It is always possible that this being is only an illusion. This is the problem that Descartes was able to solve only by appeal to the divine veracity (*Cartesian Meditations*, 116). For to show that any given predicate is really to be attributed to X is not to show that X is real. X, the object, is at the least a unity of its predicates. Is it not, however, more than this unity? Of what nature is the judgment of reality which reason passes upon some object noemata and denies to others? In order to develop this aspect of Husserl's philosophy fairly, some further details concerning his view of truth must be added.

Objects are, at the least, noematic unities. Now every noema includes a belief character of some sort that expresses the sense in which reality is attributed to the object intended. The mere awareness of this belief character does not confirm its appropriateness. Husserl first held that when the belief character is "motivated" by or "founded" on intuition, then it is verified. Thus the predication of reality is legitimized by the presence of the (real) object in intuition or immediate vision. Real being, then, is the correlate of a consciousness that originally constitutes it in intuition (*Ideas* I, 395, 399). Truth is the lived awareness of the agreement of the intended meaning with the intuition of the real being itself (*Logische*, study 6). It is the intuitively "fulfilled intention" (*Ideas* I, 401; *Cartesian Meditations*, 10f).

Perhaps it is not too difficult, if one agrees with the Husserlian notion of original evidence, to accept the proposition that objects are phenomenal, and phenomena are to a person at least what they mean. Human experience, in other words, is the experience of meanings. Furthermore, if one regards consciousness as intentional in its nature, its constitutive function, actively or passively elaborating meanings, appears not too difficult to accept. The objective world, if it is anything at all in our experience, is a meaning and like other meanings is constituted by noetic activity. Truth thus becomes not the coherence of an object with an abstract and a priori principle of thought, nor can it be the impossible mirroring by a mental state of an extramental object, nor is it merely verification of the correspondence of judgments to a judged situation as evaluated by some criterion of adequacy whose meaning and relevance is assumed by convention. Truth, rather, becomes the original perceived presence of the object fulfilling intention or expectation. When the noematic object as constituted in perception and the perceived (intuited) object "cover" each other,[4] then the latter "fulfills" the former, and the object is said to be present in its original givenness.

Here there is no question of attempting to define truth in terms of two realities, only one of which is present and possible (*Ideas* I, 186, 263). In the reduced sphere, belief in an independently existing world is suspended; truth, however, remains explicable as a covering relation among meanings and meaningful phenomena whose fundamental form is the protodoxa (certainty) founded on intuition; truth becomes the certain and lived presence of the object of reference (*ibid.* § 193f).[5] Thus the authenticity of any belief about an object is determinable only through immediate or mediate reference to that which perception presents (*absolut originären Erlebnisse, ibid.*, 220f). Phenomenology thus is a radical empiricism. Any object that is not originally given in perception or is not derived in a determined manner from something originally given in my experience must be suspect. To accept any less rigorous a standard would be to compromise the ideal of rational certainty or presuppositionlessness which so far has been our guide.

This transcendental philosophy is given a succinct statement

---

[4] *Logische*, II, study 3, pp. 50f. This theory of truth is summarized and criticized in A. de Waelhens, *Phénoménologie et Vérité* (Paris: Presses Universitaires de France, 1953), Pt. 1.

[5] Errors of observation, illusion (*Ideas* I, 226f), and accordingly, mistakes in judgments about objects are always possible, of course (cf. *ibid.*, 144, 398, 412, 420).

near the close of *Ideas* I: " 'Object,' as we everywhere understand it, is a title for essential connections of consciousness; it
first comes forward as the noematic X, the subject bearer of
different essential types of meaning and positions. It appears
further as the title for certain connections of the reason eidetically considered, in which the contained X, that unifies in
terms of meaning, receives its rational placing" (*Ideas* I, 402).
Transcendent objects—the world, nature, the sciences, whatever else may possibly be the object of experience—are constituted meanings within transcendental subjectivity. The world
originates in transcendental subjectivity. Its objectivity or reality, in short, its transcendent being, is to be accounted for
philosophically in terms of this transcendental foundation, its
arché.

Husserl's position on this matter of reality and the determination of truth about it rests, at this point, with the conclusion
that that is real which is rationally demonstrable (*ibid.* § 136),
and rational demonstration is a kind of seeing or showing. This
seeing or showing operates subjectively or in accordance with
that which is transcendentally and eidetically possible. Thus
objective reality is accessible to consciousness and yet is not
arbitrarily affected by the empirical subject.

May we not ask again whether transcendent being is completely accounted for in terms of transcendental subjectivity?
Is objective reality nothing more than a certain kind of constituted meaning presented intuitively? The objection which
Husserl himself raised appears to recur: Although I cannot
doubt that I see the thing which I see, still I may doubt that I
rightly suppose that the thing I see to be real. The difficulty
arises from the fact that illusions and confusions still seem to
be possible. After all, illusions are fulfilled perceptual intentions: that is just why they are illusory. In a sense they are
"seen," yet not really and objectively seen. Reality (the actually
existent) is not a thing which can be directly intuited or perceived, and we may well doubt that the intuitive fulfillment of
an intention should always be the sufficient index of real being.

Husserl was aware that his initial treatment of the problem of objectivity (in *Ideas* I) was open to this kind of objection, and he sought to amplify his treatment by indicating another dimension, the dimension of common experience and agreement. But this addition invited a new problem, the problem of the self and its role and the problem of intersubjectivity.[6]

§ 34. THE TRANSCENDENTAL FUNCTION OF THE EGO

Husserl sought both to deepen and to broaden this view of objective reality. The broadening brought the objectively real into continually closer contact with the life-world and with other selves. The deepening involved the relation of the objectively real to its source, the transcendental ego. This latter doctrine is central to his philosophy, indeed so central that he refers to its most fundamental branch as "egology." In examining his egological doctrine we shall note the way in which it leads back again to the problem concerning objectivity.

Since Husserl's philosophy of the ego is related to Kant's, it will be helpful to begin by experimentally reading Kant's views on the pattern of Husserl's transcendental philosophy. If one were to do so, then probably the Schematism (*Pure Reason* A137 *sq.*, B176 *sq.*) would be discovered to be the cognate of the noetic activity of the ego, constituting and ordering experience. The first three Principles (*ibid.* A158 *sq.*, B197 *sq.*), especially the Analogies of Experience, would offer a doctrine of noemata, elucidating the patterns according to which noetic activity bestowed sense. Then the section on the Postulates of Empirical Thought in General, like section IV of *Ideas*, would offer an account of the relation of these noemata to the real empirical world. What, however, is the source of this cognitive activity? A focus of difficulties in Kant is uncovered when one seeks in the *Critique* for something like the individual human ego which is both rational and empirical.

---

[6] Husserl, it should be added, was also interested in this crucial problem for its own sake and in order to complete his philosophy of objectivity and his philosophy of the ego.

Surely there is little similarity between such an ego and either Kant's merely empirical ego (the natural self) or his transcendental unity of apperception, which is formal and universal. Paul Ricoeur, who develops the parallel between Kant and Husserl at some length,[7] concludes that the rather cryptic remarks which Kant occasionally lets fall about the self's "indefinite empirical intuition" of itself, a self whose existence could not be described categorially (*ibid.* B157a, B422a), approaches the grasp of an ego that is something like a constitutive subject, the organizing center of one's life; but this approach remains unthematic. Husserl's doctrine seems to get closer to the concrete, ordering self, but it is a complex and even ambiguous doctrine.[8] At least it is clear that both Kant and Husserl were motivated by somewhat similar intentions to relate the sense-giving structures of transcendental subjectivity to the object-world by means of the active self or ego.

We have observed also that Kant's effort to maintain the life of the rational moral subject, its human activity and its pursuit of ends, in a realm separate from but coordinate with the realm of objects behaving according to Newtonian laws failed to offer a satisfactory account of the way in which the transcendental basis of value could become operative in the real world. Husserl, on the other hand, sought a transcendental basis sufficiently inclusive to provide a rationale for the whole of human experience. He was careful to avoid the series of attempts to found the objectivity of knowledge upon an unattainable external object, or upon an objective study of the

[7] See his *Husserlian Studies*, Chap. 7. Husserl, it should be added, recognized the kinship of his views and Kant's. But he recognized that Kant began with the abstract (Newtonian) phenomena whereas he began from "below," with the concrete, with phenomena as experienced. Cf. H. Spiegelberg, *The Phenomenological Movement* (2 vols.; The Hague: Nijhoff, 1960), I, 110 and note 2.

[8] See J. M. Broekman, *Phänomenologie und Egologie* (The Hague: Nijhoff, 1963), especially Chap. 6. Broekman also develops the comparison between the Kantian and Husserlian egos. On the relation to the Humean theory of consciousness, see Aron Gurwitsch, "On the Intentionality of Consciousness," in *Studies in Phenomenology and Psychology* (Evanston: Northwestern University Press, 1966), 124–40.

psyche, or even upon a transcendental self whose sole mode of access to a world opened only upon a Newtonian world.

Husserl's enriched phenomenal world was interpreted so as to found knowledge and the being of the experienced world upon transcendental structures discoverable through analysis of the phenomenal world and belonging to the monadic ego. Thus he united the transcendental and determining ground with the life-world and then with nature by way of the transcendental self. His doctrine manifests a very interesting growth from minimal requirements, or less, through increasing awareness of the role of the self in the formation of the whole range of its experience. We shall investigate the development of this doctrine only so far as required to understand the dependence of objectivity upon the constituting subjectivity of the ego.

In the *Logische Untersuchungen* (study 5) Husserl held that there is no such thing as an ego, center of its experience,[9] but in *Ideas* he speaks of the ego as living in its acts and functioning as a sort of center of reference (*Ideas* I, 143, 244). He notes, however, that the ego is unlike any experienced object in that it persists after the reductions as an irreducible residuum; yet it is not like an object, nor a part, nor a phase of experience, but it is rather like a persistent self-identical element. To underline its uniqueness he refers to it as a "transcendence in immanence" (*ibid.* § 57), but he attributes no properties to it. The centrality and complexity of the ego, however, become more and more evident as this philosophy develops.

The concrete ego is analyzable into a continuously self-identical subject distinguishable from its present cogito and from the processes and performances of its intentional activity. Husserl had observed that the self is given in reflection most directly in the present self-awareness accompanying any impression. This is the primary and given point of reference. Such a moment, however, is fleeting, but reflective grasp of it may be reiterated. A self-identical ego continuously function-

[9] The third edition of this work retracts this view.

ing as itself is always disclosed as present. This presently self-aware ego may return to a former "I" in the mode of "not-now." This "I," whose noetic activity presents its former self to its present self, whose identity with its past and future is continuous in a temporality linked by retentions and pretentions,[10] is at the least a noetic or agent unity. This continuously existing self becomes the substrate of modifications and "habitualities" (*Cartesian Meditations* §§ 31f).

"Habitualities" are the transcendental correlate of actual habits. One might be tempted to think of habitualities as the intelligible structure of habits; however, their status is not merely abstract. Rather they are selected by and belong to the ego and are not, accordingly, merely pure possibilities. They are the possibilities concretely available to an individual ego at a given time and provide a content for the abstract concept of an ego which gives form to its experiences. The monadic ego thus delineated is subject to further analysis.

This self is analyzable both noetically and noematically. It is both an originative and a continuously present self. As a continuously functioning unity of intendings, it structures its world and its own self-meaning in accord with the transcendental necessities which define its particular habitualities. Also it possesses its experience and has the identity of a rational and responsible agent. It thus mediates between eidetic necessities and concrete involvement.

The problem naturally arose concerning the origin of this transcendental agent. Husserl replied to it with a doctrine of self-constitution. Application of the method of imaginative variation revealed an originating ego constituting its own meaning to itself, the noematic ego, an eidetic possibility having definite properties, some of which must be instanced in every *de facto* ego (*Ideas* II, 110f, 310f; *Cartesian Meditations*, 70f). Every concept that is entertained must be coherent with this ego (*Cartesian Meditations*, 71). That is, not all construc-

---

[10] Martin Heidegger (ed.), *Lectures on Time Consciousness*, trans. J. S. Churchill (Bloomington: Indiana University Press, 1964).

tible meanings are constructible in any possible ego-type, just as not all constructible object-meanings are consistent with any given empirical conditions. The ego is limited in its activity and operates according to laws. If it is to come into possession of additional habits, it must undergo the discipline which opens up further habitualities.

The study of temporality and compossibility in relation to the ego revealed two very important levels of the genesis of the ego. These are the levels of passive and active genesis; they compare with psyche and thymos respectively. The distinction was discovered through the analysis of intentional activity. Husserl concluded from his analyses that some products of ego activity are the relatively late and sophisticated consequences of a more primitive activity. As he wrote, "When we trace anything built actively, we run into constitution by passive generation." [11]

To illustrate I choose the following illusion:

In the two instances the lines are measurably equal in length, and both are exactly bisected by the dots. Only, in the right hand figure, the dot seems to have moved to the left after the arrowhead was added. Has it "really" moved? Phenomenologically considered (that is, after suspending convictions about the real) the movement of the dot is not illusory. One of the midpoints is actually and spontaneously presented as displaced to the left. The displacement is judged to be an illusion only after measurement—that is, only after superposing on the phenomenon as given to perception the relatively sophisticated and artificial empirical world derived from experiences of exact measurement. The latter world and the judgments that assume

[11] *Cartesian Meditations*, 78. See also Husserl, *Erfahrung und Urteil: Untersuchungen zur Genalogie der Logik*, redigiert und heraus gegeben von Ludwig Landgrebe (Hamburg: Claassen Verlag, 1954), 75 *sq.*; and the critical study of the relation of judgment to the passively generated stratum by John Sallis, "The Problem of Judgment in Husserl's Later Thought," *Tulane Studies in Philosophy*, XVI (The Hague: Nijhoff, 1967), 129–52.

its priority are the product of active genesis by the ego. But at a lower level of the analysis of ego-activity are found "passively" constructed contents, such as the lines of the "illusion" or any perceptually appearing unitary object spontaneously recognized as such. Any object has such a constitutive history (*Ideas* II § 56). The function of the epoché and reductions is just to neutralize the prestige of the relatively "late" official worlds of common sense or of preconceived theory in order to gain access to this constitutive history of the objective world and to its origin and "passive genesis" by the meditating, perceiving, receptive ego.

Husserl was confident that the early history of the constitution of phenomena, even to the "primal instituting" (*Urstiftung*) itself, could be made to yield to analysis (*Cartesian Meditations*, 79f). As we shall see, he even attempted to trace the constitution of other selves back to the level of passive genesis. Indeed, if Husserl is to demonstrate that "transcendency in every form is an immanent existential characteristic, constituted within the ego" (*ibid.*, 84), then everything which seems so clearly to the naive mind to be transcendent to one's (natural) consciousness will have to be shown in some evident way to be the product of the active or passive function of intentional activity. The structure of pure phenomena, the arché of philosophy, will be discovered to be passively generated by the ego. This spontaneously generated phenomenal world will be found to contain the whole universe of actual objective meanings.

It may appear easy, stopping at this point, to classify Husserl's philosophy as an idealism. But this conclusion would be precipitant. Husserl explicitly points out that his doctrine is not a subjective idealism (*Ideas* I, 168); it is, rather, a phenomenological or transcendental idealism. Late in his life, in the *Nachwort zu meinen Ideen* (*ibid.*, 21), he remarks, "Our phenomenological idealism does not deny the positive existence of the real (*realen*) world and of Nature—in the first place as though it held it to be an illusion. Its sole task and service is to clarify the meaning of the world." "World" here is to be understood in the wide sense to include not only the world of objects but also that of lived events and people. Finally it comes to be understood as that background of primary institutions, the basic but unthematic unity of intentions, the *Glaubensboden*,[12] within which human life is lived, cultures are developed, and objective knowledge becomes possible. In the end it acquires a historical dimension that renders it quite difficult to classify in conventional terms.

Transcendental subjectivity is the life of the ego constituting its own self-meaning along with its phenomenal and its objective worlds. Ontology becomes the self-explication of this ego, an explication which is at the same time the "unfolding of the universal logos of all conceivable being" (*Cartesian Meditations*, 155). Is not the ego, then, given a rather heavy burden by Husserl? Is not the whole world and all its furnishings nothing more than a system of intentions radiated, as it were, by a self-constituting, noetically active ego? If so, then the aura of some sort of idealism, even if not a mere subjectivism, might seem to fall around this philosophy. At least it is not yet evident what limitations are placed upon the ego's intendings and possible accomplishments (*Leistungen*). Although this doctrine of the ego has the effect of completing and systematizing Husserl's views on constitution and of deepening them by way of the distinction between passive and active genesis, still it is not evident so far that objectivity is sufficiently accounted for in terms of the ego's constituting.

We return, therefore, to the question concerning the objectivity of knowledge. How, in effect, are the subject's constituted meanings limited so that some of them may defensibly be said to refer objectively to the real world? We saw that the management of this problem in *Ideas* was not thorough since it did not in principle exclude illusion. When Husserl returned to the topic in *Cartesian Meditations*, he showed himself not far from an everyday view, for he ended by admitting that the

[12] *Erfahrung und Urteil* § 12.

cooperation of others is relevant to the determination of objectivity. What, however, are these others, phenomenologically considered? How do they contribute to the constitution of objectivity?

In order to discover the philosophical arché which would relate the subjective to the objective, Husserl moved back from naive experience to impartially viewed phenomena, thence to the consciousness within which phenomena appear, and finally to the ego, center and origin of consciousness. He then assigned his own ego a rather heavy burden in the constitution of objective reality. It is important now to consider the grounds for assigning a similar burden to other egos as well.

§ 35.   INTERSUBJECTIVITY

A presence in the self's world which is of especial importance in self-formation, and consequently in the constitution of the world and of objectivity, is the presence of other persons. Understanding this presence presents a difficulty in Husserl's philosophy that has become notorious. Other egos that I believe to be present in my experience can scarcely be said to be given immediately in perception; only their bodily appearances are so given. However, objects of my experience have properties which would seem to be accountable only if other egos have contributed to their constitution (*Ideas* I, 420; *Cartesian Meditations* § 44). Moreover, I believe myself to be aware of other selves. But a self is a subject that experiences, and I certainly do not experience the experiencing of other subjects. What, then, do I mean by other subjects or selves? Can the other self be rendered immediately and apodictically present to me? Or can this presence be somehow derived from that which is immediate, as the ideal required?

The transcendental phenomenological reduction left me, the philosophizing ego, with the sphere of pure or transcendental subjectivity. This sphere now appears to be more complex than it first appeared. The foreign elements in it, arising from the apparent presence of other subjects, must be seen to be generated within my own subjectivity or else to be suspect. They may be under suspicion, that is, of not being phenomenologically present but of being merely unrecognized importations from the official world. At the present stage, grasp of these foreign egos must be admitted to be opaque. At least we behave toward them as if they were active (noetic) agents like ourselves, and we are scarcely able to suppose this conviction to be illusory. Still, others are not directly experienced as active egos. Are they, then, derived from phenomena given immanently? We must begin by admitting frankly that the reduction rigorously executed appears to leave the philosopher in "transcendental solitude." [13] Let us accept this apparent solitude as an invitation to consider the nature of our experience of the other. This is the problem of transcendental solipsism described by Husserl as "a dark corner" in philosophy. It should by now be evident that the problem does not concern the existence of the other but rather the origin of the meaning "other self." Ours is not the empirical problem of solipsism but the problem of transcendental solipsism (*Cartesian Meditations*, 82, 148).

In *Ideas* II and later in the fifth *Cartesian Meditation*, Husserl attempts to construct the meaning "alter ego" in a manner which will avoid the conclusion either that the other is not grasped at all as another self or that the other is directly perceived. Husserl holds that both of these alternatives are falsified by our experience. Yet we are aware of other egos.

The question concerning the nature of our experience of the other first became importunate in *Ideas* II.[14] There Husserl notes that self-experience is solipsistic (pages 167, 79ff), and that the other is reached or sensed only as apperceived through *Einfühlung* or empathy.[15] Husserl's first belief was that empathy offered original experience of the other. I evidently

---

[13] *Cartesian Meditations*, 89; *Crisis* § 71.

[14] In *Ideas* I, the problem is mentioned but only in passing. See pages 167, 420.

[15] "Die Einfühlung führt nun . . . zur Konstitution der intersubjektiven Objektivität des Dinges und damit auch des Menschen." *Ideas* II, 169.

have original perception of another's body but not of his psycho-physical person. That is, I perceive his body as a series of concordant adumbrations having a noematic unity to which I attribute an absolute existence, like my own. I am aware of this attribution by way of empathy. My sense of empathy, a spontaneous interpretation of the observed behavior of another supposed person, leads me to posit his sensorial data, his world, his personality and habits, and to expect him to react according to the laws of motivation as I have experienced them in my own life (*Ideas* II §56). Through empathy, that is, I apprehend the other as a self like myself, yet as an exceptional presence since his subjectivity is independent of my subjectivity. As is mine, his being-status (*Seinsgeltung*) is absolute. Moreover, I apprehend him as apprehending me. In just the same way as I include him in my world, so he includes me in his. Here a transcendence of a new sort is discovered. No longer do I transcend merely toward an object in my own world; I transcend toward another who also transcends toward me. I seem to be aware of getting into another's world, one independent of my own. In short, my apprehension of the ego possessing a human body is quite different from my perception of a body.

Empathy, however, is in no sense a direct and original perception or awareness of another person; rather, it offers a special complexity. However he may be felt, another person remains transcendent in relation to my experience; *Einfühlung* may point to an original experience, but it cannot complete it (*Ideas* II, 198). I must be satisfied, then, with accepting the other as someone like unto myself.[16] But the other never becomes an "*originäres Dasein*"; within my experience he never achieves *Urpräsenz* but only *Appräsenz* (*ibid.* §44). Empathy, then, does not solve a problem but rather presents one.

The fault to find with this first attack upon the problem is that its basic notion, empathy, is not fully examined and clar-

---

[16] "Der ich nicht der andere bin und nur als verständigendes Analogon für ihn fungiere." *Ibid.*, 198.

ified. It is characterized as a grasp of the motivational complex of another (*Ideas* II §§ 46f) which is developed by apprehending another's animate body functioning for him as mine does for me. How does one come, however, to know that another's body functions as one's own? Is this knowledge not merely presupposed? The development of empathy, the detail of the manner in which the feeling of and for another is constituted in consciousness, is not fully developed in *Ideas* II. Again, with such an analysis, the phenomenological ideal is compromised. Moreover, the notion of empathy as feeling for or in another, or awareness of another as being motivated as I am (*ibid.*, 228f), seems to presuppose the existence of precisely that being for which the phenomenologist is seeking to find original evidence. To see that another body or person is analogous to mine would require that the other would first have to be known as human. Then, after this prior apprehension, a grasp of the detail of the analogical relation might be expected to follow. What is now lacking is a phenomenological seeing of this prior apprehension. Husserl perceived this lack and was clearly dissatisfied with the solution of the solipsistic problem as developed in *Ideas* II.[17] He returned to it in *Cartesian Meditations*, where he attempted to work out the transcendental source of the sense of empathy and to connect it more clearly with original perception.

In the fifth meditation of *Cartesian Meditations*, Husserl uses many of the terms and notions already employed in *Ideas* II, but he approaches the problem anew by way of a second epoché which is intended to separate, within the sphere of phenomena, that which is undeniably my own—that is, the phenomenological observer's own—presentation, the primordial world. This, my primordial world, is isolated or removed from whatever may be attributed to any subject other than myself. Accordingly, belief in other selves—and therefore belief in

---

[17] So he told Alfred Schutz. See Schutz (ed.), "Edmund Husserl's *Ideas*, Vol. II," *Journal of Philosophy and Phenomenological Research*, XIII (1953), 394–413. Also see *Cartesian Meditations*, 92.

cultural objects so far as others contribute to their constitution, as well as in the public character of objects belonging to the world—is suspended. Belief in the communal aspects of the intersubjective world, previously unquestioned, is not annihilated by this epoché; it merely is not used. This belief is disconnected. My own phenomenal world, now clearly encompassed within my own subjectivity, moves on as before; each succeeding presentation is said to continue harmoniously the preceding (*Cartesian Meditations*, 107f).

There appears in the flow of my own presentations a single and privileged body, my own, provided with fields of sensation. To other bodies, perceptibly similar to mine, like fields of sensation are spontaneously attributed. I have come certainly to believe, in consequence, that each of these other sensitive bodies has its own *Ich-pol*, its subject aware of its identity and its familiar world, and its own transcendental ego actively and passively constituting a world similar to mine within a time duplicating my own temporality. What is the basis for this conviction? We have seen that the basis cannot be the sense of empathy, for this feeling is not direct perception or original evidence of the other. I do not perceive his ego. I might conclude by way of a process of reasoning that the perceptual presence of a body like mine, acting rather as mine does, entails the presence there of an ego like mine. But to recognize the other body's behavior as *like* mine is already to recognize its possible inhabitation by an ego like mine. Reasoning by analogy in this manner assumes what it is intended to conclude. Nevertheless, Husserl holds that a type of analogizing is involved in my recognition of another self. But the analogizing process which he detects in the constitution of my awareness of another is not reasoning by analogy. Rather, he concludes, it is an originative analogizing, a process of passive genesis which may be explicated in terms of "appresentation" and "pairing."

A fundamental type of awareness is perceiving by appresentation. When I, the typical perceiver, view the presented face of a box turned toward me, I also grasp by appresentation the rear face. I know a priori that the opposite face is there. In principle, that is, by an eidetic necessity, there are no one-sided perceptible objects. The opposite face of the box belongs to the (inner) horizon of the perception,[18] and the unity of the perceived face with the unperceived parts belongs to the original constitution of the noema of the object. My intention of these parts can in principle be fulfilled by turning the box around and bringing its previously opposite face to *"Urprä-senz"* (*Ideas* II § 44). In this appresentation we encounter a primordial (passive) synthesis of the perceived face of the box and the (fulfillable) pre-apprehension of the opposite face. No effort of imaginative variation can eliminate this apprehension. The essential character of lived space guarantees its sensible (if not sensed) presence. Here we grasp an essential aspect of all spatial perceiving. This appresentation is a species of passive genesis and is involved in the constitution of the objective spatial world.

In the case of the appresentation of another ego, however, we cannot turn the other's body around to expose this ego. In fact, the only body in my experience which is organic and which perceptibly includes an ego is my own (*Cartesian Meditations*, 108ff, 122). But my awareness of the organic character of the other's body and of its having an ego could be derived only from my self-experience. Husserl moves immediately to the conclusion that he has discovered an operation, which he terms "pairing," by which I relate the perceived body of the other to his appresented ego.

Pairing is a spontaneous transfer of meaning from my body and experience to the perceived body of the other. It is a species of appresentation and belongs to the inner horizon of perception. But it is unique in that the properties thus transferred

---

[18] The term "horizon" refers to the perceivable (but not perceived) and more or less indeterminate background network of events, objects, situations within which the perception or experience in question occurs. See *Ideas* I §§ 27, 44; also see Spiegelberg, *The Phenomenological Movement*, I, 161; II, 718. "Inner horizon" refers to unperceived parts or aspects internal to the perceived object in question; "outer horizon" refers to the remainder of the horizon.

cannot in principle be perceptively verified. Pairing is a necessary connection of intentionalities, occurring at the level of passive genesis. In consequence, two (or more) data given primitively and prominently in the unity of consciousness are always constituted as a pair (*Cartesian Meditations*, 112), each overlaying the other with its own sense. The two data in the present instance are the perceived body of the other and my awareness of my own experiencing ego living in and through my own body. When the spontaneous overlay (analogy) occurs, then I cannot but attribute to this other human-like body, as it appears in my phenomenal world, an animation and a pure ego or source of intentionalities like my own, an ego which experiences from his perspective a world harmonious with the world which I experience from my perspective (*ibid.*, 114, 118, 125). His world is appresented to me so long as his behavior is harmonious. On the other hand, his "organism becomes experienced as a pseudo-organism, precisely if there is something discordant about its behavior" (*ibid.*, 114). Husserl has thus moved from a noematic similarity of bodies constituted on the level of perception to a similarity of noesis (and of agent egos) which goes beyond perception.

Upon the basis of this new constitutive possibility the intersubjective and common world is instituted. My "here" is my point of reference for the other as "there"; but, since at a level of passive genesis (below the level of explicit analogizing thought) I have already constituted the noematic "other-like-me," I can attribute to him a "here" for which I am "there." And so on for other types of awareness. As they belong to me, so by a shift of perspective, they can be attributed to the other and constitute his world as he views it and as I have an appresentational access to it. The object I perceive, constituted within my own subjectivity, I apperceive also as perceivable by the other within his different subjectivity; thus I posit in the object more than is or can be originally present to me (*Cartesian Meditations*, 122). This spontaneous synthesis of our respective experienced worlds in the intersubjective world within a common objectifiable time proceeds according to an essential necessity. It accordingly provides the basis for intersubjective verification of that to which objective reality is attributed, as well as of higher types of psychic occurrences.

In the intersubjective world as thus constituted, two strata of sense must be distinguished (*Cartesian Meditations*, 124). First, there is the lower stratum primordially and passively constituted and perceived within my own subjectivity; secondly, there is the superimposed appresentational stratum which, though it coincides with the primordially perceived stratum, is experienced as given to the other ego. Here we have not two worlds, mine and another's, but rather two strata of one common or intersubjective world. To the further question of how these two strata are united, Husserl answers by extending the notion of identifying synthesis (*ibid.*, 125f). As an object upon my horizon is identified as the same upon different appearances at different times, so an object (e.g., the other's body) appearing within my own appearance system is identified as the same object appearing within the other's appearance system. Again, this analogy is not the conclusion of a process of analogical reasoning; rather, it refers to the result of an operation that takes place spontaneously, or unthematically, at the level of passive genesis.

Thus a common unified objective life-world is constituted within which men may live and pursue their interests. To this end also, the other is constituted as having me in his world. The other grasps me as a person, and every understanding of the other reveals to me some aspect of my own psychic life. The constitution of the other within my own transcendental subjectivity is at the same time a constitution of my own ego within our commonly constituted world. By such operations there is formed an open community of selves mutually interacting in complex ways and constituting the realm of transcendental intersubjectivity (*Cartesian Meditations*, 130). By some of these operations personal communication is established, and by its means sociality is organized and becomes understandable. Within sociality, cultural worlds are set up, each with its characteristic subjective type; a relevant example is classical Greek culture, whose central structural element is said in *Crisis* to be the ideal of rationality, inherited also by European man. In general, the world we live in is constituted not merely in the individual consciousness but also in an intersubjective consciousness composed of many monadic consciousnesses (*Ideas* II, 110).

One of the common elements of intersubjective life constituted within the modern world is the generally accepted method of investigating the empirical world and standards for evaluating the outcome of such investigations. Knowledge so obtained and evaluated is objective knowledge. Husserl, however, is not so much interested in elaborating or analyzing the particular standards of objectivity which might be generally accepted by scientists at a particular epoch as he is in attempting to understand how a world can come to be which can contain such standards. An essential aspect of such a world is precisely its intersubjective character. Claims to objectivity in knowing are not merely those evidenced by one's own fulfilled intentions. To satisfy the ideal, intentions must be *objectively* fulfilled. Objectively fulfilled intentions are those which are or can be intersubjectively verified. Thus intersubjectivity in Husserl's philosophy plays a part rather like the divine veracity in Descartes's. Both provide a larger context of rationality within which the individual human reason can be measured. For Husserl, this larger context underwrites, as it were, the Western ideal of rigor. In addition, this larger intersubjective context is that within which this ideal has its source.

Thus Husserl meant to reach the very important and complex conclusion: The objective world, its standards, and its methods, are dependent and derived; they are dependent upon those transcendental necessities which define the relevant subjective type, and they are derived genetically from the intersubjective world which realizes that subjective type. This latter, the intersubjective world in which we all live before we share in some specialized official world, was to become the *Lebenswelt* that figures so largely in his later reflections.

The specialized scientific world is to a considerable extent actively constituted. It is constituted by different groups in different specific ways and, unlike the passively constituted spatio-temporal world, it is not accessible to those who have not constituted a similar cultural world within themselves (*Cartesian Meditations*, 133ff). This view, nevertheless, is no cultural relativism; the same basic world is accessible to any ego (*ibid.*, 137) and requires only submission to education in its constitutive discipline to bring one into possession of it. The basic, passively constituted world and the possibilities of active constitution are eidetic necessities and are the same for each person. In addition, each is born into a particular cultural life-world and begins from infancy to construct the particular style of person and to favor the particular choice of motives which harmonizes with the style of intersubjective life (culture and sociality) of his community.

The geneses of the ego's performances, particularly in regard to the passive earlier strata, are especially difficult to uncover and to reactivate. Communal life tends to form itself into a certain type (*Cartesian Meditations*, 133), and its member egos are persuaded to accept this type naively as the only natural formation. Thus some respectable members of the scientific community regard propositions not verifiable by use of presently approved empirical principles and the methods of a favored science as figments of idealistic imagination. In consequence, for example, objectivism or psychologism may come to dominate thought. The result of such fixed attitudes is that possibilities and potentialities of the ego remain dormant and ignored. Such destructive prejudices arise from a failure to understand objectivity in its relation to its transcendental possibility and in its genesis. Just this failure lies at the root of the sickness that Husserl was to discover in European man. Phenomenology, as the constant return to beginnings, holds up to philosophy the ideal of maintaining contact with the earlier strata of the self, rather than beginning with some convenient and familiar presupposition. Thus it maintains a lively contact with the possibilities of being and value inherent within these earlier strata, possibilities fatefully concealed by the sedimentation-effect produced by the slow changes of a society.

§ 36.   CRITICISMS AND REINTERPRETATION

This management of the problem of transcendental solipsism is more ingenious than satisfying. Most Husserlian phenomenologists have not been content with it. Discontent with Husserl's management of the problem has been expressed in several ways. Ortega y Gasset, for example, holds that the radical solitude of the experiencing ego is final and that the supposed human life of the other, analogous to mine, is merely hypothetical, never more than partially confirmable by his responding to my actions in the anticipated social ways.[19] Max Scheler, on the contrary, had already attempted to argue that one's perception of another is just as immediate as one's perception of oneself.

Following quite another direction, Jean Paul Sartre has sought to destroy the problem itself by arguing that there is no transcendental ego to be isolated.[20] He believes Husserl, misled by unconscious presuppositions, did not carry the reductive process far enough. Otherwise he would have suspended belief in the existence of the transcendental ego and would have found the ego as much "in the world" as any other product of the intentional consciousness. Sartre does not, it seems to me, take sufficient cognizance of two facts. First, it is not relevant either to assert or to deny the existence of the transcendental ego. For Husserl, an existing ego would be empirical, but the whole of the existing world, specifically including the empirical

[19] José Ortega y Gasset, *Man and People*, trans. W. R. Rusk (New York: Norton, 1957), Chaps. 4–7.

[20] "La Transcendence de l'Ego," *Recherches Philosophiques*, VI (Paris, 1936–37). His arguments are clarified and extended by Aron Gurwitsch in "A Nonegological Conception of Consciousness" in *Studies in Phenomenology and Psychology*, 287–300.

ego, was suspended by the epoché. Moreover, later on in the methodical process, existence is found to be constituted in a definite way as a selection from possibilities; that which selected these possibilities is called the transcendental ego. It is easy to interpret expressions such as "consciousness of self," sometimes used by Husserl, as implying that this consciousness is a second empirical ego which is thought to be aware of the first self or empirical ego. But Husserl's transcendental ego is not a second self "outside" the first self and empirically aware of it. Any empirical awareness, whether of self or whatever, has a sense already given it. The transcendental ego, however, is that which gives sense.

In the second place, Sartre does not sufficiently recognize that the reductive process is always guided by an intention, its "transcendental guide." Were the reduction not directed by an objective, it would proceed without order or restriction to suspend any and all beliefs and assertions. One of Husserl's purposes is to understand the being of phenomena and their relation to the constituted objective world (*Ideas* I §§ 33, 49). Thus his aim in part is to understand the origin of the world and its objectivity. He achieves his purpose first by suspending and examining beliefs in existence. He then uncovers the prior being of the transcendental realm and its unifying center or ego. The actively constituting ego (as he held it to be), agent and originator of its intentions and purposes, thus becomes the originator of its world. In order to suspend this sense-giving ego, he would have had to engage in another kind of epoché having quite another objective. I think Sartre has misconceived the direction of Husserl's interests. Husserl, rather, envisaged the problem and type of desirable solution as falling between the two extremes represented by Ortega y Gasset and Scheler.

The problem of solipsism might easily appear to anyone having an essentialist or intellectualist bias in philosophy to be a pseudo-problem. The transcendental reduction, being also an eidetic reduction, seems to uncover the eidos ego as a "purely possible ego" (*Cartesian Meditations*, 71, 136f). Now clearly this eidos ego is not "alone" in any literal sense. There can be only one possible ego in just the same sense that there can be only one eidos "circle." This ego seems to be universal, evidently analogous to the Kantian transcendental unity of apperception. As Kant might have seen, the problem of solipsism is not relevant to this universal self. However, this view, which tends to identify the eidos ego with the transcendental unity of apperception, is an error. Kant's doctrine of the formal unity of apperception fails to do justice to Husserl's concern with the concrete self and its experience. Although Husserl does intend to discover the eidos ego and the essential types of perception which it comprises, still his final preoccupation is always to grasp "this ego as *exemplifying* the eidos ego" (*ibid.*, 72, my emphasis) within its own individual temporality.

In any event, the eidos ego is not a generalization or an induction from many examples, but is seen after imaginative variation worked only upon my own ego. Thus it is the eidos of an individual ego. This outcome is inevitable, since other selves are bracketed out in the fifth meditation and can be considered only after the possibility of intersubjectivity has been established. Husserl's interest centers just as much upon the individual living ego, its persistent identity, its unique temporality, and its characteristic "mundanization" of its eidos as it does upon the eidos itself. This concrete ego, called a "monad" by Husserl, is evidently neither merely abstract nor merely particular. It is the concrete and historical individual seen as instancing a constant unity of meaning which is its own persistent style of being, its own essence. It is the productive center of one's own life-world. Being a human ego, it performs in general respects like others. One may, therefore, interpret the second epoché as moving from an emphasis upon the eidetic self to the personal and individual yet persistent ego necessarily associated with its phenomenal body and the life-world.

It is now desirable to see the two relevant reductions in juxtaposition. The transcendental phenomenological reduction moves from the natural world to the phenomenal one and thence to its eidos; this eidos is understood to be transcendental or foundational and constitutive in its relation to experience. The reduction, as stated in the fifth meditation, moves within this latter realm of transcendental subjectivity to the sphere of my-ownness (*Eigensphäre*); thus it is a movement *within* transcendental subjectivity to its individual and originative center in order to discover the institution of intersubjectivity. The problem of transcendental solipsism is simply the starting point of this latter effort of discovery.

The program of transcendental idealism, guided by the ideal of rigor, requires that everything which is not transcendental ego be seen to be something constituted in the process of the concrete ego's self-explication (*Cartesian Meditations*, 86, 91). Now, I believe other concrete perceiving selves appear within my own subjective horizon. I intend them. I am not party to their perceiving; nor do I perceive their egos directly. In order to authenticate my grasp of their being, I must constitutively relate my consciousness of them to that which I do indubitably perceive. Thus, in this respect, Husserl's problem is genuine and not to be explained away on the supposition that he was the victim of a vicious subjectivism, or of an irrelevant Platonizing, or that he misunderstood the character of a universal or of abstraction.

It might now be argued that the self which is relevant to the problem of solipsism is not an eidos ego but a particular one; therefore the transcendental eidetic reduction is not the method for isolating it, since the transcendental reduction sets existence aside and the particular self which is in question must be existent. The particular ego must at the least be a cogito. However, Husserl's concern is not primarily with other selves as existent, but more generally with other selves as possessing a certain meaning within my phenomenal horizon. His purpose is to discern the transcendental foundation and the genesis of that meaning.

The difficulties in Husserl's philosophy are certainly not the difficulties of empirical solipsism.[21] Three criticisms, however, can be made within his own context of thought and observation. Notice first that the reduction expressed in the fifth meditation is intended to separate that which belongs evidently to my own experience (my *Eigensphäre*) from whatever belongs to or is in any way derived from another. This separation appears at first glance to be quite in agreement with other aspects of phenomenology—for instance, with its insistence that my perceptions and (phenomenal) bodily locus are my unique ground of certainty and in this manner differ radically from anything belonging to another body. However, as we have seen, it is asserted that a primitive analogizing apprehension lends me reason for affirming the other's body to be organic and sensitive, as is my own. May one not, on phenomenal grounds, doubt that this similarity of another's body to my own is perceived? In particular, as Maurice Merleau-Ponty and others have pointed out, I know my own body through visceral sensations, but I become aware of the other's body in a radically different manner, usually through visual perception. This recognition that the two bodies presented in these two quite different fashions are nevertheless similar would seem to be a complex recognition not reducible to "appresentation" (where, for example, one side of a perceived sheet of paper is horizontally apperceived to have another side which might be perceived through the same sense as the first side). The analogy between my sensate body and the other's body is, consequently, weakened.

Even if this special and spontaneous analogizing of the other and his body to oneself and one's own body be allowed, the self of the other is to me never more than a noematic unity, a constituted meaning intending the other noetic self which is never reached or experienced as such. Although I believe the

---

[21] However, this mistaken interpretation is sometimes found; for example, see A. MacIntyre, "Existentialism," in *A Critical History of Western Philosophy*, ed. D. J. O'Connor (Glencoe, Ill.: Free Press, 1964), 517.

other to be such a self and act toward him so, still I can never be him even if I were "there" where he is and even if my sense of empathy were ever so keen. Husserl's analysis of the generation of the sense of the other might as well be interpreted as emphasizing a "distance" between me and the other.

A quite similar criticism or comment might be directed upon Husserl's account of the unity of the intersubjective world. It will be recalled that this unity was said to be a synthesis of identity holding between two strata: my primordially perceived life-world and the appresented experience of the other. The synthesis of identity, however, is discovered originally in the unity holding within the sphere of my own perceptual life —for example, between an object intended and "the same" object intuitively perceived. But now this same kind of identity is presumed to hold between two strata of meaning: the one perceptually and originally given, and the other not so given but derived. What reason can be found within the limitations imposed by the ideal of this philosophy for supposing that a synthetic function operative within my own sphere is also operative in unifying it with another, the intersubjective sphere? In principle, I think no such reason should even be sought. (The ideal of rationality would scarcely tolerate such a *petitio principii.*) There seems to be an irreducible distance between me and others, between my world and the intersubjective one of which anyone can become phenomenally aware.

Finally, a third criticism may be directed against Husserl's effort to divide the originative solitary ego from all alien egos. The second epoché is said to effect this division. The difficulty lies in understanding the unified character of the sphere of my ownness subsequent to the division. The phenomenal world, before this operation, was given as harmonious and in accord with itself. This is the world experienced as codetermined by the foreign egos—that is, this transcendental sphere was experienced as intersubjective. That the intersubjective world is codeterminer of my own experience seems clearly to be admitted (cf. *Ideas* II, 110f; *Cartesian Meditations*, 130). Now one may raise the question whether the *Eigensphäre*, from which the foreigner and all his works were suspended, continues to be experienced as harmonious. Husserl asserts that it is so experienced (*Cartesian Meditations*, 90, 108, 114); however, he offers no reason for this conviction, nor does he lead the reader to see that it is so. In fact, my own experience from which a co-determining element has been removed would on the face of it seem to be incomplete and nonharmonious;[22] hence, it should not be experienced as human. In particular, one would be disposed to wonder how communication could go on within this reduced world of my ownness, especially such communication as is required to practice philosophy or to communicate the absence of the other to oneself.[23]

In *Ideas* II, Husserl develops the notion of an "ambient world" (*Umwelt*)—the world of persons where acts of perception, memory, recognition, and communication may occur. This is a common world developed through preconscious and conscious association and communication with other subjects. It is essentially relative to a social order of persons. Now only a person, a member of the ambient communicative world, could communicate sufficiently with himself to practice the second epoché. Yet this epoché requires precisely the suspension or nonuse of this social world as having been derived, at least in part, from other selves. To suspend use of this possibly existent world would seem to refuse to recognize it in exactly the sense in which it might be effective. Moreover, Husserl has himself developed at length an illustration of the way in which generations of experiencing, reflecting, and intersubjectively communicating egos were required to produce those convictions and concepts necessary to constitute the objective world

[22] This point is made by Alfred Schutz in "Le problème de l'intersubjectivité transcendentale chez Husserl," *Husserl*, Cahiers de Royaumont, Philosophie, No. III (Paris: Les Editions de Minuit, 1959), 335–81; see especially pp. 346f.

[23] Sallis, "The Problem of Judgment in Husserl's Later Thought," 149–52, observes in a related context the difficulty Husserl experienced in considering the world or prepredicative strata in abstraction from (intersubjectively constituted) language. Heidegger seized upon this cue.

of physical objects geometrically characterized which was available to Galileo.[24] Now, this passively constituted phenomenal life-world is correlative to my own ego. Thus it would seem that a second epoché, setting aside the foreign egos on which my own constituted ego must depend, is illegitimate. Indeed, this epoché recalls the Husserlian notion of skepticism: a methodological requirement which entails that its own theoretical foundation is impossible (*Logische*, I § 32). Clearly the ego is not independent of the intersubjective life-world.

Our three criticisms may now be summarized: Intersubjectivity was built upon a questionable analogy between my experience of my being and my experience of the other's body; the ensuing construction can be interpreted as emphasizing the distance between me, the other, and the intersubjective world; and, in any event, it tended to overlook possible incoherencies in my subjectivity when separated from the other or from intersubjectivity. Perhaps, then, the nature and unity of the total transcendental realm does not yield to Husserl's key.

We have arrived at the point where a paradox emerges. The self is said to constitute the other and thus is prior to the other; but also it can constitute the other only in a context of an already intersubjective world, and thus it is posterior to others. Hence it is both prior to and posterior to others. The phenomenal fact is that there are elements in my subjectivity which appear to be due to other persons. Husserl's ideal, however, does not allow him to make inferences to unperceived "entities," such as to other egos, in the manner which these facts seem to require him to do. But neither can he gainsay the somewhat ambiguous experiences which seem to assure us of the presence of others. Clearly an impasse has been reached.

In general, it appears that all being cannot be reduced to being clearly present to my perceiving, for the attempt to effect this reduction issued only in another version of the transcen-

---

[24] *Crisis*, 149–52; cf. Gerd Brand, *Welt, Ich und Zeit, Nach unveröffentlichten Manuskripten Edmund Husserls* (The Hague: Nijhoff, 1955), §§ 5ff.

dental problem—the problem of discovering an adequately evidenced mode of transition from my own world to the inter-subjective world. In view of this difficulty, the reasonable step may be to conclude to a rejection of the convictions that my own subjectivity is original and that intersubjectivity is derived. It may be that the world of others was not originated in transcendental solitude. Thus it may be that the origination of meanings which constitute the world is as much the work of intersubjective subjectivity as it is of my own individual sub-jectivity; or perhaps neither is original. At any rate, the two are not obviously related by a dependence-independence relation-ship. And until the matter is clarified, the goal of presupposition-lessness can certainly not be said to have been reached.

Furthermore, it is most unfortunate that intersubjectivity should not have been clearly understood, for the doctrine of objectivity hinges upon intersubjectivity. If the rational ground for intersubjectivity fails, then that for objectivity fails also. Then the bond which Husserl sought to establish between the objective world and its source in the transcendental ego is not quite evident after all.

The loss to Husserl's phenomenology, however, inflicted by criticisms such as the ones offered here might be minimized by a reinterpretation of the rational ideal of rigor. This ideal might be reinterpreted so as not to require the reduction of all being to being clearly present to my perceiving. Then the dilemma which offers the choice either of an unevidenced construction or of an impossible direct perception of the other ego might be avoided. On the other hand, the difficulty may lie deeper. Perhaps the conclusion should rather be that Husserl did not clearly apprehend the beginning of philosophy in transcen-dental subjectivity.

The first suggestion recommends merely moderating the strict requirements of the philosophical ideal of presupposition-lessness. This formulation of the rational ideal prevented Hus-serl's accepting any affirmation without the evidence of his own seeing (*Cartesian Meditations*, 151, 122). Being, within this finite perspective, is being evident to my seeing. It may be that faithfulness to this ideal brought Husserl to the point of either expressly surrendering its rigorous interpretation or of accepting the solipsistic paradox. He cannot accept the latter; hence one possibility is to conclude that we may regard his ideal as permitting, at least in the instance of the other self, something other than immediate or perspectival evidence. Perhaps, that is, we might save his doctrine by construing his ideal loosely so as to allow what I shall call "structural evidence." By structural evidence I mean some reasonable account of the possibility of constructing the meaning at issue (e.g., "alter ego") within my subjectivity, even though the constructed noema is unfillable by any seeing or experiencing of the meaning (e.g., the other transcendental ego) thus constructed. Hence, to the strong form of his animating ideal (which would allow as evidence only the immediately given phenomenon or that which is horizontally related in evident and fulfillable ways to the given phenomenon), I suggest that Husserl should be willing to add another alternative: that which is related to the phenomena or to the ego in ways which are assumed, yet which remain coherently related in all their implications to phenomena.

In other words, Husserl might allow interpretations of phenomena that refer coherently to unperceivable beings. Perhaps by this loosening of the ideal, the conflict between the phenomena of intersubjectivity and the strict demands of the ideal of presuppositionlessness would be moderated. Moreover, this loosening of the strict rational ideal seems to be in the tradition. Descartes, it will be recalled, in effect permitted such a weakening of his ideal of clarity when he admitted to Princess Elizabeth that the unity of body and soul in man could only be experienced but could not in principle be clearly understood.[25] However, the point is touchy. It is difficult sometimes to decide whether Husserl considered that the approach

---

[25] And after all, the above suggestion only extends to Husserl's phenomenology, a practice common in the sciences. For example, the physicist actively constructs the concept of an entity (e.g., the electron) which is unperceivable *ex hypothesi*, but which is coherent with all available evidence.

of his philosophy to the rational ideal is evidence for the validity of his philosophy or whether his philosophy vouches for
the validity of the ideal.

In any case, there is a grave difficulty with this interpretation.
How far can the loosening of his ideal be carried? Does it not
open the door to all sorts of constructivism? Possibly, however,
intersubjectivity itself as embodied in a tradition and expressed
in controlling purposes—e.g., the inherited ideal of rigor—will
act as a damper upon the possibilities that this loosening of the
ideal might otherwise permit. Nevertheless, a control based
solely upon tradition is always suspect; the fate of Socrates must
be remembered. A tradition may be confused, and the intersubjectivity upon which it is based may be misdirected. Husserl
himself regarded European humanity as sick, a sickness by
which he himself was victimized. How, then, could objective
evidence for this diagnosis of the then current intersubjectivity
be adduced if objectivity be a function in intersubjectivity?
Husserl makes use in *Crisis* of the ideal of the infinite rational
task in which European humanity is engaged as a sort of measure of the health of humanity. Still, it might be argued that
Husserl himself, who expresses this ideal, is a product of the
same humanity. Did he understand transcendental subjectivity?
Or is his vision also infected by the disease troubling modern
man generally?

§ 37. HUSSERL'S PREDICAMENT AND HISTORY

It does appear that the difficulties which evolved from transcendental solipsism and the need for a clear grasp upon intersubjectivity ended by placing Husserl's philosophy in a predicament: he had either to ignore an indisputable component of
his world (other selves) or to modify the guiding ideal. The
fifth of the *Cartesian Meditations*, however, does not contain
Husserl's last word on the matter; another view of it may be
gathered from his last writing. The *Crisis*, probably written
somewhat under the influence of Heidegger's *Being and Time*,
suggests that a phenomenologically oriented understanding of

Western history opens, if not upon a radical change in the rational ideal, at least upon a new evaluation of it. Then a reduction carried forward from this vantage point indicates a relation of interdependence between subjectivity and intersubjectivity. And finally, Husserl reaffirms his conclusion that the objective world is genetically derived but derived, as he latterly concludes, from the intersubjective life-world.

Husserl never went so far as to accept the conviction of some later thinkers that the Western ideal of reason had played itself out. He never lost his conviction that any new insight into reason would be continuous with European history (*Crisis*, 337). He looked forward in *Crisis* to a reformation of the ideal, not to a revolution. The *Crisis*, therefore, begins with the rational ideal as Husserl had so far come to understand it—namely, as directed toward the clear perception of what is —without assuming in advance that all that is must be mathematical in structure.

Husserl still assumed that being is being as evident to mind. But the question now requires identifying the mind to which being will become evident. Likewise in the *Crisis*, Husserl preserved what is perhaps his greatest contribution to the development of philosophy: awareness of an enormously increased sphere of phenomena. Phenomena of concern to this tradition in philosophy have, consequently, become coincident with all of that which is presented in consciousness viewed—ideally— without prejudice. Accordingly, the historical development of the phenomena accessible to men is also included in the sphere of philosophic concern. Finally, and in obedience to the rational ideal, Husserl envisaged the discovery of transcendental powers commensurate with the whole developing domain of phenomena. It remained true for him that "the only real clarifying is rendering transcendentally understandable" (*Crisis*, 193). But now a means of approach is required which would lead to a view of the unfolding of these transcendental powers. No doubt the ideal of rationality would be seen to manifest itself differently in different epochs. And in particular, since reason deals with the products of passive genesis (psyche) and indeed must take its own beginning with this prepredicative stratum of consciousness, it too must be expected to be subject to a gradual unfolding in the course of time. Rationality, too, has a history.

The broadening of the phenomenal field and of the philosophical task demanded a new method, a "universal epoché." This new methodical step is a longer and more difficult method than the reductions previously discussed. It is intended to enable the phenomenologist to analyze the world situation in which he finds himself and to see the whole scientific tradition in a cleared perspective in relation both to its arché, the transcendental foundation, and to the temporal life-world of the ego within which this tradition is generated. This new reduction is a difficult route and calls for a total change of the philosopher himself (*Crisis*, 151, 468 *sq.*); indeed, it calls for something like a radical reorganization. He writes, "It is perhaps evident that the total phenomenological attitude and the epoché belonging to it is called, accordingly, to work a complete personal change which should be compared specifically to a religious conversion. In addition, this attitude contains the meaning of the greatest change which is available to humanity as such" (*Crisis*, 140). What exactly is the character of this change which so deeply affects the person and even involves humanity? Doubtless we should see this change exemplified in Husserl himself in his transition from transcendental solipsism to an intersubjective and historically oriented philosophy which in one way or another has indeed affected a noticeable portion of humanity.

We should regard, unfinished though it is, the whole of the *Crisis* as Husserl's own effort to achieve the universal epoché. In his practice, it revealed the *Lebenswelt*, or common life-world, as the fundamental meaning of the natural life (the "*Bodensgeltung naturliches Lebens*," *Crisis*, 151). It discovered this passively generated intersubjective world always prior to any object whose constitutive and genetic processes were to be analyzed. This is the world in which we all live prior to the reflection that divides subject from object or defines the object, as Galileo did, in mathematical terms and in contradistinction from the knowing subject (*ibid.* §§ 9–11). Only a reduction *through* such epoch-marking historical developments of modern times can reactivate the earlier insights and the decisions which instituted the sciences and their objective world. Only thus can these insights be brought into a nondistorting relation to the human life in which they originated and continue to be founded.

As one might suspect, this way of approach reveals transcendental subjectivity in a different light. It is still true to say that I discover myself as a world-experiencing life (*Welterfahrendesleben*), but the world now contains other selves who contributed to its origin. Thus the difference from his earlier views becomes evident in the function taken on by intersubjectivity. After all, history is an intersubjective engagement, and a reduction through historical developments to their prereflective basis in the life-world is a reduction to a level which may still be called intersubjective, even though only individuals live through history. For the strange thing is that analysis of my subjectivity always reveals an intersubjective *Lebenswelt*. Thus, Husserl writes, "Everything becomes complicated as soon as we consider that subjectivity is what it is (i.e., the constitutively functioning ego) only in intersubjectivity" (*Crisis*, 175). Here a universal sociality or humanity becomes a sort of "space" wherein each ego-subject constitutes the common world, which is at the same time his own world. And this common *Lebenswelt* becomes the concrete context whose a priori forms determine and limit the styles of living, reasoning, the forms of culture, and the possible sciences of an epoch. Thus the intersubjective world which, as we have seen, so stoutly resisted phenomenological grasp, nevertheless seems to be identifiable as the basic and founding stratum of experience no less than—perhaps more than—the individual transcendental ego itself.

The objective world and the sciences grow out of the *Lebenswelt*. The reason which can uncover this genesis and see the sciences in their relation to the passively generated strata of human life is that broader reason which may reintegrate these same sciences and human living and thus change contemporary humanity. In short, the sciences are actively generated within the passively generated life-world and must be continually related back to that world if the misunderstanding and barbaric misuse of them are to be averted. This seeing of the sciences within their total context is the seeing accomplished by a historically understood reason. The certainty belonging to this reason is developmental; it is reevaluated as the certainty of a direction in the historical movement engaged in the task defined by the rational ideal. The philosopher is the agent of this ideal; he is the "functionary of humanity." His is the task of humanizing man.

Husserl concluded in the *Crisis* that the ideal of rational rigor was a Kantian Idea, an infinite task, one involving a totality. It was to be approached by many philosophers and scientists but never to be finally achieved in the indefinite reaches of history. This modification of Husserl's initial seventeenth-century confidence in the eventual complete transparence of experience to the self almost amounts to a reversal, for if rationality delineates an infinite task, one never to be achieved, then perhaps it may almost as well be admitted that experience is infinitely nontransparent. But such an admission comes perilously close to giving up the characteristically modern article of faith: that being is identical with being as evident to mind. If no philosopher can expect to unfold "the universal logos of all conceivable being" (*Cartesian Meditations*, 155), how can he be sure that this logos *can* be unfolded? To admit to the possible obscurity of being is a concession that may be welcomed by some philosophers, but it would have seemed to Husserl to be a surrender to fate that he could never have brought himself to accept. He drew back from a possibly self-destructive questioning of the power of reason itself. His limitation of the ideal does not go beyond a *de facto* limitation. Ideally, nothing is closed to reason, even though there may be no actual realization of this ideal, for example, in a Leibnizian god. As Husserl remarked in the *Crisis,* "The reason for the downfall of a rational culture does not lie in the essence of rationalism itself but only in its externalization, its absorption in naturalism and objectivism."

The rationalism of the European mind, Husserl held, was not responsible for the sickness of modern man; only the distortions of this rationalism were responsible. Although in a basic sense the Western ideal of rationality remains unchanged by Husserl's later philosophy, still his view of the foundational character of transcendental subjectivity is notably altered by his intersubjective and historical interpretation of the rational ideal. Since the rational ideal is an expression of the way in which humanity comes to understand itself, it must be intersubjectively engendered; thus, again, intersubjectivity would appear to be no less foundational than subjectivity, and thus Husserl's grasp upon the rational ideal can be no more clearly and rigorously based than his understanding of an intersubjectivity which undergoes historical development.

Husserl's life-long struggle to realize the ideal of presuppositionlessness by seeing clearly through the processes by which the life-world and intersubjectivity are constituted by the individual transcendental ego was not successful. The passively generated life-world and other persons seemed in some obscure sense always to have been presupposed. Perhaps this is as it should be. The nature of the transcendental foundation of individual experience, of our world, and of our common life is most difficult to divine, perhaps impossible to see upon the assumption that one of these is more fundamental than the others. It may be that neither subjectivity nor intersubjectivity can be seen to express clearly the character of the transcendental origin of experience. Neither may be more original than the other.

Thus Husserl failed fully and clearly to determine the character of founding subjectivity. In particular, he did not press his inquiry further to question the ground of its intentionality, the essence of subjectivity. Paul Ricoeur rightly emphasizes the point that in the last decade of his life Husserl's interest turned mainly toward genetic phenomenology,[26] and he accordingly tended to identify perception rather than intentionality as the essential function of consciousness. This change is important for intentionality may be empty, whereas the priority of perception entails the priority of the presence of the world to subjectivity; it entails the priority of involvement in concrete living—a circumstance which renders it all the more difficult to classify Husserl's philosophy as an idealism. The priority of engagement in the project of human living is quite in accord with the importance assumed by the life-world in *Crisis*. It also anticipates a direction which existentialist philosophers were to develop. Likewise, Heidegger's questioning of the foundations of intentionality turns in the same direction.

As Husserl repeatedly observed, discovering and understanding the beginning point in philosophy is philosophy's most difficult task. Rationality is a progressively unfolding—and possibly folding—ideal; its viewing of its own origination in the passive and prepredicative strata of psyche is its most demanding and crucial feat. To see the picture when one is inside the frame is difficult. Perhaps a view that is both clear and complete is not possible.

Husserl was aware of the basic character and complexity of the ideal of rationality and also of the curious persistence of the Cartesian transcendental problem. He strove to solve his version of the latter problem, while holding faith with the ideal, by interpreting the objectively existing world as a set of meanings which are possible only within subjectivity and as originated by the transcendental ego. At the same time, the method of reduction led him to the discovery of a far richer phenomenal world (the *Lebenswelt*) than Kant had ever dreamed of. Then with further analysis of the foundational strata of this world, he came upon an ambiguity—the status of intersubjectivity—which seemed to present another form of the transcendental problem, this time in terms of the relation of the self to others and to the cultural world. Dealing with this problem led him

[26] *Husserliana*, 204f; and cf. *Erfahrung und Urteil*, 23–28.

to the implicit conclusion that the ego and the passively generated life-world are equally primordial. But then the opacity of
this life-world appeared to demand a loosening or a reevaluation of the ideal of rationality. The guide to comprehending
such an evaluation seemed finally to be history itself, but if rationality is an historically unfolding ideal, then its demands are
infinite and may be unfulfillable in fact.

Husserl's study of the sciences led to the conclusion that their
crisis originated in the doctrine of objectivism which assigned
independent reality to objects as interpreted by the sciences.
The consequence of this metaphysics was that man's relation to
the world became an insoluble enigma. Husserl recognized the
enigma, but his transcendental idealism did not remove it.
After all, it was produced by men, philosophers and scientists,
who thought in accordance with the Western ideal of rationality. And the very same ideal had led Husserl to his philosophy.
Could it be possible that this ideal somehow led to the fateful
forgetfulness of a more original understanding of man and the
world? In any event, Husserl had been willing to relax, at
least in his own thinking, the grip of the Cartesian ideal of rational (mathematical) clarity. The consequence of his influence
upon others was a further modification of this ideal and the
opening of a perspective which appears now to be directed toward a transition into a new era in philosophizing. That Husserl
himself effected this transition cannot be claimed, but his reinterpretation of the philosophic method, subject matter, origin, and ideal were certainly invaluable steps along the way.

VI

Heidegger: The "There" and the Place of Science

§ 38. THE POSITION OF THE PROBLEM

If politics and the several voices of doom are heeded, one may conclude it to be high time that contemporary men moved out of the modern world into another—almost any other. Not a few philosophers believe they perceive in Martin Heidegger's philosophy the first vision of a new world. Has he indeed discovered the need and the possibility of forming a new world? And has he caught a glimpse of its shape?

Heidegger's original appropriation of the past has enabled him to place his own philosophy at the confluence of its several currents. From Aristotle he received the initial ontological bent of his thought, but he underwent a formative influence from the transcendentalism of Kant and the post-Kantians. Certainly a very good way of getting into his philosophy is by way of his two books on Kant.[1] At the same time he has pondered deeply the two counterweights to modern thought, Kierkegaard and Nietzsche, and has sensed the need they express for attempting to understand human existence in its uniqueness and its concreteness. Also he has studied the philosophers from the van-

[1] *Kant and the Problem of Metaphysics*, trans. J. S. Churchill (Bloomington: Indiana University Press, 1962), Pt. 4; and *What Is a Thing?* trans. W. B. Barton, Jr., and Vera Deutsch (Chicago: Henry Regnery Co., 1967).

tage point of the phenomenological perspective gained from his early association with Husserl, to whom he dedicated *Being and Time.*[2] Thus Heidegger is admirably placed for discerning the character and direction of past thought. Coming after the Romantic and early existentialist philosophers, he is well situated for sensing the need to begin philosophy with concrete phenomena as they are lived and experienced in all the shades of feeling and mood. Likewise, coming after Husserl and Wilhelm Dilthey, he is well placed for perceiving the character of the rational scientific ideal and for appreciating its effect on Western history. It is quite possible that he brings the philosophic tradition to which he belongs to its maturity. One who believes he does so, however, must reckon with those who say he brings philosophy to its end.

The history of the West, Heidegger holds, is the history of nihilism. Events since the times of Hegel and Nietzsche, both of whom saw through this history to its conclusion, show unmistakably that the values on which Western civilization had drawn in order to define man and to give meaning and direction to human life have been nullified. This general trend Heidegger describes as the "darkening of the world."[3] He certainly desires to contribute something to halting or reversing this trend. The poisoning of the environment, violence among men and nations, the pecuniary standard of value, the leadership by the masses—all these are one side of a coin that presents the intellectual side of man as the central object in a physical universe, self-destined to dominate the whole of it, yet a man whose values are merely subjective and whose history is often presumed to be scientifically predictable and controllable (at least by certain few privileged individuals).

This is the man who has, as it were, decided to seek harmony between himself and his fate and between himself and nature

[2] Trans. John Marquarrie and Edward Robinson (London: SCM Press, 1962). The page references to the seventh German edition are included on the margin of *Being and Time*.

[3] See his *Introduction to Metaphysics*, trans. Ralph Manheim (New Haven: Yale University Press, 1958), 35, 45; hereinafter cited as *Metaphysics*.

by determining his own fate and by dominating nature. Modern man would change nature and his fate in order to accommodate them to his desires rather than change his own way of being. This decision became explicit with Descartes's intention to doubt everything and his subsequent discovery of himself as a unique kind of substance, a subject situated at the noetic center of the universe and capable of mastering it through the power of applied scientific knowledge.

Heidegger would alter this decision. Rather like Kant and Husserl, he seeks to do so by returning first to the sensitive point in history, man himself, in order to disclose within the inner sources of man's being, but then also within Being itself, the basis for effecting a transition to a new vision of the self and the world. Like other philosophers in his tradition, Heidegger seeks —at least in *Being and Time*—to manage the transcendental problem occasioned by deficiencies in the basic world view by way of discovering a more inclusive context which would allow for the possible understanding of previously conflicting or confused elements. Husserl's philosophic efforts had not effected passage into a world free of crises. Heidegger, therefore, proposes a still wider context, perhaps the widest context possible, one which completely reevaluates our familiar world and appears to herald new forms of life. A prerequisite necessary for understanding the kind of transition that he proposes is to grasp the nature and status of the objective universe and of the sciences which study it as they emerge from his ontological inquiry into their transcendental bases. Accordingly, my emphasis falls upon his view and evaluation of objectivity while, at the same time, developing a discussion of his vision of man and the world man inhabits.

Heidegger's style of writing, which sometimes seems to replace sober philosophical speech with poetic and oracular utterance, has unfortunately invited condemnation of him and his understanding as antiscientific and irrational. Also, his view of the sciences and of the nature studied by science is sometimes said to be a Romantic rejection. He seems to some critics to offer a man without a natural world.[4] To more extreme critics he appears to make this offer violently and by way of a return to complete irrationality or to a kind of mysticism.[5] Some of these critics, in their milder moments, classify his philosophy as a subjective idealism.[6] My evaluation of such criticisms indicates that Heidegger does take important issue with the intellectualist ideal which has dominated Western thought. In addition, most commentators admit that certain elements present in the later expressions of this philosophy are difficult to assess. But to assume at the outset that these elements are merely "mystical" would be captious. Nevertheless, these elements are evidently alien to the rationalist mind; consequently, the particular way in which Heidegger's philosophy takes issue with the more intellectualist version of the rational ideal usually goes ununderstood. I believe it possible to show that the condemnation of his philosophy as a violent irrationalism or a mere mysticism is based upon a hasty assessment of the evidence and tends to underrate what may be the most important philosophic accomplishment of our century.

Many of Heidegger's concepts are original. Also, they are presented in an uncompromisingly novel terminology. The complexity of the ideas involved and of the relations among such notions as Being, "Dasein," existence, authenticity, the ontological sense of the world, the life-world, and the objective world make it impossible to discuss these matters separately in the comparatively simple order suggested by a mere listing. I shall, instead, after some remarks on Heidegger's relation to Husserl's philosophy, proceed through a consideration of the

[4] See Karl Löwith, *Nature, History, and Existentialism*, trans. A. Levinson (Evanston: Northwestern University Press, 1966), 103.

[5] Walter Kaufmann, *From Shakespeare to Existentialism* (New York: Doubleday, Anchor Books, 1960), Chap. 17. Kaufmann's screed of grievances against Heidegger adds up more or less to the accusation of unreason; cf. "The lack of clarity and contempt for grammar . . . border on obscurantism in Heidegger's philosophy of Being" (*ibid.*, 363).

[6] See Hazel E. Barnes, *An Existentialist Ethics* (New York: Knopf, 1967), Chap. 12.

problems that the sciences offer and the world in which they exist to a consideration of the relevant ontological structures of human-being, or Dasein, and its authentic mode of existing. This point reached, it will be possible to indicate Heidegger's management of the transcendental problem and to understand his evaluation of the modern scientific enterprise. The question concerning the transition to a possible new epoch of history will then be at least somewhat clearer.

§ 39.　TOWARD A POST-HUSSERLIAN ONTOLOGY

Although most reasonable, the suggestion that Heidegger's views on the sciences and their object-world be approached through his studies of Kant's philosophy would require more space than is available here. Consequently, it will be better now to compare and contrast certain of his views with those of Husserl and thus to lay the foundation from which our discussion can be given a direction. Consideration here of Heidegger's specific criticisms of Husserl will not be needful;[7] our purpose will be accomplished by showing briefly how the concepts of ego and world underwent a sea change when they entered Heidegger's philosophy. These changes point toward a metamorphosis of the ideal of rationality and a new envisagement of the nature and status of objectivity.

Heidegger reflected upon the ego with a mind indelibly affected by Kierkegaard. Kierkegaard said that the famous remark "Je pense donc je suis" should have been "Je pense donc je ne suis pas." But philosophers from Descartes to Hegel, with the exception of Schelling, had forgotten the existing human being; they had allowed themselves to be blinded to the obscurities of the *sum* by the glare of the *cogito*. The consequence was a series of abstract philosophies which made little or no contact with existence; these were philosophies of thought

---

[7] See W. Biemel, "Husserl's Encyclopaedia Britannica Artikel und Heidegger's Anmerkungen dazu," *Tijschrift voor Philosophie*, XII (1950), 240–80. Also see W. J. Richardson, *Heidegger: Through Phenomenology to Thought* (The Hague: Nijhoff, 1963), 178ff.

which were deficient in respect for the individual. Like Kierkegaard, Heidegger would atone for this disrespect and would
retain contact with the concrete. Accordingly, he took a critical
view of Husserl's somewhat ideal ego.

It will be recalled that Husserl regarded the egology of *Cartesian Meditations* as ontology, a study of the most basic meanings of being with which human life could be involved. His
egology was supposed to be an intentional and constitutional
analysis of the self's most fundamental performances (*Leistungen*). Heidegger takes issue specifically with this identification of ontology: For if intentionality should turn out to be
founded upon something other than consciousness, then a
description of the ego's intentional performances will not be an
exhaustive description of its being, nor would the ontology of
consciousness be identical with the whole of ontology. Now,
Heidegger was in fact concerned to determine the ground of
intentionality,[8] but his inheritance from Kierkegaard precluded
his accepting consciousness or any version of the cogito as
basic.

Despite this difference, Heidegger continues partly in the tradition of Husserl, for he accepts the latter's discovery of the
intentionality of consciousness as a signal advance in philosophy. He writes, "It belongs to the essence of the person that he
exists only in the carrying out of intentional acts" (*Being and
Time*, 73). What, however, about the nonpersonal? When
Husserl concluded that all being is conscious being, he did not
go on to consider the nothing which is not conscious being. He
did not consider that from which the ego itself emerges.
Husserl had spoken of the ego as temporally "self-constitutive,"
but he did not determine the character and limits of this
self-constitution. Also he concluded that the object-world was
dependent for its being upon constitutive performances of the

----

[8] "That the intentionality of 'consciousness' is *grounded* in the ecstatical unity
of Dasein, and how this is the case will be shown in the following Division"
(*Being and Time*, 414, note xxiii). This third Division has not been published,
although much of its material has probably been included in other writings.

ego; however, Husserl accepted this constitutive activity as self-explanatory and offered no further reason for it. Likewise, he did not show that the dependence of the world upon ego-activity entailed his presupposition that the final and most rationally justified view of the world was the objective and scientific view; indeed, his view of rationality, as we observed in the last chapter, was not thoroughly criticized. Lacunae such as these led Heidegger to a radical investigation of the self, of the foundations of its intentionality, and of its world.[9]

For Heidegger, the arché of philosophy is not conscious being nor the being of consciousness; rather, it is Being itself. But to specify the beginning by this term is ironical, for in Heidegger's opinion the basic function of philosophy is to inquire into the meaning of Being. An initial meaning, indicating Being as that which is responsible for the emergence and persistence of beings, is most difficult to describe. "That which gives possibilities" is not Heidegger's phrase, but it is not an un-Heideggerian description. (One of his expressions, "the power of world-making," will become more intelligible later.) He believes that the Greek term *physis*, related to *phyein* (to give birth to), preserves much of this meaning in both the verbal and nominative senses; it meant both an active originating and a remaining self-identically present. But then the verbal and more ontological sense was forgotten in the classic tradition. Here we shall have to hope it will be redefined in context. In order to avoid reifying the notion, it may be helpful to think of Being as light, of which one is not ordinarily conscious unless something interferes with it. At least Being in the ontological sense will always be distinguished from particular beings which belong to the "ontic" order: Thus it is "no-thing," the shadow of beings. Also it will be distinguished from beingness, the ab-

---

[9] Heidegger appears to accept the position to which Husserl partly worked his way in *Crisis*, viz., that the intersubjective character of the life-world is no less phenomenally evident than its subjective character. But Heidegger does not regard intersubjectivity as a problem in the sense accepted by Husserl (see *Being and Time* § 26). Rather he understands being with others and being a self to be equi-primordial.

stract quality possessed by all beings and all kinds of beings.[10]

Many of Heidegger's changes away from Husserlian doctrines of the ego, of the world, and of rationality are indicated by the term *Dasein*. For the most part, this term is inadequately translated by "human-being," in the usual sense of this phrase, or by "human reality." Dasein is an ontological term. Literally it means "there-being," but this "there" (*Da*) must be understood as the "place" of Being (*Sein*). That is, it forms the "place" or the situation where Being becomes apparent both in and as beings or becomes phenomenally evident. Just as Kant produced an ethic valid not for man only but for all rational beings, so Heidegger proposes to elaborate a fundamental ontology valid for any being which exists disclosively or as the "there" of Being.[11]

Heidegger also uses "world" as a more inclusive term to indicate this place where Being emerges into presence. "World" in his sense is not merely the unity of intentions, as it was for Husserl in his earlier writings. It is more closely approximated by the concrete *Lebenswelt* of the *Crisis*. Essential to a world is its being inhabited, in the pregnant sense of this term. Thus Dasein might be translated by the ontological-ontic phrase "Being-in-the-world." The point is that the Being (Dasein) to which appearances are presented is essentially linked to the place (a world) where appearances can be present.

If, now, man is a being to whom appearances are present, then he is indissolubly related to his world; he is nothing without a concrete and historical world. The expressions "Dasein" and "Being-in-the-world" clearly embody the Husserlian notion of the ego intentionally related to the object. But, at the

[10] A good account of this present meaning of Being and of its contrast with other more familiar meanings is provided in *Metaphysics*, especially Chaps. 2 and 4. Its relation with the Greek *physis* is also elaborated there.

[11] The "there" is also described by such terms as "Spielraum." See *Kant and the Problem of Metaphysics*, 74f; *Metaphysics*, 141, 164; *What Is a Thing?*, 92, 242ff. I shall continue to use the term "Dasein" in this discussion. Phrases like "shepherd of Being" and "nearness to Being" were used by Heidegger after his *Kehre*, when Dasein's receptivity (psyche) was emphasized.

same time, Heidegger's terms are intended to include not merely that of which one may be conscious, but all that to which a
being such as man can possibly be in any way related. Heidegger's term "world" is, therefore, a more concrete and inclusive term than the Husserlian *Lebenswelt*.

But like Husserl, Heidegger understands the world to include
the self in a unique sense. For the self has a "pre-ontological"
understanding of being which is manifested in the way it
intends itself. The two most fundamental ways of intending
oneself correspond to the questions of who and what one is.
Who one is, is always individual. The Dasein who behaves toward Being is characterized by first having to be this individual
self. He cannot not be his self in the world familiar to him by
birth and training. This responsibility is unavoidable; he cannot
be by proxy. *That* he is and has to be just this individual—his
Jemeinigheit—is prior to any other characterization, however
traditionally essential, of Dasein. Heidegger makes a continual
movement back and forth between this my concrete individuality in my familiar world which each one of us is (the "existentiel" sense of Dasein)[12] and the general or formal structures of
human-being (the "existential" sense of Dasein).[13] He approaches the latter question of *what* Dasein is by specifying
his essence, the ground of his possibility. This essence is his
"existence." [14]

The existence characteristic of man, the being whose purposes are or can be intrinsic to himself, is described as the
power either to be or not to be his authentic self. This power
either to be, to live in one's world as the being which one is, or
else to identify oneself as other, to disguise oneself as some-

[12] "Existentiel," thus, is correlative to "ontic"; these terms refer respectively
to the phenomenal senses of self and of non-Dasein-like beings. Heidegger seeks
to discern and express the *logoi* of these phenomena in existentials (for Dasein)
and categories (for non-Dasein-like beings).

[13] See Peter Fürstenau, *Heidegger: Das Gefüge seines Denkens* (Frankfurt:
Klostermann, 1958), 15f.

[14] *Being and Time*, 6. It is a serious, but common, mistake to suppose that
the existence or prejudice of the world which the Husserlian reduction suspended
is the same existence which Heidegger affirms to be the essence of Dasein.

thing or as someone who one is not, expresses modifications of the way in which one is open to that Being which gives possibilities. The insight and decision relative to a person's own being makes an essential difference with respect to what he is as well as to the whole structure of the world which a man inhabits and even to the character and function of the sciences of it.

The study of this being which is both individual and "exsists" is called fundamental ontology, the topic of the published portion (Divisions I and II) of *Being and Time*. It is regarded by Heidegger as preparatory to the study of general ontology, which is a "thinking" or recalling of Being as such. And it is a necessary preparation, for only a man (*this* existing individual) whose relation to his own being has become relatively transparent can expect to "think" or to have a clarified access to Being itself of which he is usually only pre-ontologically aware. But unless the meaning of Being as such is grasped in some sense (e.g., pre-ontologically), its more special disclosures and closures in human life cannot be understood at all. Thus the point, essential to understanding Heidegger, is suggested: that Dasein is "between" Being itself and its particular disclosures in the (ontic) beings of the world. Dasein, or Being-in-the-world, is the opening through which beings come to appearance or enter history. And the structures which are discerned in Being-in-the world will be those existential-transcendental structures which determine and limit the kind of world we can live in. The task of ontological phenomenology is so to describe phenomena that these structures of Being (*logoi*) become evident.

The structures which Heidegger's examination discovered in Being-in-the-World pointed to their temporal character, a fact not surprising when one recalls that Heidegger from the outset resolved not to neglect the temporality of the world and of human existence. He reached the quite un-Husserlian conclusion that human existence is essentially historical in all its aspects. An important consequence of this recognition is his reevaluation of human powers. The essential historicity of Dasein is seen to entail its finitude.

Kant had already concluded to the limited character of man's cognitive powers, but his Romantic successors had not preserved this insight, and the Humean tradition never participated in it. Husserl, too, had in his earlier work held to the infinite perfectibility of his wider notion of human rationality pursued by way of a reduction to an absolute beginning through the elimination of all unexamined presuppositions. And even in his later writing he seemed to envisage nothing more than *de facto* limitations upon human viewing. Merleau-Ponty observed, on the contrary, that "the most important lesson taught by the reduction is the impossibility of a complete reduction." [15] Heidegger would no doubt agree with this conviction—especially since it was probably acquired from him. Man is never the "world-less" Cartesian self, exempt from time and circumstance. Rather, his dependence upon a tradition forces him always to begin his self-examination and his philosophy with the already sedimented and, hence, partially obscure situation in history wherein he finds himself.

Although insights and clarifications achieved may enable a philosopher to return toward the point of his historical beginning with a new understanding of it, this circular movement cannot *in principle*, Heidegger will conclude, enable the philosopher to reach finality and perfect clarity. The intellectualist ideal, then, will have to be modified in principle. In short, the conditions of Being-in-the-world are not consistent with an unlimited claim to rationality. Also, it is not irrelevant to recall the usual consequence of making inordinate claims, whether to rationality or to any other power.

§40.   THE OBJECT OF SCIENCE AND ITS ONTOLOGICAL BASIS

In the modern world, being has become evident primarily as object. We are surrounded by objects, objects which we can

[15] *Le Phénoménologie de la Perception* (Paris: Gallimard, 1945), viii.

view clearly, analyze, measure exactly, explain, predict, control, and exploit profitably. Moreover, we often seem to ourselves to be objects just such as these, and the science of social engineering is advancing apace. Is this evaluation justified? What sort of being, we must ask, is object-being? Is it true that we, who ask this question, are —or ought—to be counted among objects? What, in short, is the relation of the sciences and the objects of the sciences to human-being? The understanding and evaluation of the objective world, the science of objects, and the scientist himself will depend upon the management of questions such as these. More than this, we live in a time when the sciences are commonly given a technological interpretation. Man and the world are regarded as human and natural resources. We must inquire, therefore, what it means to exist under such conditions as these. How does the scientific worldview come into being? What are the limits of its validity? Under what conditions does a man come to inhabit such a world?

First, let us ask, what is science? According to Heidegger, "science is the theory of reality." [16] "Reality" is the translation for the German *Wirklichen*. Heidegger connects the German term with the word *wirken*, meaning "to effect, to establish as present." And "theory," of course, he relates to the Greek *theorein*, which has to do with contemplative seeing, in particular with an intelligent viewing of the aspect of being which comes to man through appearances. Then he interprets his definition to mean that a science of facts acquires its object by "working it over" until it can be viewed as present and "real."

This "working over" is accomplished by a change in the more common and basic practical relation to a being. It modifies certain of the relations that constitute a thing as a being in the life-world. For instance, the tool character (involvement) of a being in the life-world and its "place" in a possible work-process become indifferent to the scientist (see *Being and*

---

[16] "Wissenschaft und Bessinung," in *Vorträger und Aufsätze* (Pfullingen: Neske, 1952), 45–70; hereinafter cited as *Vorträger*.

Time § 69). The iron in a hammer becomes for the chemist just the metal. More importantly, the way in which the object comes to be "seen" changes over from the kind of practical estimation characteristic of the workman to a seeing that is sensitized, prior to specific experiences, to just those aspects of the object which can become data for scientific theory. For modern science, this working over has come to be understood in the Cartesian tradition and is initially effected through the operations of measurement. By means of the techniques of measurement, the object is disposed of in a new way; it is reduced to a mathematical structure which may then be symbolically transformed and managed by mathematical methods.[17]

The Cartesian procedure is to presuppose that any object (body) belongs to the mathematical and objective world and can be exhaustively known only within it. But within this context, the object can be seen to obey exact laws which are discoverable by means of experiment. And "the experiment is that experience which in its plan and execution is guided and carried along by its basic law in order to elicit the facts which verify or disconfirm that law." [18] Science is specifically modern when it has thus conceived in advance of the possibility of using experiment to discover the laws implicit within experience or nature. When such laws are ascertained, a new relation to the object is rendered practicable. But utilizing this new relation, modern man seeks to place objects altogether according to his will in a world subject to his technology. Thus technology embodies this new relation: it profits from the predictable results of mathematically grasped laws in order to take the object into its control (*Vorträger*, 56). The being so "worked over" becomes the object which may be possessed and disposed of by mathematical-technological methods according to man's will.

[17] Husserl's *Crisis*, Pt. II may be taken as giving an historical interpretation of the "working over" process which defined the object for mechanics.

[18] Heidegger, "Die Zeit des Weltbildes," *Holzwege* (Frankfurt: Klostermann, 1957), 75.

In short, the scientist works over or thematizes the object until it can pass into the standard concepts of modern scientific theory; in this way the object comes to be subjected to calculation and control. Heidegger quotes Max Planck: "Reality is what can be rendered measurable." But in making its measurements, physics must leave behind much of that which the life-world presents. It must, for example, consider the Greek *physis* as nonanthropomorphic, a lifeless and calculable interrelated unity of separate moving bodies in empty space. Thus physics unveils objective nature, and other sciences take their cue and their ideal from physics. At the same time, physics conceals or forgets the nonphysical; it forgets the life-world.

Modern research scientists, guided in their experimentation by the ideal of exactitude and objectivity, have achieved dramatic successes. Nevertheless, they have also been said to have entered into a state of crisis. Husserl had argued that the sciences have encountered a crisis at their basis, as evidenced by the modern failure to relate the sciences to human subjectivity and to the life-world and by their consequent absorption of man himself into the sciences as if he were merely a complex natural object.

Heidegger's approach to this crisis is an effort to understand its beginning and its ontological character. He points out that physics, for example, cannot take itself as its own object of study, for its methods cannot work the whole science over into a single item within the same science. Thus it cannot investigate itself. In general, sciences are non-self-reflective. This inaccessibility of physics—or of any science—as a whole to the techniques and concepts of that science is part of its "unapparent content," or *unscheinbaren Sachverhalt* (*Vorträger*, 66).

In fact, no being as a whole is accessible to a science. For "working over" the object is precisely simplifying, specializing, "mathematicizing" it; this identifying of an object as a sum of parts is the very condition for rendering it an object for a science or, in general, for thymos. At the same time, the non-self-reflective character of science prevents any evaluation of the mathematicized object in comparison with the concrete phenomenon with which a science began the "working-over" process. Other senses in which the whole being is forgotten or exceeds the range of a science will be recalled later. The present point is to note that objective reality is haunted by this concealed or unapparent content that the methods of science unavoidably leave aside and so conceal. The scientific object is radically incomplete; ideals of scientific exactitude and objectivity may dominate a field of thought, but his field can be no more than a dependent state within a larger state. And that larger state cannot in principle be subject to scientific method and rendered perspicuous on the pattern of the smaller one.

The dependent status of the physical object becomes even more obvious when it is remembered that the processes of measurement by which the object-for-physics is determined are operations; they are purposeful activities, means to ends. The object-for-physics could not be attained without the scientists' operations. In respect to its dependency upon such operations, the object-world lies within the life-world of human activity. However, it is characteristic of the scientific attitude to contemplate the physical object in abstraction from the purposeful operational processes which elicited and defined it. In this abstraction lies its impersonality. Indeed, part of the objectivity of the object is just its fixed and public aspect, its independence of any particular worker's measurements or observations. The function of the operational definitions and measuring operations in eliciting the object, in rendering it accessible, thus tend to drop out of view. Thereby they also become part of the "unapparent content." By contrast, a part of the obligation of philosophy is to retain or regain awareness of this unapparent content.

At the present epoch in history, this forgotten responsibility needs to be engaged *ab ovo*. We need, therefore, to seek out that element of Dasein through which a world of a definite sort first comes into view.

Heidegger gives the name *Befindlichkeit* to the first and determining awareness of oneself in the world (*Being and Time* §§ 29f). *Befindlichkeit* is passive; it is a given sense of the way in which one is in his world. This sense is manifest in different modes of attunement to the world. I think we may understand these modes of attunement (*Stimmungen*) or moods as the psychic aura which prevails in a world and persuades or compels its inhabitants to submit to its dominant type of motivation. They are the initial ways in which intentionality is determined, and they provide the immediate foundation for more specific intentions.

Some mood or mode of *Befindlichkeit* is always present and performing this determining or orienting function. Certain moods are relatively permanent; others are derivative and transitory. Heidegger offers an obvious example of the latter: the mood of fear. For however long it may endure, fear is a response to a threat and tends to organize all one's intentions and behavior around itself. In general, one's whole way of being in the world is polarized in a characteristic manner by a mood. Thus moods to which the Romantics were so sensitive, but which were discarded as nonmeasurable and hence as "subjective" by most non-Romantic philosophers, play the initiating role for Heidegger. They suggest the way in which his philosophy develops that function which in many others is discharged by a doctrine of values.

To understand the fundamental orientation of an epoch, then, one must discover its dominating and persistent mood or attunement. To understand the scientific and technological era, we must discover the mood which leads the applied scientist to the laboratory or provokes nations, during an interval of "peace," to concentrate their major energies upon sending men to the moon.

In his essay "Die Frage nach der Technik" (*Vorträger*, 15–45), Heidegger inquires into the mood-basis of modern techniques. He proceeds by contrasting ancient techniques with modern techniques. Both reveal nature as changeable by man's manipulation, but they reveal its subordination to different kinds of intentionality. Ancient techniques (e.g., Greek, *techne*) rearrange the parts and energies of nature for man's use. For instance, the field is plowed and planted so that natural processes can continue; the field is only rearranged to suit man's needs. It is otherwise with modern techniques. These techniques might strip-mine the field, thus destroying it as a field in order to secure ore for smelting. And smelting is changing by processes other than those which occur in nature. These are processes which work over and release hidden energies so that they may be used in turn to release other and yet other energies. If ancient techniques merely rearrange or change the place of objects and energies, then in contrast modern techniques displace, "pro-voke" (*herausfordern*), and transform (*umformen*) them (*ibid.*, 31). Modern techniques reveal (*entbergen*) the character of nature by "ex-propriating" it. It seems to me that Heidegger's terms convey the sense of "misplacing" nature and natural objects; *herausfordern* suggests a calling forth of what would otherwise remain hidden. Objects in nature which are thus intended to be used up are called *Bestand*, "stock" or "supply," something awaiting an annihilating use (*ibid.*, 24). What is the mood, Heidegger asks, that would lead one to this persistent and systematic provoking and expropriation of the natural?

Heidegger finds no word in German—and there is none in English—to name this typically modern mode of attunement to the world. He, therefore, adopts a word which we also shall use—*Gestell* (*Vorträger*, 27). One usual meaning of this word, he notes, refers to an instrumentality for placing things, suggesting a technical operation; another meaning is "skeleton," suggesting not only a basic sort of framework but also something dangerous and fearful. The name is appropriate to the mode of attunement that directs us not merely to alter nature in order to satisfy our needs but to regard it as a calculable nexus of forces altogether disposable by our ingenuity. To this mood, things are as they are placed by theories and provoked by techniques. "Gestell" is, so to speak, the skeleton or general pattern of modern technological culture. Viewed in this mood, everything may be an instrument for freeing the energy from something else.

An important aspect of mood as elaborated in *Being and Time* is its cognitive aspect (*Being and Time* § 31). Every mood has its understanding (*Verstehen*). The understanding that is determinative of Gestell is nowhere so clearly developed as in *What Is a Thing?* (88–108). There the term "the mathematical" is used to refer to that which is taken by an epoch to be axiomatically or self-evidently true, and thus is known in advance, about the whole world. The quantitative mathematical properties of the world are, for Gestell, known in this manner. They were divined by the Greeks, but they reach clear and explicit expression with the Newtonian laws of motion. Thus these physical-mathematical laws became for seventeenth-century and much of later metaphysics the invisible but real skeleton on which the experienced world is constructed. The mathematical physicist alone has the discipline and the knowledge necessary for acquiring insight into the articulation of this reality. Only he can "work over" the experienced object and reveal its hidden but real structure. Only he, by penetrating to the secrets of nature, can come to dominate it. Thus the most powerful and efficient instrument at our disposal is scientific knowledge.

The technological interpretation of knowledge follows quite naturally to men of Gestell, men who are possessed by the Cartesian motive to become the masters and possessors of nature. But this mood, the basic (grounding) way of Being-in-the-world, comes first. Heidegger observes that mathematical and experimental science historically preceded the development of modern technology; nevertheless, they are a single growth. Neither would have been possible in a world not dominated throughout by Gestell. The "unapparent content" of modern thought and experience is all of that which is concealed by Gestell. A criticism of the modern world or an alternative to it must, therefore, be sought in the direction of that which Gestell conceals.

Heidegger affirms that a very great danger to man lies among the possibilities of Gestell. We shall want to reach an understanding of this Heideggerian diagnosis. The danger is, I believe, patent in the contemporary thesis that a machine (e.g., a computer) may be shown to be the operational equivalent of a man (see above, page 104 and note 39). For if this equivalence is accepted, it would be reasonable to dispose of men, as of machines, according to the requirements of efficiency as judged by some managerial authority. Commonly such a disposition of men is resisted—but without any very clear reasons being advanced for this resistance. Heidegger, however, offers a basis on which the man-machine thesis may be contested. This basis is to be found in his doctrine of moods (*Befindlichkeit*) and understanding (*Verstehen*) and the developments out of this basis. This doctrine can be construed as making certain modifications of *Befindlichkeit* (e.g., anxiety, charity, etc.) prior in a certain sense to Gestell and, therefore, prior to the objective world and to the sciences. This *Befindlichkeit*, however, belongs to the consciousness which the several forms of objectivism and positivism regard as "subjective" in the pejorative sense and discard.

Heidegger does not become engaged in a detailed polemic against objectivism and positivism. His aim is broader. He recognizes that any effort to criticize or to discover an alternative to the modern world must proceed first by penetrating deeper into the objective world of Gestell in which science and technology are possible. What is the structure of this world? How is its relation to Dasein to be understood? Heidegger's way of answering questions such as these begins with the life-world of daily tasks and traces the development of the object-world, topic of scientific study, out of this. The object-world, thus understood, is that which is taken over by technology as its resource or stock of energy and material. The Dasein of modern man is, then, the correlative to this development. The next few sections will elaborate the notions of world, its relation to Dasein, and to authentic Dasein. Thus a context will be elaborated for understanding the danger offered by Gestell and for evaluating the sciences.

§ 41.   ON THE ORIGIN OF THE REAL OBJECT

Science, then, is the theory of reality. Technology is a method for calling forth and transforming the stock of reality according to will. Can some way be discovered for grasping the "real" object within its world and in its concreteness? Is there a way back to the initiation or origination of the man of Gestell who is concerned with bringing the object into the scientific context and finally within his own control? The way back, Heidegger holds, is through phenomenological reflection or thought about the logos (meaning) of the being manifested as ordinary phenomena.[19] This thought proceeds by one's giving oneself over to such radical questioning as the times render possible. Doubtless Heidegger has not yet completed his whole account of the way back to the ontological or transcendental sources of experience. We for our part must be content first with a brief and general account of the emergence of the object, as developed mainly in *Being and Time,* and then of the world within which the object emerges.[20]

Just as a thing can become apparent as an object with a specific atomic structure only to the specialist who is trained in nuclear physics, so a something emerges in the first place as a distinct being only to someone for whom the being *can* be there in the world. That is, the scientist's training is to the scientist rather as the human ontological endowment—Dasein —is to the human being; it enables him to function as the

---

[19] "Ordinary" phenomena (*Being and Time,* 93) I take to be phenomena as rendered evident to a reasonably unprejudiced observer. They may also be called "ontic" if, as here, the intention is to use them as beings through which one may approach the primary phenomenon, Being.

[20] See *What Is a Thing?* and my review of it, "Heidegger on Bringing Kant to Stand," *Southern Journal of Philosophy,* VII (Spring, 1969), 91–103, which discusses Heidegger's account of the object as related to Kant's philosophy.

being he is. We have seen that an ontological consideration of physical objects and objectivity begins with their first emergence and transition onto the human horizon. Also it must begin with the being who possesses such a horizon and, hence, to whom beings can emerge or be recalled.

Consider, by way of an analogy, a transition over a physical boundary—say, by means of a jump. The actual jump is a being. We shall assume that the appropriate mood, in which the intention to make such a jump is grounded, is possessed by Dasein. Also we assume that the intention to make the jump is given. Then, in addition, the act is rendered actually possible by means of a rather elaborate, though habitual, process of selecting the solid ground to leap from, measuring the distance by eye, choosing the place to land, selecting and flexing the necessary muscles, engaging in preparatory breathing, and the like. Then the leap occurs. The factual world, including one's body and its whole region, are used as tools to effect the intention. All in all, one may say that the jump is born into a place prepared to receive it. A man can jump just because he can prepare the "place" into which the jump can come to pass. We take the leap to be typical. Any human act is possible just because and to the extent that its happening can be so prepared. Furthermore, the actual preparation for an act, such as that just described, consisted of other acts. They, too, required preparation in order to come into being. And shall we say that those earlier acts required yet prior ones? If the man who intended the leap and made it is not excluded by reason of some prejudice, perhaps we may find in him the metaphysical (non-ontic) possibility or the kind of being through which the intention to jump can make the transition from its beginning, through its preparation, and into the lived world actively and in fact. Heidegger's philosophy moves toward insight into the coming to pass of beings through the conditions for their emergence into the human world.

Any being comes "there" into our world or emerges into the horizon of our awareness in virtue of an advance preparation, as suggested by the analogy just used. Making this preparation, which throws open the horizon for a certain kind of experience in advance of the actual experience, is one aspect of the function of Dasein. Dasein is the opening where beings can be disclosed and acquire meaning (*Being and Time*, 176f). Dasein must, then, be structured so that this functioning is possible. And it must be "motivated" to use this structure—that is, it must care in some fashion for Being and its manifestations. It is this power, this "care" (*Sorge*), rather than some specialized view of beings already geographically there, that endows us with humanity. The structure or character of this Dasein, our Being-in-the-world, can to some extent be revealed by phenomenological reflection and analysis.

Our analogy of the jump over a boundary bears reference also to another ontological characteristic of Dasein: its limitations. To make the decision to leap in one direction is precisely to decide not to leap elsewhere. One course of action tends to exclude others. The value of other possible jumps is thus lost. Opposing moods, projects, actions must wait for other times for their realization. We have already noted that the temporality of our opening upon beings is one of the ways this finitude was brought home to Heidegger. Being is accessible to man only in time. The opening prepared for the emergence of beings (and for man himself understood as a being) is historical; in different epochs, different aspects of being have become disclosed. Correlatively, other aspects have remained hidden. The reign of the attunement of Gestell in the modern world, for example, would conceal as much as it reveals. Indeed much of Heidegger's ontology converges upon the view that Dasein is finite and can never disclose to us more than a limited perspective upon Being. Thus all disclosing of possibilities is also a closing off of them, a concealing. All coming into being is at the same time a passing away into nonbeing; this insight is fundamental for Heidegger's philosophy.

Physical objects, as we now know them, did not come to pass all at once upon our horizon. The present way of "working

over" beings in order to gain access to their hidden mathematical structure so that they might be controlled was itself prepared by earlier and now obscure stages of change. In leaving
behind these earlier stages—pre-Homeric, Platonic-Aristotelian,
Cartesian—into which earlier men were thrown, much has
been lost and forgotten, even of the originally limited disclosure. To understand the origin or emergence of physical
objects, we must first distinguish the earlier levels of the power
of encountering things and also attempt to recover—to "re-
peat"—as much as possible of that which has been forgotten.
Heidegger's progress toward this clarifying repetition goes from
Dasein, the transcendental foundation of the world of human
activity and life, through the work-world and then to its modified form, the object-world.

§ 42.   WORLD AND REALITY

The topic of the relation of man to the world in which his
fate is worked out is alluded to in some of Plato's views and,
as we observed earlier in Chapter 3, in views associated with
the seventeenth century and the Enlightenment. This topic
becomes thematic in Husserl's philosophy and receives a crucial
development in Heidegger's.

As the jumper prepares his leap, so Dasein prepares the life-
world of instruments and tasks. Heidegger analyzes the work-
world of ancient techniques in terms somewhat reminiscent of
Aristotle and works out a doctrine of the "significance whole"
(the worldhood of the world) through which Dasein transcends
into the world of its concern (*Besorgen*) and of which Dasein
itself is the *Worumwillen*, the for-the-sake-of-which. Then within this sphere of praxis, the object-world comes to be defined
by the expedient of disusing certain of the tool-relations—for
instance, the relation to an end. It is as if the tool were broken
and so dropped out of the purposive movement of praxis; still
the tool remains unused, looked at with regret or curiosity.
Now if this curiosity becomes impersonal and persistent, then
the object may become the topic of scientific inquiry. Thus

a thing comes to be real (objective) in relation to an object-judging subject. The real-world is derived from the work-world by a kind of abstraction, or by only a partial use of the work-world.

This thumbnail sketch may be sufficient to recall the details of this complex doctrine to the reader's mind. Those who want a full account will find it in Division I, Chapter 3 of *Being and Time*.

It is possible now to see that the meaning of "existence" is relative to the context within which the term is used. Existence, in general, refers to that necessary character in virtue of which something can be said to be in a particular world. Existence in the object-world means having an actual locus in the abstract space and time that belong to this world. Spatio-temporal co-ordinates might be assigned to an object and its existence plotted in a world-line. In the life-world, however, existence refers to occupancy of work-region or to having a function in a project of making. Finally, the ontological meaning of existence is closest akin to the etymological sense. Existence in this last context might be understood as the "place" where subjectivity penetrates objectivity. However, the objective world has been shown to be derivative. Thus it is better to observe that existence in its basic sense refers us to Dasein's essential character as the opening through which Being becomes evident in beings. This opening, Being-in-the-world, is reminiscent of the Kantian transcendental subjectivity and to a lesser extent of the Platonic receptacle. Heidegger also uses existence to name Dasein's complex directedness, both toward Being and toward beings within the world.

Objects conceived as physically existing—that is, as occupying loci in an infinite space and in an indefinitely prolonged clock time—constitute "reality" as viewed in the modern era (*Being and Time* § 43). Objective reality is the topic thematized by the sciences. This reality offers a view, but only one view, of Being; it reveals Being as object. But it conceals other respects in which Being can appear. This concealment is likewise referred to as existence (cf. *Metaphysics,* 64). Concealment is the negative sense of existence, its falling away or its inclination toward nonbeing. We shall discuss this aspect of it in greater detail later.

Here the point needing emphasis is that an objective being is a real object only to an object-judging subject. To think of being primarily as object, then, is also to overlook any other function than this object-judging function. Thus this view tends to conceal not only the life-world of activity but also the Dasein which gives that world its structure. As Being-in-the-world is concealed by Dasein's directing care specifically upon its work, the particular task to be done, so the life-world of activity and Dasein as artist are concealed by one's self-limitation to theoretical seeing. Being tends to be concealed by revealing the life-world, and the life-world is forgotten or concealed by fixing attention upon the object-world.

Is there ground for supposing Heidegger to be antiscientific in this view of the status of the world as open to theory? Of course not. Rather, Heidegger has taken as his task to point to that which has been concealed but which must be rediscovered and seen to complement objective theory and the world which is its object. The discovery of Dasein as mediating between the ontic and the ontological is just the discovery of a means of access to an understanding of the intention of science and of its natural or objective world. Heidegger's is no irrational rejection of science, theory, and technology, but a reasoned opposition to accepting as final and basic any view whose bases and functions have been forgotten.

The ideal of objectivity and precision in formulating theories of reality is a worthy ideal surely, but it is so only because the sciences and their objects are human enterprises and are derived from the life-world and its intentional structure, which in turn are grounded upon Being-in-the-world. A part of Heidegger's purpose is to show that and how the sciences and their objects are thus conditioned. The inescapable suggestion is that unless the derivative and conditioned character of this rela-

tion is understood and appropriately evaluated the consequences for human life and thought could be disastrous. If,
however, this derivative character be grasped in an appropriate perspective, then other problems, specifically the transcendental problem, may cease to be quite so obscurely trouble-
some.

§ 43.   THE STRUCTURE OF CARE AND THE CARTESIAN
        TRANSCENDENTAL PROBLEM

The management of the transcendental problem moves through
two main stages; the first of these has to some extent already
been elaborated. The point has been made that the object-
world is derivative from the life-world of mankind's work and
activity and that both of these latter are rendered possible by
Dasein and the structures through which it "ex-sists" into the
world. Human health and well-being, or even being, are functions of the ways in which this derivation is understood. What,
in fact, are the ways in which this understanding is exemplified? Do they offer an adequate solution to the transcendental
problem by unifying the traditionally separate subject and
object? Is Heidegger's solution an advance over the possibly
similar proposals of Kant, Schelling, or Husserl? Or, if his
solution is different, is it merely a species of irrationalism?
We shall first review certain elements of the ontology of man
so far developed in order to open the way to a consideration of
these questions.

Heidegger views man's relation to the world not as the relation
of a rational animal somehow responsive to a pre-existent
rationally ordered universe but as a relation that is identical
with Dasein. Man as an embodiment of Dasein is the means by
which meanings, whether rational or other, are given both to
himself and to other beings.

According to Heidegger, Dasein is not, of course, an empirical subject. It is "in" the world only as mediating between
the ontic and the ontological; it is that through which the
world is given its unified structure of worldhood, and, conse-

quently, it may be said in this mediate sense to be the source or arché of the meaning given to the worldly beings. Since Dasein functions as the mediating source or the beginning of the meaning assigned to beings, whether to subjects or to objects, the concept of Dasein suggests a solution to the transcendental problem.

In addition, a second stage of Heidegger's consideration of this problem will have to be concerned with the character of Dasein in the sense in which it is not only unifying but is itself unified. Otherwise Heidegger might, as Kant did, rediscover another form of the transcendental problem recurring within his "solution." That is to say, he might have found the unity of the knower and the object of its knowledge in Dasein as Being-in-the-world, only later to discover that Dasein itself cannot be understood as one being. In order, therefore, to place the present solution in proper perspective, it will later have to be related to the senses in which man's being is a unified, limited, and finite being.

Consider an illustration of meaning-giving. We say that a house is not a home except in so far as the house is given a meaning by one's dwelling in it and caring for it. Quite possibly, however, this consequence of one's care is not recognized until the home has been destroyed or until, for some reason, one has left it. Similarly one's life-world is such in consequence of one's living and working in it and caring for these activities.

But one might ask—as Husserl did not—why care? Why does Dasein project a world? As the place of a tool in the work process does not become evident until the tool is broken or inoperative, so the role of world is not evident until the familiar world itself is somehow cancelled. Heidegger in several famous passages describes the fading away of the world in the attunement of anxiety (*Angst*; see *Being and Time* §§ 40f). For anxiety is fear, but it is a formless fear; it comes from no specifiable source; it is of nothing. In this basic attunement one is alone, and the world loses its familiar presence. One feels *unheimlich,* uncanny, alien. Beneath the familiarity of the world is thus revealed a threatening worldlessness. One may, therefore, suspect that the everyday world usually projected is a protection against this strange worldlessness. Still it can be asked: what of worldlessness? Why desire protection against it? The answer is not far to seek: The end of one's world is death; anxiety in the face of the nothingness of death requires no apology. Furthermore, a sort of worldlessness is suffered by anyone who is masquerading or leading an inauthentic life, a life not his own (*uneigenlich*). Dasein projects a world precisely in order to be itself. It cares for the world because it cares for itself, indeed *is* this care. Thus the phenomenon of anxiety brings the everyday empirical self face to face with the more original self which cares for self and world indivisibly. One may say, then, that the phenomenon of self-world is a primordial and unitary phenomenon.

The problem of the relation of the ontic (empirical) subject to the object is, therefore, not so much resolved as transported to the prior phenomenal plane where self and world are, at least under certain conditions, experienced as one. This experience may become the topic of analysis, an analysis which will exhibit the structure of Dasein *qua* care and will throw light upon the ontic separation of subject from object and perhaps also upon the estrangement of modern man from the technological world.

Dasein, accordingly, is said to be care, but care is not easily defined. Moreover, since care is not an object and in no way has the character of any object definable within a conventional universe of discourse, it may appear not to be definable at all. Nevertheless, care is not merely a vague notion; it can be placed within its limits and these limits can be seen to have a phenomenological basis. In this sense, care can be understood. Its limits are first expressed by the ontological terms: existence, facticity, and fallenness.

Existence used in this ontological manner must be taken in the etymological sense to which allusion was made earlier (see

above § 39). It also means "to stand out" as a ship stands out
to sea. It has much the same import as the term "transcendence" used in the preceding section, only it is specifically limited to Dasein's transcendence into its own world.

The transcendence of Dasein is also limited in two additional ways; these are indicated by the terms "facticity" and "fallenness." Facticity refers to the predetermined character of the
context within which Dasein finds itself. It alludes to the way
human-being is involved with and necessitated by other beings
and is dependent upon their being just as they are (*Being and
Time*, 82, 174). Facticity is to Dasein as factuality is to non-
Dasein-like beings. The primary instance of facticity is a man's
being thrown into his world and time without any choice on his
part and without any reason why this context rather than
that. One is born into an elaborated world and into an epoch
of history. The absolute contingency of this fact simply cannot be controlled or rendered transparent (*ibid.*, 136). Moreover, the circumstances of the given environment limit one at
every turn. The beings among which one is thrown are what
they are. Facticity is a denial of any sort of fancied power to
originate or directly to control or to alter their nature. It is the
representative in Heidegger's thought of the ancient fate
(*anagke*) and effectively prevents classification of his philosophy as an idealism.

The third way in which Dasein's transcendence is limited is
rather more subtle, but it is also indicated by the etymology of
the word "existence." Heidegger points out that existence de-
rives from the Greek *existasthai*, which he translates to mean de-
parture from permanence (*Metaphysics*, 64) and refers it by
way of a grammatical metaphor to a declination away from the
primary Being. At its extreme, this declining will end in nonbeing. This declination I interpret to refer to the "falling" of
Being and Time (§ 34B).

Falling, regarded as a constitutive element in care, must not
be identified with inauthentic Being, although clearly there is

a relation between the two. Care, whether authentic or in-authentic, is always falling since "falling belongs to care itself" (*Being and Time*, 341). It is, therefore, reminiscent of the internal fate which has been associated with Romanticism. Heidegger so vividly describes one sort of fallenness in terms of "unrooted" idle talk, superficial curiosity, and identification with the impersonal mass man that many interpreters tend to see in these phenomena the whole reach of fallenness (*ibid.*, 210 *sq.*). This view, however, is incorrect. Falling may be better interpreted as the necessity of Dasein for caring for other beings. Men's dependence, their needs and deficiencies, force them to practice the arts and to be concerned with the detail of daily living. This inclination either toward the work-world or toward the object-world is at the same time an inclination away from Being. Since Being is that which offers (finite) possibilities, an exclusive devotion to the current life-world or to the object-world is also a rejection and a forgetting of other possibilities which may be offered.

Acceptance of and active engagement in the world is scarcely a matter of choice; rather, it is the consequence of thrownness and of the limited ways in which Dasein can accept and deal with the facticity of its worldly involvements. Dasein must be involved with other beings; it must be concerned with the beings, their roles, and the minor and major purposes required by the demands of daily life. These insistent tasks cloud over or conceal Dasein's vision of its own individual possibilities for Being. In consequence, Dasein is diverted or falls away from its own Being. Its vision of itself as the end—or essential for-the-sake-of-which that defines its world—is liable to a tragic distortion. This distortion is experienced as an alienation of man from his world. Today it is conceptually expressed in many ways: for example, as the Cartesian subject separated from the object-world, as the positivist man-as-object estranged from man as he knows himself subjectively, or as the technological culture by which man expected to dominate the world but by which he appears to be wholly dominated. In short, according to Heidegger's view, modern man can scarcely be said to have a very perceptive grasp upon his fate.

Fundamentally, falling is an inevitable inclination to lose sight of the truth of one's Being. It is a dimming of the understanding of oneself, of one's possibilities and one's limitations. This failure to grasp one's Being with transparency and clarity is a source of guilt, surely, but an ontological source, one which belongs to Dasein's finite character. For Dasein is not possessed of an infinite understanding to which the whole of Being and of beings could be simultaneously transparent. Dasein's unavoidable engagement in the life-world, which is already a falling away from its Being, places a limitation upon the possible intelligibility of its world. Obviously this doctrine is not a run-of-the-mill irrationalism; in no sense is it a surrender to unreason. Rather, it is a thoughtful reinterpretation of the phenomena presented by human life to the effect that no ontological defense can be discovered for the presupposition that being is or can become completely intelligible to men. Heidegger thus takes a decisive step beyond Husserl. The rational ideal acquires in his philosophy a limit not merely in fact, but in principle. The finite character of Being entails that the revealing of one being is always also the concealing of some other.

Heidegger's own questioning led him back by way of the experience of anxiety to the phenomenon of his own oneness with the life-world, a phenomenon whose logos is care and the structure of care. Analysis of this structure led to his interpretation of the current metaphysical and epistemological separation of subject from object in terms of a blind or inauthentic fallenness. Thus an ontologically prior unity gives rise to a derived duality of subject and object, but this duality appears to be basic and irreducible from the point of view of a Dasein which is unaware of its own falling. That this solution of the transcendental problem is neither a repetition of old attempts nor a recourse to irrationalism or idealism I take to be evident. But it does belong to the transcendental type of solution, and it does lead to a limitation on rationalism. That this solution is in every respect complete is another matter, one to which we shall return in subsequent sections.

From the present-day perspective of Gestell, the typically modern scientific world-picture could become current only under the circumstance that a single view of man as the knowing subject and of objects as illimitably knowable, given the correct method, should come so to dominate the scene that no other view could offer competition. Thus Dasein as Being-in-the-world became lost, forgotten. The world of familiar objects ranged against subjects came to appear to be the total and given world. Likewise, all the philosophical problems concerning the relations between these two metaphysical ultimates—subjects and objects—became insistent, but insoluble. The next and final step of this development arrived when it appeared possible and advantageous to some philosophers to re-define the subject exclusively as a peculiar and complex sort of object. Thus human subjects could become the objects of a science.

Man regarded as a peculiar object which can somehow get into sufficient touch with other objects to acquire objective knowledge of them and to control them is now the popular view. Governments support it. Just this apparent ultimacy of man's separation from the world is presented by Heidegger as a sort of ontological illusion which follows in part from the intrinsic limitations of men's being, the inclination toward fallenness, and in part also from his avoidable failure to question his being in such a way as to keep those limitations in sight.

§ 44.   THE UNITY OF CARE AND THE RELATION OF AUTHENTICITY
        TO OBJECTIVITY

Dasein is in the world as caring for it. Ontologically it can be said that Dasein cares to lead (to "shepherd") Being to evidence as beings. This same care has already been described as a structure of existence, facticity, and fallenness. Can these three elements be seen in some further sense to form a unity? It is likely that this unity would be exhibited in several modalities. In fact, one of the more widely discussed phases of Heidegger's philosophy elaborates certain modalities of existence in terms of the authentic-inauthentic distinction. Furthermore, the way in which Dasein unites subject and object is a function of its existence. An understanding of Heidegger's thought on these points is important for the present discussion, since it leads to a firmer grasp of his views on objectivity.

Since Dasein and the world are correlative, it follows that as Dasein becomes inauthentic or authentic the world tends to become altered accordingly. To explicate this point and its consequences, let us first consider authentic care and its meaning.

Dasein's care may be directed upon the object-world, upon the tool-world, upon other people, or upon its own existence. Clarity in this last mentioned kind of understanding is termed "transparency" (*Being and Time*, 186). A most important aspect of transparency is its connection with the for-the-sake-of-which, for this is Dasein itself; and Dasein needs self-understanding, for only when possessing this understanding can it exist as just itself.[21] This existing toward its own Being or being just itself is authentic existence. The content of this formal and abstract expression, however, is obscure. What is his own Being? How does Dasein experience itself and its limits?

The reference to the for-the-sake-of-which might recall the Platonic conviction that one's first function in life, as well as that of the state, is self-care. Is Heidegger repeating this Platonic belief? Not, surely, as Heidegger understood Plato. One of the Platonic approximations to a doctrine of the self, one which is only adumbrated in the Dialogues, is that the self in its most real sense is a form. The young Socrates alludes to a possible form of man in the *Parmenides*, and the *Republic*

---

[21] "Das Verstehen wirft sich primär in das Worumwillen, das heisst das Dasein existiert Selbst." See Heidegger, *Sein und Seit* (10th ed.; Tübingen: Max Niemeyer Verlag, 1963), 186; *Being and Time*, 186.

develops a doctrine of the several interlocked functions of man as referring to a complex form or essence. Platonic learning is coming increasingly to embody the human essence. Now Heidegger, in his essay on Plato,[22] expresses the view that Platonic forms, and surely the forms involved in the human essence would be included, are only reifications of the "correct" or conventional ways of seeing. The Platonic ideal man, then, would be merely Plato's intellectualist conviction given a persuasive setting in an artificial, two-world, "ontological" context.

Even though Heidegger firmly rejects the Platonic realistic ontology, interpreting it as a reification of the contemporary correct ways of seeing, still the what-man-is retains its position in Heidegger's philosophy as a decisive factor of Dasein's concern and the chief defining element in the world. It is, however, difficult to say just what Dasein is. The difficulty may be purposeful, for Heidegger desires to avoid being victimized by a single set of possibilities for man, such as those offered by fifth-century Greece, or by twentieth-century Germany. In any event, Heidegger's study is ontological and not anthropological. What, then, can be specifically said of man's Being? Perhaps nothing specific. Dasein is that "space" (*Spielraum*) in which Being becomes unconcealed; it is the stage on which beings, including the several historical visions of man himself, appear. But Dasein is not any one of these beings and is not exhausted by any one of these visions. Dasein is rather that which is continually to be questioned or probed in "anticipatory resoluteness" so that his own possibilities will become appropriately manifest. Heidegger's questioning led to his developing two kinds of characterizations of authentic Dasein, a negative and a positive one.

The positive characterization concerns Dasein's function as the scene for the manifesting of Being. We have already considered, in this connection, the doctrine of world. In his later writings Heidegger developed this strain in the direction of

[22] *Platons Lehre von der Wahrheit* (Bern: A. Francke, 1947).

poetry or myth. Man "is the shepherd of Being," for instance, or "Man is the clearing in the forest." [23] He is that through which being appears and is transformed into history. But the interpretation of these expressions is difficult. Perhaps they had best be left as myth, remembering that myth is that into which our insight can continually be deepened, and remembering, too, that myth is the product of psyche or the poetic power to which men have commonly returned upon occasions of menace or in the anxious times of transition.

Dasein, then, is that which refuses the routines of a single interpretation of itself and its world; rather, it continually contemplates such myths about itself, aware of their function in preparing for other ways of being and for poetically making new worlds. "Man dwells poetically upon this earth," as Heidegger remarks, quoting Hölderlin. Under such circumstances, the appropriate attitude of Dasein toward itself is interrogative. When, according to this interpretation of Heidegger's difficult sayings, Dasein is preoccupied specifically with the questioning understanding of itself and with throwing itself into novel possibilities which open up new worlds revealed by such questioning, then it is on the way to becoming itself authentically. Then its world can appropriately be said to take the ruling element of its structure from the for-the-sake-of-which, which is Dasein itself.

How can we know, however, when Dasein is genuinely and not merely romantically, superficially, or irrationally preoccupied in this manner with its own Being? To answer this question, Heidegger developed the negative interpretation of Dasein's whole Being. Such a negative account will be recognized to be inevitable if the terms used to describe existence be recalled. Existence—Dasein's kind of transcendence—was observed to be directed toward just that which the man at any time is not. As constantly engaged in this kind of movement,

[23] "Letter on Humanism," trans. Edgar Lohner, in *Philosophy in the Twentieth Century*, ed. William Barrett and H. D. Aiken (4 vols.; New York: Random House, 1962), III, 270–302.

Dasein can also be said at any moment not to be that which it is. Jean Paul Sartre plays elaborately with these paradoxes. They are also present in Heidegger and arise from his fundamental conviction that Being, that which gives possibilities, is always both revealing and concealing. He treats the concealed aspect of man's Being in terms of such negative notions as nothingness, guilt, conscience, and death. And he finds that the ontological sense of these negative elements is phenomenologically expressed in authentic Dasein's understanding of its own existential limits.

This preoccupation with limitations or finitude is quite necessary, for without a firm grasp upon limitations, the possibilities which genuinely belong to human-being may escape us; inappropriate or impossible ones might be attempted. Then the *Worumwillen* which defines worldhood would be misidentified and the world would be distorted. Accordingly, Heidegger worked out a view of human limits based upon interpretations of the meanings for man's existence of the phenomena of guilt, anxiety, and conscience.

In anxiety, it will be recalled, the world becomes strange, unhomelike (*unheimlich*), and seems to fall away; thus anxiety points to the end of the power to be in a world. But the end of the power to be in the world is death. Awareness of this end or ontological limit can become a constant and formative element in one's understanding of one's projects. Likewise, the silent voice of conscience is a communication and refers Dasein back, through the sense of guilt, to the beginning of his Being, his arché. Guilt, understood ontologically or as belonging to care, expresses the way in which Dasein is aware of its thrownness. Acceptance of this guilt can also be a formative element in Dasein's self-understanding and self-care. Let us consider these interpretations more closely.

Death, opened to us in moods of anxiety, must not be understood in this context as an event; neither is it the bushido doctrine of the Japanese warrior which requires that he be always prepared for death by the sword; nor is it the folk wisdom which reminds us that "golden lads and girls all must, as chimney sweeps, come to dust." Rather it is described as something inviolably one's own, not to be outstripped (*unüberholbar*), and nonrelational (*Being and Time*, 294 *sq.*). I understand its not being "outstripped" to be a reference to the impossibility of transcending it; this description is a recognition of the peculiar and limited character of human transcendence: its existence. Not all possibilities are open to the human-being. I understand the nonrelational property of death to be a recognition of the finite character of the world into which Dasein exists. For the world, as we have seen, is a relationally structured significance-whole. The nonrelational aspect of death is a reference to the boundary or end of Being-of-the-world, as physical death is the termination of one's real world.

Also death is a cancelling of relations with others (e.g., of solicitude). Thus death brings one to oneself alone. This reference to death being one's own is an emphasis upon its personal, concrete, and ever-present character, its *Jememigheit*. One cannot die by proxy any more than one can exist by proxy, although one may try to conceal these limitations. No preoccupation, no one, not even the human species, can alleviate or diminish this mortality, for it is a possibility that belongs always and essentially to the existence of each individual. This last recognition removes some of the generality and remoteness of the discussions of the world which all of us inhabit and of the existence and fallenness which belong to Dasein as such. Death in the ontological sense is the name for the final limitation upon the kind of Being that belongs to each man. Death marks the boundary of the human.

An additional sense in which human life inclines toward nonbeing comes to the fore in Heidegger's later writings. Here he elaborates upon Dasein's function as the place where Being comes to appearance. Being is brought out of concealment by Dasein. To reveal Being, to bring it into history—this function is the end of human-being. Whenever this end is achieved, Dasein has completed its task or has reached the end of its function.

But since it is always and essentially disclosing Being, Dasein's completion or end is present at any instant. Thus any instant as much as any other is an instant of nonbeing or death. In this sense also Dasein is continually existing toward death. Again, authentic existence consists in the constant anxious acceptance of this function and this end. In particular, such an acceptance determines the quality of one's anticipation of the future.

Another limit upon the Being of man is revealed by an interpretation of the phenomenon of conscience. Conscience attests to guilt. Guilt is an element of Dasein's care which always comes to him from his past. In this sense it is not the consequence of breaking a taboo nor the violation of a moral boundary (*Being and Time*, 328). Rather, guilt is ontological and refers to the negative aspect of care. Heidegger recalls the connection of the German *Schuld* (guilt) with indebtedness of some sort. In the present ontological instance, I interpret the indebtedness as owing for one's Being. No man is self-creative; thrownness into the world and to death is a primary given element in facticity, and it can never be clearly understood and controlled. Acceptance of this dependence of one's own being is expressed in awareness of it as a basic and ontological debt; it is a recognition that one owes for one's Being. Birth is a symbol of this non-self-creativeness. The world into which one is born is not a house which one has originated and built al together alone.

Heidegger expresses the kind of ontological negativity intended by this sense of guilt by saying that care is "the null Being-basis of a nullity." [24] This statement, as I take it, is the inverse of the expression that Dascin is the meaning-giving basis of the world. It makes the dual point that human-being is not the absolute source of meaning and, also, that the intended world by itself is a nullity. The intended world is not an independent being; moreover, it is possible only as a concealing-nullifying of other possible worlds and even of Being itself. Yet,

---

[24] "Nichtiger Grundsein einer Nichtigkeit." *Sein und Seit*, 305; *Being and Time*, 353; cf. *Being and Time*, 328ff.

Dasein and the world, in their different ways, depend upon that Being whose power to reveal remains concealed. Anxious, silent acceptance of this ontological dependence or guilt is summed up in the notion of resolution. Thus "resolute anticipation" describes the understanding and acceptance of limitations at the beginning and end of one's kind of Being. One becomes aware of those limits, particularly the initial limit, in listening for "the silent voice of conscience." For this voice is the expression of the absence of Being; it constantly speaks to one of what one is not or cannot or will not be. Such a sense of one's limits in the anxious voice of conscience is a distinguishing mark of authentic Dasein. Likewise, this anxious voice, containing an ever-present reference to Dasein's past beginning and future end, expresses the peculiar quality of authentic time.

Heidegger seeks to gather up the several analyses of Dasein into a unity. He discovers the ground of this unity in temporality (*Being and Time*, 352; cf. § 69). To understand Heidegger, we must assume or see that temporality is a unity. Now, Dasein can be understood to be essentially temporal; hence it is essentially undivided, however superficially this unity may be exhibited in inauthentic man.

The world is primordially disclosed in time. That is, the relations constitutive of worldhood are made possible by the appropriate phase or "ecstasy" (out-stretching) of temporality. For instance, Dasein can be the for-the-sake-of-which because it stretches out into the futurality of time. The in-order-to depends upon there being a present. And the world as thrown, or as factually existent, and the world as that to which one applies oneself are possible because of pastness.

Similarly, the elements of care and the awareness of the limits of care depend upon analogous phases of temporality. Care exists toward the future and finally toward death, the end of its possibilities. In the present, it falls away from its own Being in its concern with being or with objects in the world, but it is modified in this fall by the anxiety in which the world seems to fall away and by the voice of conscience in which guilt is recalled. Care's facticity and its thrownness are with it from its pastness and are witnessed by conscience remembering the debt for its Being. Thus the three ecstasies of temporality—futurality, presentness, and pastness—bring the several aspects of Being-in-the-world and of care together into a temporal unit. This unity tends to be the ordering element of the life of authentic Dasein, but it is overlooked or minimized by inauthentic Dasein. Nevertheless, the unity of Dasein is the unity of the same temporality which is the condition of the appearance of Being.[25] The transcendental problems of the unity of man and the unity of man with the world, then, are given solutions which vary existentially with respect to one's state of authenticity. (The question remains, however, whether all the steps in this variation have been adequately conceived; this point will recur in § 46.)

The anticipatory decision to be ready for anxiety and to listen for and to meditate the call of conscience is a rejection of the project of achieving a clear and perfect knowledge of the whole of the cosmos, or a complete technical mastery over the objective world and over other men. It is a renunciation of the project both of Cartesian rationalism and of the kind of scientific and technical domination that was projected by such philosophers as Comte or Marx. It is a rejection, too, of the infinite longing of Romantic poetry and of the infinite claims made for man—for his reason or for his feeling—by Romantic philosophers. Rather, man's relation to his fate is conceived as a function of his authenticity. And authenticity exacts anxiety for oneself remembering one's susceptibility to fascination by the inauthentic promise of unlimited power over the objective world and over others. Heidegger offers this attitude as an appropriate one for estranged man who would live his own life in an age of technology. In spite of the fact that the

---

[25] A basis is thus provided for understanding man, Dasein, to be essentially historical, that is, to be genuinely affected by the time through which he lives. If man is an essence in the classical sense, obviously he cannot be so affected, nor can he if he is only a grammatical fiction or an arbitrarily posited entity or function.

world of workaday occupations and of other people makes demands upon Dasein and diverts man's care away from his own possibilities, Heidegger holds that the resolute anticipation of Being within human limitations can be continually renewed or repeated. He writes, "Where else does care (*Sorge*) go, if not in the direction of bringing man back to his essence again?" [26] Awareness of the falling aspect of care, or of the inclination of self-knowledge to become dim or to remain concealed, might lead one periodically to bring one's own Being back into meditative question. Then, in fact, one would be existing as that being whose own Being is at issue. When this habit is preserved, Dasein's falling is more nearly resolute and authentic. There appears to be no reason why this attitude should not be approached whether a man's everyday role be of a scientific, practical, officially poetic, or even a professionally philosophic nature.

§45. EVALUATION OF SCIENCE AND TECHNOLOGY

The evaluation of the sciences and technology that follows from the philosophical standpoint set forth in this chapter emerges when three elements are related. These three are science and technology, authentic Dasein, and Dasein functioning as the for-the-sake-of-which. When these three are appropriately juxtaposed, some apprehension should develop of the nature of the danger which is said to lurk in Gestell. Then science and technology may be evaluated in terms of their relationship to man. The several sections immediately preceding have sketched the perspective within which the three elements may be appropriately juxtaposed.

First, we should eliminate an objection. In opposition to the critics who say that Heidegger exhibits a Romantic rejection or devaluation of science, we must observe that science and technology are not ontologically independent beings. They are founded within the world, and their evaluation must be related

[26] "Letter on Humanism," 274.

to this dependence. Let it be emphasized that the sciences and technology could certainly be pursued by authentic Dasein. There is no reason in this philosophy for concluding that the sciences of nature and their utilization are inauthentic in their own right. To the contrary, they are beings within the world and are dependent upon it. The structure of the world, it will be recalled, is revealed in Dasein. And it is Dasein, not technology, which may properly be either authentic or inauthentic. Dasein, by misunderstanding its own being and misplacing itself in inauthenticity, may render the whole world inauthentic in a derivative sense. Under these conditions—but only in this derivative sense—could the sciences be judged to be inauthentic. We must conclude that Heidegger's evaluation of the sciences is determined by what he believes contemporary man has made of them rather than by their independent character.

Heidegger's criticisms and warnings are addressed to contemporary man and are provoked by his recognition of the danger inherent in the modern outlook (Gestell) on the world. The danger follows from the fact that men today are not merely preoccupied as of old with the tool-world and other workers in order to provide the basic necessities of life, together with a modest supply of luxuries. They are tempted to become entirely absorbed—Heidegger's term is "fascinated" (*benommen, Being and Time*, 316)—by the very demanding universe of objects studied and manipulated by the sciences.[27] Hence a much more compelling temptation follows to interpret the self on the model of some being other than Dasein. To interpret the self on the model of an object, however, is to attenuate, perhaps even to lose, authentic Dasein. And Gestell, understood in abstraction from Dasein, seems to offer a limitless perspective upon nature. Also, again understood in abstraction from other and latent possibilities of Dasein, Gestell seems to open the *only* reasonable perspective upon nature. Finally, the astounding

---

[27] "In general, we are involuntarily linked to technique, whether we passionately affirm it or passionately deny it." See *Vorträger*, 13.

successes of this view of the world seem to confirm its infinity and its unique appropriateness.[28] The threat of Gestell, in short, is the seductive promise of infinite power over the world upon one condition: the forgetfulness of Dasein. And modern man continually yields to this temptation. No doubt in our time we should be reminded of the machine model, the computer model, or the rat model of the human being, or the model of the impersonal organization man. In other words, modern man, tempted away from an understanding of his own distinctive being, has been persuaded to "work over" himself—and others —as the technical scientist works over the useful thing, in order to reduce his being to an object and to subject it to scientific examination and then to technical control.

This interpretation of the self on the model of some non-human object and the acceptance of persons as resources are instances of falling. And falling, as a dimension of care, is inescapable. However, the falling which loses sight of its direction of movement, so to speak, is the falling of inauthentic Dasein. The appropriate effort is not to avoid falling, but to avoid a blind and inauthentic falling.

Thus the point is not that these nonhuman models of the self are unequivocally and in every respect false. All of them have their interest and scientific importance. They lead astray, however, when they become predominant and so fascinate those who study them that these students forget the powers and limitations of their own being, their Dasein. For then thrownness, human finitude, individuality, freedom, and mortality are denied or overlooked, and the appropriate price for such denials must eventually be exacted. Heidegger observes, in fact, that the world is too much with us and we lay waste our powers to be ourselves by concluding unreflectively that we are objects of quite other than the human sort.

The most serious consequence of visualizing oneself upon the

[28] In this sentence I use "success" in a popular sense. Seen over a longer time range, these successes may be failures even when measured by popular standards; cf. Barry Commoner, *Science and Survival* (New York: Viking, 1966).

model of some nonhuman or non-Dasein-like being becomes evident when it is recalled that the crucial element in the structure of the world is the for-the-sake-of-which, Dasein himself. In changing his view of himself, Dasein is changing the crucial factor in the worldhood of the world; thus he changes his world. And now he has become a "human resource" within the world rather than its determining or final factor. Consequently, the contemporary world has become a world virtually without man; at best it is a world in which men are estranged from their own humanity.

Thus Heidegger sees the danger associated with Gestell not in science, nor even in technology, nor in machines as such, but rather in man who has lost his insight into man and behaves toward himself and to others as though all were non-Dasein-like objects.

The loss of insight consequent upon accepting Gestell not as one revelation but as the total and final revelation of Being leads also to the end of philosophy. The skeleton or death which lurks within Gestell is precisely a threat to Being, in particular to man's Being. For the man who thinks of himself as an object, perhaps as a useful but replaceable cog in a social machine whose purpose is either beyond all ken or else is identical with someone's wishes, is no longer functioning with authentic Dasein, disclosing Being with anticipatory resolution. He is no longer the shepherd of Being but is seeking to escape from the freedom of disclosure. Philosophically, he no longer apprehends himself as mediating between the ontic and the ontological; rather he struggles with the problem of the relation between mind and body or between subject and object, or he stands aside altogether while he clarifies the words in which such problems are sometimes phrased. Or he moves on to the last stage: He serves the state by designing attractive ideologies useful for capturing and exploiting the masses.

This evaluation of the sciences and technology points to the contemporary philosophical task; this is the problem of discovering where we are situated *vis à vis* the modern attunement to the world with the eventual purpose of countering the blindness with which Gestell is more and more commonly accepted. Is there, then, some method for recapturing a more human, a more authentic, Being-in-the-world?

§ 46.   FROM GESTELL TO GELASSENHEIT

The current self and our Western convictions about human nature, Heidegger seems to say, have been caught up in routines which effectively blind us to the alternative possibilities which an understanding of Dasein might reveal. Man, absorbed by Gestell, has disappeared into the object-world; his present predicament repeats the absorption of the Humean self into space. In his later writings, therefore, Heidegger appears to direct his consideration upon the kind of change which might lift contemporary man out of the repetition of routines now become meaningless and open the way to a more authentic existence and to a renewed vision of his fate. For example, he suggests that our energies be devoted to what he calls "thought" or "recollection" of Being (*Andenken*). This thought of Being, however, has been difficult for him to characterize. It seems to be a turn to a sort of docile contemplation of Being, a "letting be" or "releasement" (*Gelassenheit*). Releasement, I suggest, is an initial mode of attunement to the world which is quite opposite to the mood of intellectual and technical domination of Gestell. Releasement is described as the patient waiting for the silent voice of Being. This receptive waiting of psyche is held to be the appropriate function of man, for only by this waiting is Dasein effective in bringing Being to appearance. Only thus does man become the shepherd of Being. One aspect of this contemplation is difficult to understand; the initiating function seems to be taken away from man. The "thought of Being" is as much a thinking done by Being through man as it is man's thinking of Being. (In this regard, Heidegger is reminiscent of the ancient Greeks for whom the gods, to whom they had access through psyche, were as much a center as were the things of this world, to which they had access through thymos.)

Many readers of Heidegger have trouble in following him in this turn (the *Kehre*). Some regard it as a turn to mysticism; others take it to be a decision for idealism. Heidegger's turn falls into its proper perspective, however, when placed in relation to his reading of history. Likewise, a key to understanding it is provided by the threefold structure that we have already seen in the analysis of care, of the world, of temporality, and of Dasein's existential limitations.

According to my understanding, Heidegger reads Western history as a decision, dating from Socrates and Plato, to regard man as the decisive factor in being. This decision remained for a long time more or less implicit until it emerged as the cogito in the philosophy of Descartes, as the I-principle (the "I think . . .") of Kant, and as the Romantic belief in the infinite productiveness and self-creativeness of the ego. In the Humean and scientific traditions this Romantic belief in the creativeness of the self is rejected as unrealistic or as outright "nonsense"; nevertheless, the same decision is even more effectively present in positivism and allied philosophies, though in an altered guise. It is present as "subject-ism" or the resolution to subject the whole of nature to man's technological control. The dominating assumption of this mode of attunement might be expressed in our phrase: Being is identical with being as evident to mind (thymos). Now, the emphasis placed upon Dasein's receptivity, so noticeable since the *Kehre*, is to be interpreted as an explicit turn away from this characteristic decision of Western philosophy whether expressed within an idealistic, realistic, or positivistic context. Rather it is a turn toward the identification of Being as that which gives possibilities or as that from which intuitions or inspirations may be received. Heidegger rejects the anthropocentrism of tradition. The major central position is held in his philosophy by Being, although man might still be said to be a minor center in so far as Dasein, functioning in and through him, brings Being to evidence as beings. The famous *Kehre* is simply a turn to Being as accessible through a deepening understanding of Dasein.

The analysis of this turn, which at the same time is evidence of Heidegger's continuing anti-idealism, may be carried forward by exhibiting the moments in the renewal of the care structure. The renewed and authentic Dasein shows a change in the character of his temporality. It manifests, for example, an acceptance of facticity. This acceptance is exemplified in understanding pastness as "repetition," or by way of an interpretation which uncovers and reactivates meanings previously sedimented and forgotten. Dasein's orientation to the future may be thought of, I suggest, as a new interpretation of the *Worumwillen*, the for-the-sake-of-which. The function of authentic Dasein is explicitly understood to be the unconcealing of Being. Thus it is aware of existing as the opening in which Being, the power of world-making, comes to evidence and expression. The world is for the sake of Dasein, but authentic Dasein is for the sake of Being. This particular acceptance of facticity and this orientation to the future are united in the receptivity of "releasement," which most obviously rejects the self-centeredness of tradition and yields instead to the way possibilities are given by Being in the "moment of vision" (*Being and Time*, 338). Just as Heidegger interpreted Kant as placing thought (conceiving) in the service of intuition, so now Heidegger is to be interpreted as placing intuition or receptivity in the service of Being. And thus Heidegger points away from the ego-centeredness of the modern tradition (Gestell) and seeks to effect a transition to a new vision of man, whose existence is centered both upon Being and upon his own Dasein function, a vision which resolutely accepts his fallenness, his finitude, and his thrownness.

How, in terms of this book, is the change in human-being to which Heidegger points to be understood? Certainly his movement is not toward an idealism. Rather all three of the factors involved in this change are to be placed in the service of a Being which by no stretch of the imagination could be identified with a Hegelian absolute or with any other idealist ultimate. More positively, this contemplative waiting upon a nonobjective and nonideal Being might be described as a waiting upon inspiration. It might be regarded as a modern expression of the function of the ancient psyche. Indeed, much of Heidegger's ontological thinking might be associated with the same psyche, for this thinking is not translatable into precise formulae. It is not, like the thinking most cultivated in Gestell, a problem-solving or a manipulative kind of thought (thymos) directed upon subjects and objects. Rather it is a receptive thought which waits and listens, hoping to recollect or to become aware of some hint or inspiration from that Being which is prior to the distinction between subject and object. It is only questionably—and questioningly—intellectualist. Rather it seeks to include ratiocinative and mathematical thinking within a larger context of possibilities, the totality of which cannot in principle become evident to finite mind. Moreover, the way in which Heidegger's thought includes objective thinking is crucial. As our account of his philosophy of the sciences and of the objective world indicated, he does not Romantically reject objective thought nor does he derogate from the objective world. Indeed, his philosophy seems in some respects to be close to the view for which this present study stands, namely, that receptive and contemplative thought should always be closely interrelated with the more intellectualist and precise thought.

My claim is that the primary function of philosophy is to be the intermediary between inspiration and rational rigor, between insight and exactitude, between psyche and thymos. Can Heidegger be claimed as a philosopher in this sense? Not, I think, if he is proposing that philosophy give itself *exclusively* over to a meditative waiting upon Being.

Consider how Heidegger describes this meditative and receptive thought or "releasement" in his book *Gelassenheit.*[29] First, as implicitly concluded in the preceding sections, this kind of thought can be achieved only by Dasein, whose vision has

---

[29] (Pfullingen: Neske, 1959), trans. John M. Anderson and E. Hans Freund, under the title *Discourse on Thinking* (New York: Harper and Row, 1966).

been rectified by becoming authentically itself. Second and especially to the present point, it is a "will-less" and non-representative thinking (the Scientist in the "Conversation . . . about Thinking," included in *Gelassenheit*, experienced difficulty in conceiving and conceding this point). More positively, "releasement" is a waiting which is a "release into openness" (*Gelassenheit*, 68) or an acceptance of the coming forth of truth upon the initiative of Being (*ibid.*, 81). But just this unconcealment of Being, as intimated also elsewhere (e.g., in the essay "What Is Metaphysics?"), is the "naming of the holy," a naming specifically distinguished as the poetic function. But the philosophic function is said *not* to be the poet's.[30] Heidegger does not clarify the distinction between the two.[31] And he does hold that both share in maintaining a docile and receptive attitude toward the coming or unconcealment of Being. Both, then, are engaged in meditative thought. In general, as it is written in *Aus der Erfahrung des Denkens* (1947), "We do not come to thinking; rather it comes to us." This receptive thinking comes to us as the poetic word which is the *Da* of the renewed and authentic Dasein; "poetically man dwells upon this earth." *Gelassenheit*, as Paul Ricoeur remarks, "is the gift of poetical life."[32]

In the terms of the present study, this receptive, will-less, nonrepresentative, meditative thought about Being, in which authentic Dasein engages, is a contemplation that seems at first to require an identification with psyche alone. It is something like a highly developed form of Platonic recollection. At the least, it would necessitate releasement from the concern with

[30] "The thinker utters Being. The poet names what is holy," from "What Is Metaphysics?" in *Existence and Being*, trans. Werner Brock (New York: Henry Regnery, 1949), 360.

[31] A point made also by Ludwig Landgrebe in *Major Problems in Contemporary European Philosophy*, trans. K. Reinhardt (New York: Ungar, 1966), 143f.

[32] "The Critique of Subjectivity and Cogito in the Philosophy of Martin Heidegger," in M. S. Frings (ed.), *Heidegger and the Quest for Truth* (Chicago: Quadrangle Books, 1968), 62–75.

beings which is demanded by the highly specialized and complex tasks presented by industry and research today. Thus it would certainly put an end to fascination exclusively with problem-solving thought and its technological utilization. The emotions with which it is associated are the tranquil and contemplative emotions opposite to those associated with the aggressive-defensive attitude of Gestell. Would a poetic self-surrender such as this also require a surrender of philosophy?

If the philosopher were resolved altogether to forget the discipline of precision and to listen only for the nonrepresentative voice of Being, would not philosophy have reached its end? Would not the philosopher become lost in the contemplative or in the prophet who, if he spoke at all, would speak only with the voice of poetry or of myth? This is the mystical strain which some critics find in Heidegger's later writings. And it must be admitted that of late he speaks primarily for Being and as the representative of psyche. It is sometimes difficult to find the relation of this psyche to precise and communicable doctrine. At least to this extent, there is some color to the accusation of mysticism.

If this criticism of Heidegger be correct, then indeed the Kantian-phenomenological tradition in philosophy may seem to come to an end with the meditative thought of Being, although this end is quite the opposite from its end in the Humean tradition. The latter concludes with so much information about beings that our computers cannot keep up with it nor can our Humean analysts keep it analyzed, whereas the former concludes with an almost unspoken inspiration of Being itself, inviting men to a change of soul through a mystical contemplation of their source. I shall not attempt to determine in detail here whether this criticism of Heidegger is correct or not. But I myself cannot accept it;[33] Heidegger clearly states that the later philosophy is not to be construed in separation from the

---

[33] Though I once did: cf. my "A Brief Introduction to the Philosophy of Martin Heidegger," *Tulane Studies in Philosophy*, XII (1963), 106–51.

earlier writings. The *Kehre* is not a turn away from the earlier and nonmystical philosophy. It is a turn toward a thinking which is complementary to objective and ratiocinative thinking. If Heidegger were charged with not working out the detail of the relation between these two kinds of thought, perhaps he might reply that not all tasks can be accomplished at once, or that much of this detail is already present in his writings. Still the question is difficult and commentators are divided.[34] I shall go no further than to observe that Heidegger points the way from Gestell to Gelassenheit, but it is difficult to discern all the steps which must lie along this way. The need for this discernment indicates, no doubt, Heidegger's own version of the transcendental problem. To describe "releasement" so as to eliminate the unintended overtones of an irrational mysticism or "misology," to clarify the movement of transcendence from Gestell to this releasement, and to specify the relation between the use of the mind characteristic of Gestell and that characteristic of releasement, these are the tasks required if a complete solution of the present transcendental problem is to be reached.

Meanwhile it is worth observing that the pass to which some of Heidegger's hostile critics believe he has brought philosophy is much more properly illustrated by the antirational position adopted, for example, by the Russian existentialist Lev Shestov. Shestov carries to its extreme the Romantic rejection of the

---

[34] Richardson, in *Heidegger: Through Phenomenology to Thought*, 241ff, believes this turn involves something new yet coherent with Heidegger's development. But other views are also to be found: cf. James Demske, *Sein Menschen, und Tod* (Freiburg: K. Alber, 1963), Chap. 5; also John Sallis, "La différence ontologique et l'unité de la pensée de Heidegger," *Revue Philosophique de Louvain*, LXV (1967), 192–206. Cf. also Heidegger's letter contained in Richardson, *Heidegger: Through Phenomenology to Thought*, xvi, xxiii. Of course justice cannot be done in this chapter to the subtleties of thought involved in the *Kehre*—for instance, to the disappearance of the term "Dasein" in the later writings. Heidegger's thought, however, continues to circulate around the two foci: that through which Being comes to appearance, and the Being which so comes. But the second of these (Being) tends to withdraw, suggesting, if the Copernican metaphor be retained, a "parabolic" course of thought. Heidegger's later preoccupation concerns the lighting process itself whose source is thus withdrawn, but it continues to concern also that which through releasement can be sensitive to this process.

ratiocinative and scientific mind.[35] Heidegger, however, certainly would not discard reason and all its works in favor of a "freedom of ignorance." He might even observe that the need for scientific and technological knowledge is entailed by our finitude. Moreover, reason and knowledge are parts of the human-being and can become authentic.

§ 47.   THE COURSE OF REASON TO HEIDEGGER

The possible authenticity of reason brings again to the fore the fact that an alteration in the ideal of reason is demanded by Heidegger's evaluation of Gestell and of releasement. This is an alteration which would render reason's finitude explicit. Its finitude is related to Being. Being, it will be recalled, reveals itself to Dasein only upon condition that it be also concealed. Being thus can no longer be assumed to be identical with being as evident to mind. Man's fate, Heidegger seems to say, can never become completely evident to man. Rather it becomes evident partially and differently in different epochs of history. In the present epoch of Gestell, finitude, dependence, receptivity tend to be concealed. They need not be completely concealed, however, and an appropriate gift from the philosopher in these times of transition would be a thinking that recalls the forgotten functions of psyche and communicates a sense of Dasein's finite existence and an awareness of its dependence upon the gift of poetical life. Heidegger's philosophy thus occupies an important place in the history of reason. His

[35] Shestov identifies man's original sin as the desire to master the cosmos by means of reason. He counters this fatal choice, whose consequence is death, with a reminder of the possibility of faith. This faith bears a resemblance to the releasement offered by Heidegger. It is a "thinking forward" which tends to silence; it is nonobjective and does not reject mystery. It comes as a gift to the receptive mind and "delivers man in an incomprehensible way from the chains of knowledge." See Lev Shestov, *Athens and Jerusalem* (Athens: Ohio University Press, 1966), 317. The dangerous aspect of an exclusive choice of this mystical faith is its quiescence. Assuming that this is the choice that has prevailed in many nations of the East, one can suspect a relation between it and the hunger, disease, superstition, and inadequate social organization to be found in some of these nations.

place, for present purposes, can most easily be designated by means of a concise review of the stages in the development of this idea.

The characteristically modern context of thinking is dominated by the Cartesian ideal of rational clarity—the ideal of thymos and of psyche in the service of thymos. This Cartesian ideal was made possible originally by Plato's genial intuition of the mathematical harmonies embodied in the cosmos and in man. Such an ideal, however, when successfully used, can entice the thinker into a bifurcation. In Descartes's persuasive formulation, it did so. Whatever was most clear and distinct to the mathematically disciplined mind was awarded the metaphysical privilege of superior reality. That which was less clear to the mathematical mind became subordinated, less real, "subjective," and was finally ignored, forgotten. This Cartesian interpretation was carried to its all-inclusive and most one-sided extreme by positivism. Although Kant's rethinking of the role of the subject in experience rendered possible a reevaluation of the ideal of Cartesian clarity, it led immediately only to Romantic irrationalism. Still, this irrationalism is a determination by the rational ideal, yet only a negative determination. Then the way was opened by Husserl's philosophical explorations to a reevaluation of this ideal; he concluded this ideal was only to be approached, never to be realized. But it was Heidegger who actually revised the rational ideal, a revision which is incorporated in his principle of the finitude of Being.

Heidegger's revision is not an irrationalism. Neither Cartesian rationality, the sciences, nor technology are rejected by this revision. Rather they are included within a wider horizon which seeks also to include that which Cartesian rationality, the sciences, and technology must necessarily ignore. The Heideggerian doctrine that the Being which reveals also conceals seeks to include in principle within the philosophical purview both that which is clearly "seen" and that which any definite decision, any clear view, must perforce exclude. It is an attempt to remember the forgotten. We may understand this widening of the horizon of reason as a movement to include psyche, freed now to live its own life on earth, sensitive to the intimations of fate, and alive to the dramatic ironies of history. And no doubt the greatest irony of history arises from the fact that the reason which clarifies also obscures. Nothing can be illuminated unless a shadow be cast.

VII

Where Three Ways Meet

§48. THE POSITION AT THE PRESENT

Philosophy, as here defined, is the interpretation of the transitions over the significant boundaries or crossroads of human life and concern. The boundaries with which we have been mainly preoccupied have been of two kinds—those which have separated historical epochs and those which occur within a philosophy and seem to compromise its coherence. Transitions over such boundaries made or attempted by several philosophers have now been examined. Where have we arrived? Have we come to an impasse in recognizing the opposition between the Humeans and the transcendental tradition? And have these two strains come to their respective ends? Or are there other possibilities which indicate other ways through the labyrinth of history?

If we glance briefly back over the way we have come, perhaps the choices that we now face may be seen more sharply and the future of philosophy may be envisaged. Then something of the character of the boundary that philosophy now faces may be anticipated. This anticipation will be facilitated by using the metaphor of the labyrinth to suggest the character of the choices which the future may offer.

270

§ 49. PHILOSOPHY DIVIDED

The Golden Age of Greece was a time of transition out of an epoch when fate seemed to be a blind determination. And though it is scarcely true to suppose that as man became more rational, fate became less irrational—since rationality itself and its relation to the world are problematic—still at least the partial intelligibility of fate and of man came to be entertained. But even Plato, whose Academy was dedicated to the god of intellect, experienced difficulty in understanding the all-important transition from particulars of the world to the forms of intelligibility apprehended by the intellect—terms which delineate one expression of the transcendental problem.[1] Likewise, another obscure problem, that concerning the relation of the nascent sciences of the world to man's good and to his fate, was persuasively conceived by Plato in terms of the means-end relationship. However, this persuasive force was not destined to outlive the medieval theological context for long.

Descartes, who sought to lead man out of the finite, quantitative, and moral world of the medievals into the infinite, quantitative, and impersonal universe of science, found his great problem to lie in understanding the relation of the self to the new environment which the sciences were to dominate. The Humean philosophers ushered man into the modern world altogether by adopting the self into the physical universe as an object among objects. The Kantian tradition, however, elected the more difficult passage. It chose to preserve the uniqueness of the self by seeking to understand the self's peculiar relation to the world, a choice which was to require a new envisagement of the whole being of man and of the world.

Of these last two opposing philosophic strains, the first may be broadly described as an all-inclusive scientific rationalism,

---

[1] At the least, however, Plato provided many of the conceptions which could be utilized more or less directly for reaching a solution of the problem; cf. the extremely interesting use of these and similar concepts by Professor Charles Bigger in his *Participation: A Platonic Inquiry*, Chaps. 5 and 6 especially.

the other as tending to become a poetic antirationalism. Surely recognition of this dichotomy is not new. But the obviousness of the division should not be allowed to mask its importance. Perhaps there has always been such a contrast of convictions in our history; the opposition of Democritus and Plato will be recalled, or that between Gassendi and Descartes, as well as the one between the positivist and the transcendental traditions of more recent times. Such contrast expressed in ancient terms reflects an emphasis now upon thymos and now upon psyche, now upon impersonal discursive reason and now upon poetic inspiration as the appropriate instruments for dealing with human fate and interpreting movement into the future. Do these two alternatives exhaust the situation? Our study points, at least dimly, to others. These other alternatives begin to emerge, however, only when one contemplates the contemporary contrast. It will be useful, therefore, with one final stroke to mark this opposition more briefly and as sharply as possible.

The Humean strain, culminating in scientific humanism and the analytical philosophy of the Anglo-American countries, limits man's mind to preoccupation with discursive reason seeking technologically to master the cosmos and other men. It views man as an object among objects, his good as achievable by alteration of an external world, his history as subject eventually to control, his fate as "external." Its critics speak of this philosophy as objectivistic, and since it delivers man over to a world without man, they predict its catastrophic fall in the irrational and violent return of the forgotten psyche. In contrast, the transcendental strain, culminating in the views of some contemporary European existentialists, tends to discover in psyche or in poetic inspiration the primary function of mind seeking insight, wisdom, and a sense of oneness with others and with "the prophetic soul of the wide world dreaming on things to come." It views man as a unique being, his good as achievable primarily by alteration of himself, his history as manifesting his possibilities, and his fate as "internal." Its critics speak of it as a subjectivistic philosophy, concerned with man without nature, and they predict its catastrophe consequent upon its destructive neglect of the sciences of the world and its intellectual isolation from the forces of progress.[2]

An important part of the history of this contrast is put into a nutshell by the observation that the Western development of reason has disclosed its two components, psyche and thymos, related in its different epochs to man and to the world in characteristically different ways and with different emphases. Typical of contemporary times is the virtually complete separation of these components in the two dominant philosophic strains. Such contrast defines the present position of philosophy. And this present position is paradoxical. The first extreme, developing primarily the discursive reason, thymos, led to a doctrine which denied the unique being of the self who, however, is continuously and individually self-affirming or self-denying; whereas the second extreme, especially developing the intuitive mind, psyche, led to a doctrine which tends to deny discursive reason, but can deny it only by using it, and thus reaffirming its value. Placed in this crisis, in what direction can philosophy now move?

[2] A remark will not be amiss upon the way in which the contrast between these two philosophic traditions is sometimes viewed within university departments of philosophy. The Humean philosopher thinks of himself as a professional man, a specialist in certain rather well-defined intellectual techniques, mainly techniques of clarification, who can best offer his services through an institution, such as a university. And he regards a university as an institution devoted to research and training in the more intellectual specialties required by society in the interests of security and maintenance of the status quo. In contrast, the other type of philosopher thinks of himself as a nonspecialist who seeks to pursue and to understand human change and self-care. He regards the notion of being a professional philosopher as ridiculous. (A professional lover of wisdom is no less ridiculous than other professional lovers: a gigolo of wisdom!) He has until now often followed the calling of a professional teacher in a university, and he thinks of a university as being, or as seeking to be, an institution almost unique in the modern world, one whose primary and sufficient purpose is to provide an environment favorable to the discovery of self and to growth in self-knowledge. The same tension is discussed in several contemporary contexts by William Braden in *The Age of Aquarius* (Chicago: Quadrangle Books, 1970), 5 and *passim*.

§ 50.   PHILOSOPHY AND HISTORY

A crisis occurs when essential elements of a culture come into conflict with the result that the identity of man and the ends which he pursues are brought into question. A crisis of this sort led primitive man to seek continuity and security in the protective power of the gods. It impels the philosopher to seek an intelligible continuity or at least a rhythm in the movement of history. It then urges him to discover, if possible, the ground or reason for this continuity or rhythm.

The present-day critical point appears first to require of the philosopher a decision. In what general direction of thought will the continuity and intelligibility of human change be most likely pursued? To answer such a question we may look again at the epochs considered here and attempt to determine whether any guide is suggested by the course that has been followed.

The irrational forces and dark questions which haunt humankind may seem to have been penetrated from time to time by various intuitions, metaphors, concepts. And yet in the course of events each of these instruments of illumination has lost much or all of its power. Is philosophy, then, altogether subject to the irrational forces of history in the manner of other elements of culture? If so, philosophy is merely another of those things which come and go with the succession of the epochs of history. If the kinds of philosophy which can be seriously entertained at any time are already determined by the culture, then philosophy would seem to be nothing more than the history of philosophy. But if it is identical with its history, it may well be nothing more than a cul-de-sac in the labyrinth of human time. The ideal of the finitude of reason, for example, like that of its infinitude, may be merely an abbreviated way of referring to such a cul-de-sac.

Perhaps, however, an escape route from this skeptical conclusion is opened up by the philosophy of history, for a philosophic understanding of history may exhibit the apparent relativism of a philosophy to its culture as the outcome of a principle which transcends the contingencies of any particular time. However, an overview of such philosophies of history is suggestive; it is suggestive of the dependence of philosophies of history upon the very same history which they seek to illuminate. Is history itself a movement toward the complete actuality of existents? Is it a device for the salvation of man? Is it a progress through which pseudo-problems are eliminated and genuine problems and conceptual instruments continually clarified? Is it a progressive adjustment between basic productive activity and social organization? Is it a series of gifts (*Geschicken*) which both reveal and conceal Being? The philosophies that elaborate such questions and yield affirmative answers are themselves expressions of the presuppositions and trends which are exhibited more widely within their own respective times. None has achieved permanence. Again we touch upon the quicksands of historical relativism.

The present essay, however, has elaborated upon at least one constant, one function not confined to any particular one of the epochs or philosophies that we have studied: namely, the definition of philosophy as the interpretation of transitions. More than a mere abstract or even analogical unity of philosophy is thus designated. For in the first place, any interpretation is in fact regularly affected by those which have preceded it. And in the second place, this affection can be observed to follow a recurrent pattern. These points, already illustrated in the preceding chapters, may now be considered more generally. It is not impossible that some degree of guidance through history may be acquired by means of an understanding of the pattern to which I refer and by a determination of one's position within it.

Philosophies are the outcome of the dialogue between reflective men and their inheritance. Even those philosophers who believe that past philosophy is irrelevant to progress in their specialty have been led to this conclusion by the communication between them and the philosophies which they inherit and have studied. But surely the clarity and effectiveness of any philosopher's communication with the tradition varies over a large gamut. Ideally, perhaps, a philosophic interpretation of any given epoch would be hierarchically related to those of the past epoch in that it would remember and use the philosophies of the preceding epoch. These, in their turn, would have remembered and used those of the preceding, and so on indefinitely far back. Thus, ideally, philosophy might grow in the manner of a tree, retaining past growths as resource and strength. Philosophy, however, is not in fact cumulative in this sense. Philosophic insight is not an assured heritage. Each philosophy includes the preceding only so far as communication has been efficient. And communication between the generations is notoriously poor.

In addition, it is most important to recall that the very absence of any attempt to communicate with the tradition is itself a significant communication. At the least, such a communication expresses a negative evaluation of the tradition and seems to justify the ignoring and forgetting of that which is thus negatively evaluated. Such negative communications can be heavy with consequences. This opinion needs to be elaborated and applied.

Communication between generations of reflective men is explicit and critical, no doubt, but it is also implicit and pervasive. This latter, the implicit and pervasive influence of the past, is not within control. These hidden communications and failures of communication represent the tyranny of the past. The ignorance and forgetfulness which are the conditions of this tyranny precipitate crises and sometimes take on the threatening aspect of an avenging fate. No doubt the inevitable drift to cultural crises is a very complex phenomenon in any epoch. The present essay has been concerned with such crises mainly in regard to that aspect of the tyranny of the past which has been termed fate.

"Fate" has been used to name a compulsive and irrational force in history. This force has not been so irrational as to go without recognition. We have observed it in both external and internal guises. External fate was once imagined as an impersonal disposing power, determining both gods and men, and opposed by man only through the assertion of his dignity and Promethean freedom. The modern external fate, however, is envisaged as the "ironbound" or determined laws which describe the whole of nature. But these laws are knowable to men. By use of this knowledge, men may, and should according to the knowledge-is-power ideal, subdue the whole of nature to their inclinations. We have seen this program become paradoxical when men came to envisage themselves, and even their knowledge, as parts of nature and when the ideal of knowledge-is-power-over-nature came to be interpreted as knowledge-is-power-over-knowledge.

On the other hand, internal fate was understood by philosophers as the will of God for man, a will from which man fell but to which he might return by way of a personal rebirth. Modern times have understood the internal fate Romantically as the compulsive forces arising from the depths of the self. Perhaps these forces are the consequences of denied and repressed, or of unrealized, needs and impulses. However, they are held to be eventually accessible to the mature man who, by way of personal change, may come into possession of his own powers.

Parallel to these two versions of fate are two prevailing metaphors through which man has sought to penetrate his fate and to understand himself and his world. We have, in this respect, considered the beliefs that had their origin in man's attempt to understand his artistry and himself as material having definite possibilities for becoming that which the artisan intended or for becoming that which, as it were, its own nature intended. So pervasive were the concepts which issued from this matrix that they became obvious common sense and dominated the ethics, politics, cosmology, theology, and common sense of the Greek and medieval epochs. Other concepts, other possible views of the world and the self, were placed in the shadow by this and were all but forgotten. We have also considered the crucial recognition and criticism of the more or less implicit communication of the beliefs which formed and preserved this earlier culture. We observed the recollection or discovery by Renaissance philosophers of other analogies which placed physics upon a new and successful footing. Then we noticed the victory of these new notions in domain after domain of life and thought, until finally man himself and his society came to be understood in their narrowly intellectualist image. Again, analogies of this basic kind define and limit the way in which the world appears. That which they cannot adequately translate is necessarily ignored and becomes forgotten and consigned to the irrational; this forgotten material came to be manifested as the obscure compulsion that we have termed external fate. And thereupon it may become, in the fullness of time, the provocation to catastrophe. In other words, we can scarcely avoid the conviction that irrational forces dog our "progress" whether toward the Millennium or merely toward the future.

More particularly, the persistence into contemporary times of the doctrine and problems of Cartesian dualism suggests strongly that it is man himself who is not adequately included in the concepts derived from the modern physical analogy. The concepts designed to interpret and control the cosmos have let man himself, his human-being, slip through their net. Man himself thus becomes a most obscure element in the modern fate. We now have seriously to face the prospect that progress in the sciences has at the same time entailed a retrogression in humanity. There is at hand evidence enough to argue that the fate of modern Western culture, wherever it impinges on man, is internal disaster: alienation and nihilism. The growing conviction that this disaster is now overtaking us has led in certain quarters to something like a recollection and a rebirth of values and views closely related to Romantic philosophies. There is, however, among others this important difference: that these values have not been supposed to be defined by some natural and intuitable drive to the infinite.

A similar area of contrast and tension emerges in the effort to determine the nature and possible functions of that characteristic human endowment: the mind. The problem, as it has been engaged in these chapters, concerns the relation between the kind of knowledge which is human virtue and the kind of knowledge which is power and is pursued by the scientist and engineer. The contrast to which I refer is suggested by the meanings of "know" in these two phrases: Heifetz knows how to play the Beethoven violin concerto; this young Ph.D. knows how to solve problems in acoustics. Socrates initiated inquiry into the contrast between these two kinds of knowing in the *Phaedo.* And in the *Timaeus,* Plato indicated a solution; he argued that an intellectualist knowledge of the cosmos could become the means to self-knowledge and harmony of soul. Then, however, the central figure of Christianity pointed to the uniqueness and exclusive importance of self-knowledge when he spoke of himself as "the truth and the light." But modern times turned toward a quite different ideal, the ideal of thymos, and identified the knowledge which is virtue with intellectualist and scientific knowledge. It also identified the liberating function of knowledge with technology; it was interested only in freeing the energies of nature. On the other hand, there is the possibility, suspected by the Romanticists, that these last two identifications are merely a forgetting or a denial of the existence of the kind of knowledge which changes and liberates the human-being. This liberating knowledge is more like the unconceptualized inspiration of the poet than the conceptual knowledge of the engineer. Romantic philosophers and poets suspected that the rejection by the Enlightenment of the knowledge which liberates the human-being would altogether eliminate the possibility of a culture centered upon the whole of man, his being, his changes, and his growth. This rejection is like a forgetting of the human-being and is sensed as an absence or an alienation. The elimination of necessary elements from the culture in which men must live always reaches a limit of toleration. In the past, the misunderstandings of, and consequent violation of, humanity have issued in crises. Such crises may be illuminated by a philosophy which is sensitive to their recurrence, even if the content of that philosophy is the off-spring of its times.

§51. THE DRIFT OF HISTORY

Such rather general reflections, which develop out of the more particular ones of the preceding chapters, point, I believe, to something not unlike a pattern in the recurrences of history. Such a pattern may be simply stated in a triad of terms: for-getting, crises, and discovery or recollection. The understand-ing of these terms can be developed by reference to fate and to the human mind (psyche and thymos).

The blindness which inadvertently loosens the destructive forces of history has repeatedly been called a kind of forgetting. This metaphor is useful, but it must be recalled that there are two kinds of forgetting. There is, first, the forgetting of that which was once clearly in mind. Many arts, many styles of liv-ing, for example, have in this sense been forgotten; they are no longer practiced, though they may still be appreciated. Secondly, there is a forgetting of that which might have been in mind but was not explicitly grasped. This failure to grasp a principle—the contrary to Platonic recollection—may be a failure to apprehend and use the structural elements necessary for the formation of a world of a certain sort. For instance, we do not understand, and probably could not adequately grasp, all the structures necessary for living in the world of the ancient Egyptians. (If we did so grasp them, we would be living in that world.) Now, it should be obvious that living in any one world entails the "forgetting" of infinitely many other pos-sible world structures. Platonic forgetting is as inevitable as Platonic recollection is necessary for founding any world. I think we may say, more generally, that the Platonically for-gotten is to the recalled and used in any culture as the knowable or perceivable world is related to the world actually known or perceived. The relation involved here suggests the relation between the depths of a person's psychic life—his total possibility—and his everyday actual self.

It is important to become aware of this Platonic forgetting. This awareness is revolutionary; it amounts to substituting the ideal of the finitude of reason for the Cartesian ideal of infinite clarity which has hitherto held sway in the modern world. What the recurrent convulsions of humankind seem to teach is that the relation between man and his world is not arbitrary. The forgetting of certain possible world structures can be disastrous for the living of a viable human life. (This is the forgetfulness which is "punished" by the fateful and sometimes violent revulsion against the deficient world.) A culture confidently founded upon such essential omissions will surely be surprised by crises.

History also suggests, however, that revolutionary crises can, if guided with philosophic vision, become archaic experience. An archaic experience, it will be recalled, is not only an experience having the character of a first temporal moment; but it is also first in the sense of evidently embodying a principle. An archaic experience marks the close of one temporal epoch and the initiation of another just because it is a time of insight into or recollection of that which may serve as a principle or an arché. An epochal crisis of history is a return to a beginning, to a source, in this dual sense.

At the point of such a beginning, the epoch immediately past appears not as the only way of life but as the consequence of decisions to which there were alternatives. It appears as the realization of one set of alternatives out of many. The future likewise appears as an opening rich in possibilities. But since all possibilities cannot be realized at once, this future urges a new decision. A beginning, then, is an initiation into a new but still limited future which is yet to be enacted, brought to its maturity, and finally brought to its own fateful conclusion.

What I am endeavoring to suggest is that the arché, which becomes evident upon a successful return to the beginning, is an initial inspired grasp of values, a novel view of life, or perhaps the vision of a new form of society. At any rate, it is a fruitful recognition of seemingly irrational and forgotten possibilities partly implicit in an older form of living and thinking. In time this beginning may be developed and more clearly formulated. But a genuine beginning requires as its decisive phase the reception of an inspiration. Such an inspiration, if it has revolutionary significance, is the as yet dim and initiatory recollection of a new world.

Since this return in response to aporia to a beginning or arché, which is the reception of a new and initiatory inspiration, is a perennial or transcultural occurrence, it may still be spoken of in mythical terms. Plato's recollection of the world and of the good man as essentially structured by the same intelligible harmonies is a typical illustration of the return to a beginning. Descartes's mathematical inspiration of 1619 is another; Kant's Copernican turn to the transcendental offers a third illustration. Such oracles point to the way through history; the interpretation and explication of them give rise to philosophies. These philosophies are in many respects relative to their times; only so would they respond effectively to the problems and insights which called them into being. But the pattern of events to which they respond is more general. This pattern is the structure of the history that brings men to the problems and frustrations which fate has in store for them, and brings them likewise to the source or insight which may lead through the crisis to a new beginning. Of course the times may also be poverty-stricken and unphilosophical. Then no new beginning becomes evident. Then men persist in their routine five-year plans and risk nothing uncustomary.

Fate now seems to have brought Western peoples to such an impasse. The alienation of many workers from necessary industrial work, the evident emptiness of economic success, the presence of misery amid plenty, the uncontrolled population increase, the loss of the individual within the mass, the poisoning of the environment, the fear and threat of global war, the reduction of poetry to advertisement and propaganda, the prevailing value-nihilism, all point to the absence of some essential world-structure. As I write these words on July 21, 1969, the walk of two men on the moon has just ended. What is the meaning, in this context, of their extraordinary technological achievement? Most of the first reactions were expressed in terms of exhilarated self-congratulation. Immediately there were predictions of journeys to other planets, even of the eventual "conquest" of the whole universe, perhaps of other galaxies. In Brazil an enterprising real estate operator is said to have sold lots on the moon! These reactions are limited to plans for quite similar explorations. They anticipate walks on Mars, deeper and yet deeper penetrations into outer space, and more efficient exploitations of the knowledge gained thereby. Such an interpretation of the moon-walk is the obvious and conventional one. It sees the meaning of the event in more and more astounding repetitions of essentially the same event. Thus it is the prisoner of the present cultural routines. It lacks the inspiration that could turn the present crisis into a new beginning. Moreover, many philosophers are no less the prisoners of cultural routines; they are concerned only to assist the scientist and engineer in their present tasks or else to clarify contemporary common sense.

Another and perhaps more revolutionary interpretation of the moon-walk could seek first to penetrate to the initial motive for such a journey and return; thus it could discover in the journey an as yet unseen meaning. But it is difficult to discover the duck in the rabbit. Consequently, the more pessimistic among us expect only more rabbit-walks. Nevertheless, a few could see how to convert the exploration of outer space at the same time into an exploration of inner space. These few could conclude, with the help of poetry, that the visit to the moon, that barren and inhuman wasteland, is symbolic. They could conclude that such a visit may be a way of telling ourselves where we presently are. Through such reflections and prompted by anticipations of the co-implied fate, men could become fruitfully aware of the analogy of man to the universe (or at least to the moon) and thence turn to something like self-conquest. If that time were to come, the pattern which may condition all being in history, the pattern of forgetfulness, crisis, and insight, could again become evidently relevant.

Meanwhile, for a philosophy which is concerned with philosophy's own position and function in history, this transcultural pattern itself is explicitly relevant and merits reflective attention and interpretation. Three elements of it have been elicited by the present section; one of these is the forgetfulness induced by any exceedingly successful, and hence very persuasive, world-view. This persuasiveness blots other possibilities from mind. Such forgetfulness is unavoidable and lends an inexorable quality to the fate that awaits. For instance, the unquestioning success which attended the Cartesian ideal of rationality was ominous. This ideal of complete rational illumination was deceptive, and its triumph was an invitation to crisis. That crisis is now upon us. But the crisis which is attended by explicit awareness of this pattern may become an archaic experience; it may become the advent of inspiration to the receptive psyche.

History is the dramatic struggle between the receptive active mind of man (psyche and thymos), which can return to the beginning and can also use the inspiration therefrom, and fate or that which any definite inspiration must omit but which remains darkly communicated, "forgotten," only to return in the guise of future crises. A decision concerning the philosophy appropriately to be pursued during a time of crisis should be prefaced by the recognition that a genuinely philosophic decision can be made only upon condition that this historic struggle and the pattern which devolves from it be anticipated. The ontological principle, that the being which reveals also conceals, is precisely such an anticipation. The often repeated pattern, to which I have drawn attention and which offers a kind of guidance through history, is an exemplification of this principle.

§ 52. END OR BEGINNING?

Such a conclusion returns us again to the present division of the ways and to the question whether philosophy has reached its final phase. The explicit alternatives seem to offer philosophers the choice either to make their exit by the door labeled "science and technology" or by the door labeled "contemplation and poetry." Must, however, all of us elect to relate ourselves to the conditions of human life either by changing the external world or by changing our inner selves? I think we need no prophet come from the future to inform us of the desirability of a mutually determining relation between the alternatives which have now come into view or else of the need for discerning a new beginning for philosophy. For we do not desire to fail in the present crisis and to suffer the fate with which, according to Plato's *Symposium*, Aristophanes' angry gods threatened men: to cut them into quarters so that they would have to go about on one leg and with half a wit. It is more difficult, however, to specify relations among the data at our disposal which will not be merely a reenactment of the persistently forgotten and a continued attachment to present routines.

How might a new and fruitful beginning be sought? One suggestion which has received attention of late is that the representatives of the leading philosophic traditions should enter into a dialogue. The expected outcome would, no doubt, be an amalgam of the clarity and precision attributed to the Anglo-American tradition with what is loosely termed the "life-relevance" attributed to the European tradition. What, however, might be expected of such an amalgam? Is it not likely to be merely another loosely knit eclecticism? In any event, the question of the possibility of a dialogue between two such radically opposed factions must first be resolved.

"Dialogue" has become a suspiciously popular word today. It may be that the demand for more dialogue merely betokens our concern about its lack and our fear that none may be possible. "Dialogue" is surely the most wistful term of the times.

A dialogue is at the least a species of transition. It is quite true that large groups of peoples may differ almost radically and yet hold the convictions and values which enable them, for example, to engage in economic transactions despite these differences. But shared beliefs and values must be of a more basic sort if they are to be used as the medium for a creative exchange of philosophic ideas. Nowadays, however, when men are linked each to each mainly by money, it is difficult, perhaps impossible, to discern ideas of this basic kind held by both the two traditions which we have emphasized. At least the present study has discovered little of significance which both groups share. Even the questions raised and discussed by either of the two groups seem to the opposite faction to be nonsense ("What is the meaning of being?") or to be trivial ("What do I mean when I say: 'The wallpaper is yellow' ?"). And where the background from which questions are asked, the questions themselves—as well as the kinds of answers anticipated—are so different that it may well be doubted that there is enough in common between these groups to render a dialogue possible or profitable.

Furthermore, analytic philosophers of all persuasions are disinclined to question the basic assumptions of our technological and progressive culture. Logical positivists often desire to be mistaken for scientists and seek to reduce the views of opposing philosophers to meaninglessness. Language analysts, as a rule, take for granted the commonsense clarity of the empirical tradition and treat their philosophical opponents like flies in bottles or invisible beetles in boxes, muddle-headed idiots in need of therapy. Both groups play their games as modern war games are played: they play to win; and winning requires the total elimination of the opponent. The question goes unasked whom the analyst would play his philosophic game with should he win definitively.

Perhaps, then, we shall not be well advised to conclude that the transcendental problem now facing philosophers is the discovery of a mode of transition between the positivistic-analytic tradition and the European phenomenological-existentialist tradition.

In any event, another possibility commands attention. A different locus of the contemporary transcendental problem is suggested by the intimate bond which unites man, his world, and his culture. We who live on the fault between two worlds, whose minds are molded by all the persuasive means of these schizoid times, can scarcely avoid reflecting within our own minds the two extremes which this book has endeavored to set forth. Is it not reasonable to suppose, therefore, that one should deal first with the opposition of these extremes as it occurs within oneself? For a person who comes to reflect upon the crisis which has emerged in the present, the transcendental problem is already set. He must undertake to discover the meaning of this split between the object-world, topic of the sciences and their mode of problem-solving thought, and the life-world with its more intuitive and sometimes poetic kind of thinking in the particular way in which this opposition is reproduced in his own makeup and thought. He must, in other words, institute a dialogue within himself between thymos and psyche.

A dialectic of this kind could be initiated by dissolving blind allegiance to the ideal of Cartesian clarity and entertaining instead an ideal of the finitude of reason. It could then proceed by forming descriptions of the common phenomena or elements of the contemporary life-world phenomena such as the experience of distance, of lived time, of things, of the self, of others, and the like as they are presented today—with an eye to determining how one could move to a more subtle experience of them. Such a procedure could also lead to more complex and abstract thought about the phenomena and their foundation. Thus some elements and aspects of concrete experience, which the contemporary rational consciousness has forgotten and so consigned to the irrational, might be laid bare. And thus the philosopher could discover in further detail where we now are with respect to the relation between living experience in and of the world and exact thought about it. Thereupon, the philosopher would be likely to develop a sense of possible new and creative interpretations of these phenomena and a new awareness of the world, an awareness that would include the scientific and technological world in a more just relation with human living. I suspect that the effort required to see this new relation would drive thought back to a renewal of its contact with the transcendental ideas. Another outcome might be a clarified grasp upon the neglected passive and receptive function of mind. These and other interpretations could then anticipate, or determine anticipatorily, the conditions for making a transition to and for living within what may be a newly emerging world.

Obviously we cannot at this writing proceed with these suggestions. The task of making such descriptions and interpretations must be reserved for a future enterprise. Nevertheless, the kind of internal dialectic between inspiration and discursive reasoning which could issue in such interpretations may appropriately be related to a metaphor which has already served us on several occasions. This metaphor bears in part upon the past but also upon the future of philosophy. A brief examination of it will help to designate the attitude and the approach for developing philosophy along the way to which I refer. I have in mind the figure of the labyrinth. The same figure of speech may also help further to point up the use and function of the present kind of historical study. But it must be emphasized that my elaboration of this metaphor is intended only to be summary and suggestive.

§ 53.   THE LABYRINTH OF FATE

The figure of the labyrinth, already commandeered a number of times in this essay to refer to the tangle of problems with which history presents us in our world, is serviceable again now that we need to represent the possible choices to which history has brought philosophy and which affect the direction of future movement. It is relevant likewise to recall its connection with symbols used earlier in this book. One such symbol is the art of weaving—the art which gave a first meaning to fate, as we observed in Section 3 above. To the ancient weaver the crisscross of threads presented a labyrinth through which he had to weave his way aright if the pattern ordained by the determining authority was to emerge. Another symbol that bears more directly upon our own world is the pair of crossed lines which could either define Cartesian coordinates or else allude to the religious emblem. The pair of crossed lines also refers to the place or places in a labyrinth where a decision must be made if one is to move through the maze and its confusions. One desires to choose the more preferable direction of movement. Here the point is reached where one may choose either or both meanings of the cross. These alternatives suggest, I believe, the character of the present labyrinth.

This present labyrinth, the place where fate and history have delivered us and from which we must move, is the space of modern thought. If this figure be accepted as a symbol for the complex and interinvolved problems that face modern man, then the question must occur: Does this labyrinth have an exit? One attitude leads to the view that no exit exists. There is, according to this attitude, no alternative but to accept the world in which we find ourselves. And this world is the object-world, the only one in which men may work out their fate; hence it would seem to follow that men would do well to learn to find their way efficiently around this complex. And happily enough, they possess the key to its intricacies in mathematics, for mathematics is admirably suited to manage problems concerning choices of turning.

Perhaps eventually the whole labyrinth can be considered to be a single vast problem whose transformation is to be seen not so much in Cartesian coordinates, whereon many of the curves of nature can be mapped, but more generally in the sophisticated computer capable of solving any problem which can be expressed with exactitude—that is, expressed in a binary system. This yes or no thinking is just the kind required to find one's way around a maze. That there are no problems save those which can be computerized is thus an easy to make supposition. There is, furthermore, a temptation to imagine that the practical and objective world of men's involvement can be considered to be an enormous computer which generates problems. This computer is linked with the governmentally organized, collective, mathematically thinking mind which stands as a second computer resolving the problems generated by the first. The mental and the physical worlds of Cartesian tradition thus become two interdependent and linked computers. The mental computer also performs the secondary and Humean-philosophical function of criticizing, simplifying, and improving its problem-solving techniques. One suggestion which quickly comes forth from this analogy is that problems which cannot be programmed must be pseudo-problems. No doubt the question whether there exists an outside to this labyrinth is just such a problem, for the reference to an outside cannot be entered on the computer program. If so, then the question is not whether the labyrinth has an exit; the point is that such a question makes no sense within the labyrinth.

Another attitude is maintained by those philosophers who would reject the modern world, they being convinced that there is an escape from that labyrinth. I do not refer to suicide. The exit which I have in mind is, so to speak, the same place whereby men entered it. This place is that which in man enabled him in the first instance to elaborate the vast network of institutions, objects, and technologies that constitutes our everyday world. And that which has enabled man to elaborate this context is his human-being, his Dasein (his horizon of transcendence) used in the service of thymos and its technological world. Instead, then, of continuing to use their human power to elaborate this complex computer-world with all its frustrations and problems, men could turn away from it altogether to the "will-less" and waiting contemplation of the Being which is the source of that world's possibility. The Theseus in this instance who can move through the labyrinth is the mystic hero who returns to its source. His power depends upon the exclusive cultivation of the psyche or the power of poetic receptivity in man. This is also the alternative offered by some myths and by the other-worldly element in religions; it is the way of self-sacrifice and renunciation. A modern version of it is expressed in the Romanticism of the nineteenth century; this version is a vague pantheism which, happily, is mostly passé. Its clearest recent version is expressed by Shestov.[3]

The options so far presented here are exclusive: either one interpretation of the labyrinth or the other, but not both. And men have often elected either one or the other exclusively. Still, there are arguments against either one over the other. For instance, choice of the first is scarcely reasonable since the question is whether to remain within the labyrinth, and this question is not a labyrinthine problem. Also, to suppose that one can at any point return to the source and achieve a complete renunciation of the modern world and all its works may be quite blind. Moreover, a decision in favor of such a renunciation does seem to involve not only a failure of courage but of charity as well. Both of these kinds of efforts suggest an avoidance of fate, whether through "adaptation" achieved by the tacit acceptance of bourgeois comfort and respectability or through total retreat achieved by some sort of mysticism or Yoga-like discipline. Certainly neither of these ways would have been chosen by a tragic hero, whether Greek or other. And they do not exhaust the possibilities.

One could at first be inclined to believe that a new world could come into being if the problems solvable by discursive reason were given over to computers, thus leaving men free to cultivate psyche and its inventive, inspirational, and contemplative powers. But such a world seems scarcely to be possible. Just as the ancient world could free a few for living a cultivated and human life only upon condition that the many would bear the physically enslaving burdens of life, so this third plan would require the minds of many to be devoted ex-

[3] See note 35 of Chap. 6.

clusively to developing, maintaining, and operating computers and the other machines necessary for preserving the lives of billions of people. Only the few, then, would be freed for the life of psyche.

Probably a viable third alternative will be seen to lie in the more strenuous and paradoxical direction of both accepting and rejecting the modern world; this alternative would hold that one can simultaneously be both within and without its labyrinth. This is the alternative which seeks to combine ratiocination with poetry, routine with inspiration, thymos with psyche into the whole man. Tradition has for a long time held up this alternative before the world as its guiding yet vague ideal. The unifying process was alluded to in the preceding section in terms of a dialectic between thymos and psyche—a difficult notion. And now surely it must be added that there is no more weasling a word in the language than the term "whole" in the phrase "whole man."

For our purposes I suggest that an illustration of wholeness is offered whenever a person has achieved a genial insight and has followed it by a detailed application or by communicating it through the routines of language. One illustration of this kind of achievement was offered in our first chapter by reference to Poincaré's mathematical discovery and its development. Poincaré to some extent was able to unite his extra- and intra-labyrinthine halves, and thus he reached a certain wholeness with respect to his mathematical powers. May it not similarly be possible to achieve revolutionary insights into human wholeness and its powers of becoming itself? The effect could be a genuine human change. A quite suggestive illustration is the continuous movement out of and back into the Platonic Cave. The Socratic hero must be understood to be always in motion between these two worlds. Here the movement is the thing, the movement unifying the two worlds and at the same time the intra- and extra-chthonic parts of man. The same becoming is again suggested by Plato's account of the philosopher-king and also in his conviction that the mathematical understanding of the cosmos could be made to serve the human good. This good, however, has since the Renaissance come to seem even more obscure than it may have appeared to Plato. The Romantic theme of the salvation of the depths is relevant; relevant also is the possibility that some of these depths will forever remain hidden, for, as Heraclitus remarked, so deep is the human logos.

Human unity and wholeness have not yet been adequately defined. And the fate of past philosophies indicates that no neatly and traditionally defined essence of human-being will circumscribe its transcendence for long. Perhaps, therefore, the new age should be conceived to be a time of continuous self-transcendence. If so, then it must also be a world which continually reinterprets and reassumes the old.

The human past cannot be inherited; it must be rethought or re-created. This effort of re-creation of the past cannot but be selective; hence it must omit or ignore much of the past and must, therefore, reckon with the hidden irrational and compulsive forces to which the name of fate has been given. Historical philosophical studies suggest the inevitable resurgence of such forgotten and irrational forces as powerfully as does the study of the unexpected consequences and self-frustrations of modern technology. To accept this view, that re-creation and understanding of the past are in principle necessarily selective, is to accept a special form of the basic insight of Heidegger: that Being which gives possibilities is itself finite and cannot let some possibilities come into the open without concealing others. There is always an end to possibilities; the existence of all simultaneously is impossible.

The persistence of fate forcefully suggests that men will continually have to engage in transitions among worlds. This need to make such transitions points to the sense in which one may be said to be both within and without a labyrinth. A world is a labyrinth. When a person (or a culture) is engaged in making a transition from one world to another, then he is in the in-between state, both within and without a world. Furthermore, if a world is a situation wherein a person may work out his fate, and if fate is always in some degree obscure, then the needs involved in being himself will continually require a change of worlds. Fate assumes its dark and menacing aspect just when it is obscured by the world in which a man currently lives. Fate's darkness is the effect of a world-obscurity. The function of philosophy is to detect the crisis, to see the kind of transition needed, and to interpret the change-over into a world which, for a time, will be less obscure or less stultifying.

An evident present need is for a better grasp upon the elements involved in such revolutionary change. We have dealt with these elements in the terms of customary world, thymos, forgetfulness, fate, crisis, psyche, being or arché, transition, interpretation, and new world. A consideration of these terms invites, I believe, an awareness of the absence of that which the customary world conceals. This awareness may also contain a hint of the world which is to come. Hence this third attitude of both accepting and rejecting the modern world seems to moderate the revengeful aspect of fate, the violent return of the forgotten. And thus it may convert the threat of tragedy into comedy.

Viewing it in this way, I think it obvious that the end of modern philosophy need not be the end of philosophy. At least it is evident that a one-sided decision for a Cartesian exactitude of thought in an experimentalist approach to nature, when extended to include man, invites a tragic catastrophe. In terms of this essay, it invites the forgotten psyche to return in the guise of a revengeful fate. Perhaps this vengeance consists in the lostness of learned men in the maze of minor problems. Or it may consist in the self-frustration arising from so many of our achievements—for instance, from self-protecting devices which threaten the world with total destruction. (Perhaps, indeed, it is true that a secret battle report from the technologists' war against nature reads as follows: "We have found and identified the enemy: He is ourselves.") On the other hand it is not evident that a desirable avoidance of this fate would be achieved by means of a complete and passive surrender to psyche.

The movement in history from mythos to logos and back again, together with the correlative transition back and forth within the mind from that function which is capable of insight and inspiration to that which is capable of disciplining, communicating, and using insight seems to be one of the permanent factors in history; we are only in this becoming. Philosophy exists in the interpretation of such transitions.

Index

Alienation, 57–58, 60, 89–90, 100, 118, 245, 255, 259, 279, 282

Analogy, 8, 18, 39, 42, 61, 66, 69–70, 76, 83, 88, 105, 118, 191–93, 195, 202, 205, 236, 257–58, 278, 288; of being, 42; of man to universe, 284; of objective world to computer, 258, 290

Anglo-American philosophy, 71, 107, 109, 272, 286

Anthropocentrism, 21, 142, 261

Anthropomorphism, 41, 43, 48, 50–51, 65, 73–74, 79–80, 84, 90, 93, 142, 144

Anxiety, 170, 242–43, 246, 254, 255

Arché, 28, 114, 141, 175, 180, 186, 188, 210, 222, 242, 251, 281 82

Archetype, 160–61, 163

Aristophanes, 285

Aristotelianism, 5, 11, 37–40, 76–77, 80, 82, 84, 87–88, 95, 105, 125, 177, 216, 238

Aristotle. *See* Aristotelianism

Association. *See* Idea

Atomic events, 95, 119

Atomism, 94, 101

Attunement, 231–32, 237, 242, 259–61

Augustine, Saint, 28

Authenticity, 219, 224–25, 243, 248–49, 256–62, 264

Bacon, Francis, 107

Balzac, Honoré de, 65

Befindlichkeit, 231, 234

Behaviorism, 109, 148, 150

Being, 5, 26, 51, 55, 58–59, 64, 70, 81, 178, 205, 212, 218, 221, 223–24, 227, 234–35, 237, 239, 241–42, 290; as absolute, 86; analogy of, 42; as creative, 105; as finite, 245–46; as human, 114, 118, 126, 133; as infinite, 30, 59–60, 142; as intelligible, 70, 81, 261; as mediating, 138; as opening, 239; originating, 63, 222–23, 262–63; and "power of world-making," 222, 262; as rational, 7, 122–23, 209, 267; as supreme, 40, 42, 141; as transcendental, 142; as "that which gives possibilities," 222, 249, 254, 261. *See also* Transcendental

Being-in-the-world, 223, 225–26, 233, 239–40. *See also* World

Bergson, Henri, 110

Bigger, Charles, 26

Boundary, 18–19, 270

Byron, George Gordon, Lord, 169

Care. *See* Dasein

Carnap, Rudolf, 33

Cartesian problem, 176; coordinates of, 33, 70, 112, 166, 289; tradition of, 228, 272–73, 290. *See also* Descartes, René.

Cartesian spirit, 64–65, 268

Categorial principles, 144